ECONOMY AND SOCIETY

This study aims to explain the relationship between economy and society. The author, Robert J. Holton, argues that the relationship is one of mutual dependence, in which political and cultural arrangements influence the functioning of economic life, just as much as economic contingencies influence the shape of politics and culture. This argument is pursued by means of a critical historical survey of major social scientific traditions, including economic liberalism and political economy.

The author moves on to discuss the differentiation and reintegration of economy and society, the viability of the market as an economic institution, the centrality of power in economic life, the significance of economic values and economic culture and the globalisation of economy and society.

This study is a major landmark in economic sociology. It draws upon the author's previous work in both sociology and economic history. It is of interest to a wide range of teachers and students of social science, including sociologists, economists and political scientists.

Robert J. Holton is Associate Professor of Sociology, Flinders University, Australia.

ECONOMY AND
SOCIETY

Robert J. Holton

London and New York

First published 1992
by Routledge
11 New Fetter Lane, London EC4P 4EE

Simultaneously published in the USA and Canada
by Routledge
a division of Routledge, Chapman and Hall, Inc.
29 West 35th Street, New York, NY 10001

© 1992 Robert J. Holton

Typeset in Baskerville from the Author's wordprocessing disks by
NWL Editorial Services, Langport, Somerset

Printed in Great Britain by
Mackays of Chatham PLC, Chatham, Kent

British Library Cataloguing in Publication Data

A catalogue record for this book is available from the British Library.

Library of Congress Cataloging in Publication Data

Holton, R.J.
Economy and society/Robert J. Holton.
p. cm.
Includes bibliographical references and index.
1. Free enterprise. 2. Liberalism. 3. Economic man.
4. Markets. 5. Capitalism. 6. Economics. I. Title.
HB95.H646 1992   91–42680
306.3 – dc20   CIP

ISBN 0–415–02909–0
        0–415–02910–4 (pbk)

For Polly and John Holton

CONTENTS

FIGURES AND TABLES

FIGURES

TABLES

ix

ACKNOWLEDGEMENTS

This study has been five years in the making. Particular thanks are due to colleagues and students in the economic sociology program at Flinders University of South Australia for their comments and criticisms. Ray Jureidini, Ross Boyd and Joan Carr have played a most important role in acting as a sounding-board for the ideas that make up the greater part of this study. I am also grateful to Sue Manser for her skill and unswerving commitment to accuracy in preparing the manuscript for publication.

This study was written while on outside study leave from Flinders University. The delightful working conditions in the Kentish countryside on Tong Farm contributed immeasurably to its completion.

The book itself is dedicated to my parents without whose encouragement and support I would never have embarked on a career as academic and author. Their experience in balancing the economic, political and cultural aspects of household organisation has been a subtle but enduring influence on me.

R.J. Holton
Little Tong, Kent
January 1991

Part I

INTRODUCTION

Economic issues are a major concern for contemporary individuals, households, communities and governments. Economic growth and decline, wealth and poverty, employment and unemployment, productivity and inefficiency, freedom of choice and inequalities of economic power – these represent some of the most pressing reference points by which the welfare of individuals, households, communities and governments are judged. While there are major differences concerning the priority that should be accorded economic matters, no-one can ignore their importance in modern life without being branded a hopeless utopian.

For large portions of the world's population in the Third World, economic issues are a matter of immediate material survival, of life and death. Even in the Western world, where material survival is, for most, more secure, economic issues dominate the agenda for everyday life and political debate. Rich and poor are inextricably implicated in economic life, even though their life-chances differ considerably through inequalities in control over economic resources.

Beyond the material struggles and exigencies of everyday life, economic questions are intimately bound up in the ways we understand the structure and dynamics of social life, and in debates about what kind of economic arrangements best advance human welfare. During the twentieth century these concerns have been expressed in the analysis of capitalism and socialism (or communism) as rival economic systems, and in public policy debates about the relative merits of free markets and public planning. Such debates raise questions about the actual operation of economic institutions such as markets, private property rights in economic resources, public planning agencies, and about the ways such institutions relate and interact with political and cultural institutions. Many questions arise as a result. These include the relative merits of capitalism and socialism, or markets as against welfare states, in generating economic efficiency and a just distribution of economic resources. Key values such as 'freedom', 'justice' and 'equality' are critical yardsticks against which the performance of economic institutions are judged.

Underlying these debates is the spectre of economic development as a dynamic yet destabilising process, that outstrips the capacities of human agencies to control it. The fear of social life being dominated by apparently uncontrollable economic processes has become intensified by the increasing reality of a world economic system. The anxiety is that global economic institutions and processes have become more powerful than either nation-states or social movements seeking to regulate economic life in accordance with individual, or community or national political objectives.

The analysis and debate of economic issues is shared – albeit in different ways – both by those inclined to measure human welfare primarily in material terms such as income and productivity, and by those who believe that economic considerations should be subordinate to 'higher' social values, such as equality, justice and environmental protection. This reminds us that economic analysis is far more than a technical matter, for it raises many of the most important values about which individuals and governments feel most passionately. Economic arrangements will always be matters for evaluation and moral scrutiny.

The present study is, however, not intended to resolve such matters of moral evaluation and political choice. The aim is rather to provide a survey of the principal ways in which economic life may be analysed and understood. Within this survey particular attention is given to the relationship between the economy and other aspects of society, such as the political system and cultural values. This book is centrally concerned with theories of economy and society. Such theories seek to explain how the economy and the wider society interact, how far economic forces determine the shape and fate of society, and how far social forces outside the economy proper in turn influence the course of economic affairs. These general themes are pursued through an analysis of key theories of economic institutions such as markets, property rights in economic resources and systems of production and consumption, together with the cultural meanings and values that have become associated with economic activity.

The importance of economic matters in contemporary society is of course reflected in the emergence of specialised bodies of social scientific thought, associated above all with the rise of economics as a distinct profession. Economists have sought both to understand the functioning of the economy, and to advise individuals and governments on how best to secure their economic welfare. At the same time economists have not succeeded in achieving an effective monopoly of discussion over economic issues. There are two reasons for this.

First, much economics has been highly abstract and mathematical in character focussing on arcane technical issues rather than economic problems as they are perceived in policy-debate and everyday life. Leontief (1985, pp. 29–30) in an analysis of articles in the *American Economic Review* during the 1970s, reports that 50 per cent were purely mathematical containing no empirical data at all, while 22 per cent contained 'cooked up' data not assembled in a systematic manner. Of the few articles that were based on direct empirical analysis, several concerned laboratory experiments on pigeons and mice, rather than observations of human beings. This state of affairs has left something of a void which other social scientists, including sociologists and political scientists, have sought to fill alongside a minority of economists.

A second reason for the lack of effective monopoly control by economists over economic discussion is the willingness of non-economists to tackle head on the relationship between the economy and the wider society. This includes the interactive relationships between the economy, the political system and broader cultural values and norms. As we shall see in Chapters 4 and 5, these matters have only recently and belatedly been picked up in a systematic manner by mainstream economists, and only through the application of narrowly economic (rational choice) assumptions to social and political life. The present study, written by a sociologist, takes as its premise the failure of mainstream economics to offer more than a partial account of how the economy works. This failure is largely related to a parallel failure to explain the interactive relationship between economy and society, except in excessively narrow ahistorical terms. Another way of putting this is to say that an analysis of the economy and its place in society is too important to be assigned to economists alone.

1

DEFINING THE ECONOMY
A historical, multi-dimensional approach

WHAT IS THE ECONOMY? TOWARDS A PRELIMINARY DEFINITION

It is easier to produce a check-list of the major components of economic life, as conventionally described, than to get social scientists to agree on a settled definition of what the economy actually is. One such check-list recently suggested by Richard Swedberg (1987, p. 5) is outlined in an expanded and amended form in Table 1.1.

This represents a valuable 'common sense' inventory of institutions and issues commonly regarded as constituting the economy. What it does not indicate is the common quality that

Table 1.1 Check-list of economic phenomena

Consumption and production
Productivity and technological innovation
Markets
Contracts
Money
Saving
Economic organisations (e.g. banks, insurance companies, corporations)
Life in the workplace
Division of labour and occupational segregation
Economic classes
The international economy
The economy and the wider society, including government, social movements and cultural values
The impact of gender and ethnic factors on the economy
Economic power
Economic ideology

---

distinguishes this list from the non-economic aspects of society. Put another way, if the economy is to be regarded as a part of a wider whole, what is it that differentiates the economy from that which lies beyond? Is it some common element in the listed set of economic phenomena themselves? Or is it some overarching human need or challenge that all these phenomena seek to satisfy?

Historically, the terms 'economy' and 'economic' derive from the ancient Greek terms *Oikos* and *Oikonomia*, which refer to a self-provisioning extended household. The *oikos* sought to satisfy its members' needs by supplying food, clothing, shelter and sociability from within itself with little or no exchange with others. The analysis of household provisioning in this sense is rather foreign to the contemporary check-list of economic phenomena listed in Table 1.1, although it does live on in an attenuated way in notions like home economics concerned with cooking and other forms of domestic management. The tracing of linguistic derivations in this way does not, however, get us anywhere close to modern conceptions of the economy as a distinct part of society with its own purposes or functions, distinct from those of the other parts.

The ancient Greek *oikos* can be regarded as a base unit of the social system, in which the household was simultaneously an economic, cultural and political institution, and the male householder the foundation of political and patriarchal authority. This type of institution differs from modern conceptions of the economy in two ways. First, it combines a wide range of social functions, including political and cultural affairs alongside economic provisioning. This contrasts with the modern tendency to generate specialised economic institutions. Second, its economic outreach does not include exchange with other households through mechanisms such as barter, markets and so forth. Again this contrasts with modern economic systems of exchange as distinct from self-sufficiency. We must therefore look elsewhere for an answer to the question 'What is the economy?'

The most widely used approach to defining the economy is to identify it with the performance of a specific social function distinct from other non-economic functions. The foremost strategy for defining a specific economic function makes use of the distinction between the 'ends' or 'objectives' of human action on the one hand, and 'the means' used to achieve such 'ends' on the other.

Within this framework, the specifically economic function centres on the means used to satisfy human 'ends' or 'wants', rather than the creation of those wants or ends in themselves. This definition is often elaborated to associate the economy with the satisfaction of *material* wants, rather than other kinds of wants. This emphasis on the material, however, is hard to sustain since it is difficult to distinguish material wants from other kinds of wants, without making rather arbitrary assumptions. Put more concretely, it seems arbitrary to limit the economic function to the production of basic material necessities such as food, clothing and shelter, to the exclusion of goods and services which reflect social status and which convey symbolic messages about those who possess them. Purchase of a Rolls Royce or a Ferrari is not only a matter of satisfying a material want for transport, but is also implicated in other kinds of wants, including possession of status symbols of success, power and wealth. To sever one kind of want from another seems highly misleading, especially as the definition of what constitutes a basic want or a luxury varies between cultures and across history. For many in the Third World simply owning a car is regarded as a luxury.

If it is not possible to limit the definition of the economy to the means necessary to satisfy purely *material* wants, it is possible to be more precise about the specific types of material means involved. This is appropriate because the economy cannot be indiscriminately associated with the deployment of any kind of means to reach a given end. If the 'end' in question is religious salvation and the 'means' chosen is 'prayer', the deployment of prayer would not typically be regarded as an 'economic activity', unless some subsidiary assumption is made, such as the belief that the level of financial contributions accompanying religious devotion had a bearing on the spiritual outcome. Even then, this hypothetical transaction would not be regarded as a mainstream economic activity unless religious bodies turned the sale of devotional means of salvation into a regular and continuous activity, or unless the majority of supplicants attended church just to participate in the transaction.

The initial definition of economic activity focussing on the deployment of 'means' to realise 'ends', can be made more precise by focussing on land, labour and capital as essentially *material* means by which the economy operates. Whereas the economy functions by deploying material means to satisfy wants, the remainder of society can be thought of as functioning both to generate and articulate wants, and to deploy means other than land, labour and capital, e.g. prayer, love, friendship, in satisfying them.

Before we proceed any further with this type of functional definition, it must be stressed that reference to 'function' does not imply the invariable success of economic institutions in satisfying wants. To say that the economy functions to satisfy wants using certain types of means should not be taken to imply invariable successful performance of this function. This point requires emphasis in order to avoid the functionalist trap of assuming that wherever economies exist, this must reflect successful performance of economic functions. After all, world history is littered with examples of famine and economic depression, while the much-vaunted economic dynamism of previous world leaders such as seventeenth-century Holland or nineteenth-century Britain no longer perform at the same level as today's vanguard economies in Japan, the USA or Germany.

A leading example of a function-based approach to defining the economy is provided by mainstream or liberal economics. This typically adds a further essential component to the means–end approach to the economy, by positing a chronic *scarcity* of means by which to realise our ends. In this view it appears we never have enough means to satisfy all our wants simultaneously. Thus economics, the study of the economy focusses, in the words of leading economist Paul Samuelson (1976, p. 3), on 'how people and society end up choosing, with or without the use of money, to employ *scarce* productive resources that could have alternative uses, to produce various commodities [sic!] and distribute them for consumption now or in the future among various persons and groups' (Samuelson's emphasis).

This emphasis on scarcity and choice of means presupposes that we want to get the most from our limited means. As such the definition of the economy approximates to the popular notion of 'economising' or being economical with our resources.

10

This emphasis on the problem of scarcity and the need for prudent choice has recently received a major boost from the emergence of widespread concern over environmental problems facing the planet Earth. In particular, much stress has been placed on the finite nature of the earth's physical resources, and the consequent need to treat physical resource utilization in the light of the depletion of scarce and often non-renewable resources. This problem of finite environmental resources provides a new dimension to the conventional economistic emphasis on scarcity, by encouraging a cautious and prudent choice of economic techniques with a view to resource conservation. This environmentalist support for 'scarcity'-based definitions of economic activity is a somewhat unexpected one insofar as environmentalists and economists often draw rather different practical conclusions about the scale and dangers of resource depletion. These differences do not, however, undermine the importance of the common focus on problems of choice under conditions of scarcity.

A number of criticisms have been levelled at scarcity-based definitions on the grounds of narrowness of conception, and of limited historical applicability to economic life. Polanyi (1977) and Sahlins (1972) for example argue that many tribal or ancient societies do not possess insatiable appetites or wants, and hence do not suffer from the perception that the resources necessary to satisfy this multiplicity of wants are in scarce supply. Sahlins' discussion of stone-age economics in hunter–gatherer societies is particularly interesting in this respect. On the basis of anthropological evidence drawn from hunter–gatherer groups such as the Kalahari bushmen or Australian Aborigines, he claims that wants in such societies are very simple and the means are generally at hand to satisfy them. This interpretation appears to fly in the face of the perception by members of modern societies that hunter–gatherers live in conditions of extreme destitution, on the precarious margins of subsistence. Sahlins, however, insists on the paradoxical point, that hunter–gatherers, while they have a very low standard of living, may nonetheless feel comfortable with their lives in the sense of not feeling deprived of goods and services that they lack. What looks like abject scarcity to an outsider is experienced in terms of satisfaction by hunter–gatherers able to migrate in search of food and sociability.

11

This discussion warns us that the formulation 'unlimited wants–scarce means' is very much a product of cultural circumstances rather than a universal feature of human society. For the hunter–gatherer wants are scarce and means often plentiful. The drive to satisfy a multiplicity of wants through scarce means is not, according to Sahlins, a basic component of human nature. 'It is not that hunters and gatherers have curbed their materialistic "impulses", they simply never made an institution of them' (1972, pp. 13–14).

As a result of this type of criticism of the 'scarcity' definition, Polanyi has argued that there is a fundamental conflict between what he calls the *formal* definition of the economy, based on notions of scarcity of means and the drive to economise resources, and the *substantive* definition of the economy based on specific historical patterns utilised in the deployment of material resources to meet wants. The German sociologist Niklas Luhmann (1982), however, argues that this response to the scarcity definition is too negative. Properly reformulated, Luhmann believes it is possible to reconcile the two approaches that Polanyi regards as incompatible.

For Luhmann 'scarcity does not mean the same thing as the rarity or lack of objects, nor does it refer to deprivations or distress' (1982, p. 195). Rather he sees scarcity as a reflection of our inability to meet all our wants at one and the same time. We must therefore choose between the temporal priority of different means. Thus 'we can specify needs and the means of satisfying them only to the extent that we can defer some of these needs and guarantee their satisfaction in the future' (1982, p. 194). In this way, Luhmann claims an important distinction between actions we take now in the present (such as investment of labour and resources, or consumption of existing goods) rather than actions which are deferred to the future (such as saving designed to provide for future consumption). Applied to hunter–gatherers, this suggests a choice in terms of action between whether to hunt now and consume later, consume now or hunt later, or perhaps to store now in anticipation of future consumption, or as a response to seasonal variation in the returns of hunting. We cannot choose all these options simultaneously. Different options are therefore scarce in a special temporal sense.

Luhmann's reformulation of scarcity in terms of the generic

problem of choice among competing ends suggests that it is possible to reconcile scarcity-based definitions with functional conceptions of the economy based on the relationship of means to ends, and the deployment of material means to satisfy ends. There is no unbridgeable gulf between the scarcity-definition as such and other functionally-based approaches, as Polanyi claims (1977). The main problem with the scarcity definition is not its inapplicability outside market economies, but rather that it is not an exhaustive conception of the economy. Put another way, the analysis of scarcity is not in itself sufficient or comprehensive as a basis for analysis of economic life.

One of the problems with the liberal economic approach to scarcity, focussing on the deployment of 'scarce' means to reach given ends, is the obscurity with which it treats the remainder of society. Where, for example, do the 'ends' or objectives of economic action and choice come from, and are they so clearly separate and distinct from economic life?

The problem with this is the assumption that the economy can be defined in a vacuum, so to speak, without clarification of the other social functions which may exist alongside the economic function. The difficulty here is that the remainder of the social fabric is bracketed out and taken as a 'given' when the economy is under analysis. By treating the social context as a stable 'given', a profoundly ahistorical character is also imparted to economic analysis.

It is of course true that economists as individual social observers usually do realise the interactive nature of relations between the economy and the wider society. However, in terms of systematic analysis incorporated in economic theory, very little direct assistance is available to analyse relations between economy and society. Three main responses have emerged, but none has proved very satisfactory.

The first argues that the surrounding social context is not amenable to scientific analysis or to sociology. This is either because the ultimate basis of individual action is regarded as so complex as to be unknowable, or because it is regarded as having a psychological or physiological basis, refractory to social analysis. For many economists therefore it is impossible to discover why individual wants or ends are as they are. Indeed, many regard sociological attempts to pursue the existence of social patterning of ends as an artificial fabrication or the imputation of patterns that goes well beyond the evidence. In extreme form this argument denies the existence of society as an overarching entity. What exists is only individuals making choices. This view is politically expedient to those who believe in the ideology of the free market and free-standing individualism. The major problems with it are the entirely arbitrary dismissal of the possibility that social wants may indeed be socially patterned and the failure to consider the possibility that individualism is a product of social circumstances.

A second response to the problem of where society fits in relation to the economy is to admit society, but only on a very limited basis. One way of doing this, suggested by the Italian social scientist, Vilfredo Pareto, is to institute a division of labour between the rational and non-rational aspects of social life. The economy is concerned with rational functions, such as the choice of efficient courses of action in the market, whereas other parts of society deal with non-rational concerns influenced not by calculations of efficiency, but by desire or moral values.

There are, however, serious problems with this approach too. These apply, not only with respect to the validity of regarding non-economic matters as immune from rational calculation, but also with the rigid separation of economic and non-economic concerns as if they did not mutually influence or condition each other.

A third, more recent, and more interesting response is to apply the apparatus of economic theory developed in the first instance for an understanding of markets to a range of non-market institutions such as governments or the family. This approach, is reflected in the work of the Public Choice school (Buchanan and Tullock 1962; Buchanan 1986), in the new institutional economics (Williamson 1975), and in the work of writers such as Gary Becker (1976, 1981). This response is more radical than the other two in that it colonises the remainder of society for conventional economic analysis. We are therefore provided with 'economic' theories of democracy or of the family and the household.

One initial problem with this approach, as far as the definition of the economy is concerned, is that only one social function is proposed, namely the 'economic' one. All aspects of human

14

behaviour are thereby rendered similar in that they are seen to be dominated by the self-interested search for means to reach given ends. To take one example, the conventional sexual division of labour within a marriage, between male bread-winner and female home-maker, is interpreted in economic terms, as a self-interested alliance. Marriage becomes the rational 'means' whereby males whose ends are to hold down paid employment, form an effective exchange with females whose 'ends' are to become housewives.

There are many problems with this approach as applied to the case of the family, not least the failure to analyse why male and female sex roles emerged, and why they are also subject to change. We shall examine these problems in Chapters 3 and 4 of this study. For purposes of definition of the scope of the economy, however, this general approach is deficient in that it reduces all of society to one set of economic functions, without analysing and rebutting alternative theories of society and of the relationship between economy and society. Instead, its proponents assume that economic explanations, if they can be found, are intrinsically superior to other explanations. Hence there is no need to look beyond 'economic' explanations, in order to determine whether better explanations can be found elsewhere. In this view the economy is equated with human nature itself. This whole position is therefore very controversial as a result of its failure to engage with other rival approaches.

TOWARDS A HISTORICAL, MULTI-DIMENSIONAL APPROACH TO ECONOMY AND SOCIETY

In the discussion so far we have outlined the search for a definition of the economy in terms of the performance of a specific set of social functions designed to solve certain types of problems encountered in human society. We have also identified the conventional economists' definition of the economy in terms of a specific link in the chain linking the 'ends' (or objectives) of human action with the 'means' utilised to achieve them. A further distinctive feature of this approach is the problem of scarcity, that is taken to lie at the heart of the economic problem. This school of analysis, however, is deficient in failing to provide an overarching account of how the economy, thus conceived, fits in with the wider society. This inadequacy is further magnified by a tendency to be ahistorical.

The economistic approach has, in fact, been challenged by a number of writers over the last hundred years. Its critics include Karl Marx, the historical economists in the late nineteenth century such as Gustav Schmoller and Werner Sombart, the classical sociologists Max Weber and Emile Durkheim and, more recently, the economic anthropologist Karl Polanyi and his associates. It is Polanyi's critique that forms the point of departure for an alternative way of conceptualising the economy able to address certain deficiencies in the economistic account.

Polanyi certainly accepts a functional view of the nature of the economy. However, he also argues for the need to analyse the economic function historically, and to develop analytical tools that are trans-contextual rather than dependent on one particular economic pattern such as the market (Polanyi 1977).

At its most general level, Polanyi's theory treats the economy in any given society as the mechanism by which resources are mobilised to satisfy wants. As such, the economy involves interaction with the physical environment and with other parts of society. The resources brought to bear include land, labour and capital. However, the manner in which they are mobilised is regarded as historically variable rather than uniform. Thus Polanyi posited four main modes of integration by which resources have been collected, produced, stored and distributed to meet human wants during the course of history. These are summarised in Table 1.2.

Table 1.2 Polanyi's conception of four distinct modes of integration of economic activity

1	RECIPROCITY Wants are satisfied through exchange of goods and services within a closed tribal or kinship system designed to reaffirm the interdependence of all members through performance of obligations.
2	REDISTRIBUTION Wants are satisfied through centralised control over resources, achieved through means such as imperial domination.
3	HOUSEHOLDS Wants are satisfied through self-sufficiency.
4	MARKETS Wants are satisfied through market exchange.

Source: Polanyi (1977)

In this account markets are merely one of four types of economic system without any privileged status as bearers of a higher rationality. Similarly, each of the four rests on a distinctive mode of exchange which is not reducible to any other. This means that the market model of exchange by self-interested human agents seeking a 'rational' choice of scarce means to meet their aims, is not seen as the key model underlying all others. Instead, Polanyi introduces issues of obligation and power into the constitution of economic relationships.

According to Polanyi, economists have neglected the first three types of economy in favour of a market-based economy, as the basis of their conceptualisation of the economy. As such, they have neglected the way in which the economy has been *embedded* in wider social relations wherever reciprocity, redistribution and the household have been dominant. Instead, economists have focussed on the market which is the sole type of economy sharply *differentiated* from the remainder of society. (The concept of embeddedness and differentiation are represented diagrammatically in Figure 1.1.) For Polanyi, it is this narrow ahistorical approach which has enabled most economists to bracket out 'society' and 'history' from their definition of economics. He believes this bracketing out cannot be sustained.

The analytical task raised by this discussion is first to identify what all economies, whether embedded or differentiated, hold in common and then to explore the historical dynamics which bring

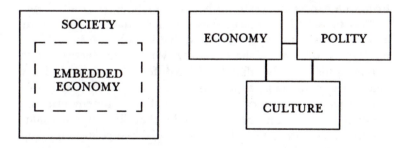

A. ECONOMY EMBEDDED   B. ECONOMY DIFFERENTIATED
   IN SOCIETY   FROM SOCIETY

Figure 1.1 Economies: embedded and differentiated.

different types to the fore. For Polanyi, this second strand in the analysis focussed on the process whereby the predominantly embedded economies of the ancient and medieval world became challenged in the eighteenth and nineteenth centuries by the differentiation of the capitalist market-based economy from political and cultural institutions.

Polanyi's conception of the embedded economy simply means that the institutions that perform the economic function of resource mobilisation with respect to land, labour and capital are multi-functional. If we take the example of reciprocity based on tribal relationships, Polanyi's argument is that the tribe is just such a multi-functional institution. It functions simultaneously as an economic institution mobilising resources to feed, clothe and shelter its members, and as a cultural institution providing meaning and a sense of community cohesion between its members. Hence when tribal members exchange goods they do so not only for purposes of material survival and access to a wider range of goods, but also to reaffirm the social bonds between them. In this sense, economic relations are embedded in broader social relations. Contrast this with markets, where the mechanisms of price determination and calculations of cost–benefit do not carry in any direct way cultural or political significance. Markets, according to Polanyi, are not designed to reaffirm social bonds between those who use them. Indeed, it does not matter whether producers and consumers know each other or are members of a common community. Here economic relations are differentiated from wider social concerns, rather than embedded within them.

This model of the market-based differentiation of economy and society is not unique to Polanyi, but is built into virtually all modern definitions of the economy. What is distinctive about Polanyi is his insistence that the sharp differentiation of economy and society entailed by a 'pure' market system is not sustainable in reality. On the basis of a historical analysis of nineteenth- and twentieth-century Europe he concludes that differentiated market economies generate such extreme social and political tensions that new types of 'embedded' economies emerge. These include welfare states in which the function of social protection re-emerges to take precedence over that of market independence.

We shall examine, in Chapter 2, the accuracy of Polanyi's historical scenario of embedded, differentiated and re-embedded economies. For the moment our concern is with the implications of his analysis for the provisional definition of the economy.

Above all else, Polanyi argues that a generic or universal definition of the economy cannot be sustained on the basis of the historically distinctive market model. Use of the market model by economists and by some Marxists, however, has obscured the extent to which most economies at most stages in human history have been embedded in wider social relations. It follows that economic life cannot be abstracted from the wider society, even for analytical purposes, without severing the key role of social influences in constituting economic relations. We should not think of the economy as an autonomous realm in which politics or the community 'intervenes' or 'interferes' as if from outside. Rather, extra-economic influences contribute in constituting and reproducing economic relationships, just as they are influenced by them.

To give one example, the economic institution of wage-labour in which individuals sell their labour-power to an employer in return for a wage, did not arise historically as a result of purely economic market-based influences. Nor has it survived for purely economic reasons. While wage-labour may under many circumstances provide a more economically efficient means of labour organisation, its origins and reproduction have depended on favourable forms of political underpinning, including political and legal support for the limitation or abolition of non-wage based employment alternatives such as peasant farming or voluntary unemployment through the welfare state.

The main thrust of Polanyi's argument is therefore that the economy cannot be defined in abstraction from the remainder of society. On the contrary, the economy can only be successively defined and understood in terms of a theory of the relationship between economy and society. It is this insistence which has attracted the wrath of those economists who believe that society is in fact the economy writ large.

What further light, then, does Polanyi shed on the relationship between economy and society?

The concept of embeddedness enables Polanyi to make a very strong case for his proposition that the economy can never be defined in abstraction from the wider society. However, when we come to the market, and the differentiation of economy and society, Polanyi says comparatively little about differentiation as an enduring social phenomenon in the modern epoch. This is because he wants to insist that pure differentiation, as projected by adherents of *laissez-faire* and market freedom is impossible. But what if the check to *laissez-faire* only partially reverses the differentiation process?

A problem arises for Polanyi's discussion here, in terms of the relationship between economic functions and economic institutions. Under reciprocity, redistribution, or the household, he can claim that tribes, empires or the *oikos* operate in their different ways as multi-functional institutions. They combine economic with other functions. But what of modern Western societies, where the extreme differentiation of the pure market has been limited by the expansion of state intervention? Are there still single-function institutions performing economic functions (such as factories, banks and stock-exchanges), while political functions are performed by governments? If this were true it would mean that the economy had no intrinsic political, cultural or moral components to it, while the polity or cultural practices of any society have no fundamental economic aspects. Or has the trend towards social protection and de-differentiation recreated multi-functional institutions, creating for example a new moral economy and a politically regulated market?

We do not offer a historical or empirical resolution of this question at this point, although such issues will be discussed later in the study. For the moment we are concerned with the implications of this set of questions for the definition of the economy.

The sociologists Talcott Parsons and Neil Smelser (1956) have attempted to resolve the relationship between social functions and their connection with the institutional fabric of society, by distinguishing between analytical and empirical aspects of social life. Their argument starts off with the familiar general idea that the economy is to be defined in terms of a specific social function, performance of which is of critical importance to the successful development of a social system. They also conclude, like many other analysts, that the *specific* nature of this function (which they call the adaptive function) is bound up with the deployment of resources such as land, labour and capital to meet human wants or goals. This incorporates the functions of production, in which society acts upon nature, and the exchange of goods and services for consumption.

Like Polanyi, and unlike most economists, Parsons and Smelser then go on to try to identify the other non-economic functions that exist alongside economic functions, and which interact with them. Whereas Polanyi limits his discussion to the non-economic function of social protection, Parsons and Smelser identify three additional functions. These are:

1 Goal-attainment: involving the political articulation and implementation of goals
2 Pattern-maintenance: involving the institutionalisation of values into stable cultural patterns
3 Integration: involving the creation of a balance between the other three functions (i.e. including the economy) so as to manage conflict and tension.

Parsons and Smelser see these four functions as analytical features of social systems whether large or small. By a social system, they mean any relatively self-subsistent entity, that is any entity that can achieve autonomy from its environment, whether it be a nation distinct from other nations, or a firm or corporation distinct from other corporations and from government. What, however, does this term 'analytical features' mean?

Parsons and Smelser use this term to make the point that the four functions are not located in four entirely separate sets of social institutions. They are rather abstractions from reality, abstractions designed to reduce the complexities of social life to four key or functional problems underlying social life. Having made this abstract theoretical point, Parsons and Smelser agree that in reality, all social systems, including major institutions such as governments, corporations and cultural communities, are concerned with various combinations of *both* economic and non-economic functions.

Governments, for example, while concerned with political 'goal-attainment', cannot at the same time avoid economic issues such as the fiscal basis of government activity, or the destabilising effect of unregulated market forces on community cohesion, except at their peril. Similarly, apparently 'economic' institutions like banks are implicated not only in economic resource mobilisation, but in other social functions. To remain viable, banks must clearly focus on the profitability of investments, loans and other services. Yet they may also become involved in 'politics', through relationships with government over the regulation of financial markets, the setting of interest rates and so forth, and in cultural institutions, in terms of the positive promotion of values such as saving and home-ownership.

Parsons and Smelser argue that purely economic issues can be distinguished, but only analytically by abstracting from the more complex multi-functional reality of the real world. Here actual institutions, while they may be primarily concerned with one function, tend to be implicated in wider multi-functional networks which combine 'economic' with 'non-economic' functions. The analytical question of the definition of the economy cannot be resolved simply by reference to economic institutions, because purely economic institutions rarely, if ever, exist.

What Parsons and Smelser help us to add to the definition of the economy is an awareness that real-world institutions cannot be so neatly separated into economic and non-economic categories. We cannot therefore conceptualise the economy without reference to *analytical* problems. It is these concerns, rather than a particular category of empirical objects, which define the economy.

The classical sociologist Max Weber recognised this problem in promoting what he called 'social economics'. Weber argued that intellectual disciplines were founded on analytical questions rather than empirical divisions distinguishing various phenomena (Weber 1949). To tackle the question of how and why economic arrangements had developed as they had therefore required analysis of a wide range of social phenomena that could be shown to have a bearing on the analytical issues identified as 'economic'. Social economics, in other words, looked at phenomena that were economically relevant from an analytical point of view. As such, it rejected the view that some phenomena were intrinsically and exclusively economic while others were not.

Weber's social economics failed to convince the economists of his day as a program for a new kind of economics. The essence of his approach, however, has resurfaced recently in the rebirth of economic sociology, designed to theorise the relations between economy and society (Swedberg 1987). This study is intended as a study in economic sociology, or social economics.

2

THE DIFFERENTIATION OF ECONOMY AND SOCIETY

In Chapter 1 we examined some ways in which social scientists have defined and conceptualised the economy. The premise behind this analysis is that all societies – whether ancient or modern – have economies, even though the substance of economic life may change considerably over time. Put another way, the presumption is that all societies, to remain viable, must somehow attempt to mobilise the resources of land, labour and capital to meet human wants. While it is true that humankind does not live by bread alone, it is equally true, speaking meta-phorically, that humankind cannot live without bread.

In this chapter we shall look more closely at the issue of differentiation, a key concept introduced in outline in Chapter 1. In the first part of this analysis we shall identify a number of different dimensions to the process of differentiation, which emerges as a multi-layered rather than one-dimensional phenom-enon. In the second part of the chapter attention will shift to a scrutiny of the historical and theoretical adequacy of Polanyi's account of the Great Transformation whereby originally embedded economies became differentiated from and then reintegrated into social life.

THE PROCESS OF DIFFERENTIATION

The process of social differentiation has a number of distinct but interrelated dimensions. At the most macro level it refers to a *differentiation of social functions*. On the assumption that social life involves some kind of complexity in which more than one key function is required, we may legitimately speak of functional differentiation. There is no consensus among social scientists about the nature or number of functions involved. The most conventional way of understanding this process, however, is by means of the differentiation of 'economic', 'political' and 'cultural' functions, the latter two being concerned with government, and with the institutionalisation of meaning, identity and social solidarity respectively. The economic function is not, therefore, the only function, and it is not necessarily the most important one either. Social scientists in fact remain undecided as to whether one such function is necessarily of primary importance, or whether the search for primacy should be abandoned in favour of a multi-functional approach. Such an approach need not imply that the various functions are always and invariably of equal importance, since primacy at any given moment may depend on the complexities of the specific historical context.

We have already provided one example of a multi-functional approach to social life, in the four-function paradigm developed by Talcott Parsons, and applied to the economy by Parsons and Smelser (1956). In Parsons' case, however, multi-functionality did not prevent a tendency to regard cultural explanations as primary (Parsons 1966, p. 113). This discussion may usefully be compared with an alternative multi-functional approach proposed by Michael Mann (1986) in which social differentiation is discussed without any commitment to a general causal prime mover.

In the *Structure of Social Power Vol. 1* (1986) Mann outlines four differentiated sources of power, namely ideological, economic, military and political. This multiple approach is linked to power rather than social functions because Mann believes that social functions can never be successfully performed without being institutionalised in networks of power. However, Mann's four power sources arise in a similar way to Parsons and Smelser's functions, as key needs or problems facing any kind of social life. Ideological power, for example, derives in part from the fact that human beings 'require concepts and categories of meaning' and also in part because 'shared normative understandings are required for stable efficient social co-operation' (Mann 1986, p. 22). Military power, meanwhile, 'derives from the necessity of organised physical defense' (1986, p. 25), while political power 'derives from the usefulness of centralised, institutionalised, territorialised regulation' (1986, p. 26). Economic power, finally, derives, according to Mann, 'from the satisfaction of subsistence needs through the social organisation of the extraction, transformation, distribution and consumption of the objects of nature' (1986, p. 24). As with the other attempts to define the economy, discussed in our introduction, Mann links economic activity with the satisfaction of a particular need or function.

In reaction to numerous attempts to claim primacy for one particular function or need, Mann goes on to argue that no one source of power is generally predominant. Like Max Weber, before him, he rejects previous forms of reductionist theory, i.e. theories seeking to *reduce* social life to one prime mover – whether economic or cultural or whatever. For Mann, as for Weber no such general overarching theory has proved adequate to deal with the complexity of social life. He therefore prefers a multi-causal approach since any or all of the multiple source of power are capable of being socially effective at any one point in time. The four sources of power are thus irreducible to one common denominator that stands above them all.

This type of multi-functional, multi-causal approach to differentiation stands in marked contrast to earlier prime mover debates between materialists and idealists. As applied to the economy, in particular, it challenges the economic reductionist thrust implied in Marx's famous base–superstructure theory, in which causal primacy was assigned to the material or economic base, on which foundation the remainder of society, the political, religious and legal superstructure stood. It also stands in marked contrast to another type of economic reductionism entailed by economists' emphasis on self-interest as the foundation of social behaviour.

Functional differentiation is therefore a key aspect of the analysis of social differentiation, one that raises very profound issues for the theory of the economy and society, and especially for the analysis of causal relations between economy and the other parts of society. If some version of what we have called economic reductionism cannot be sustained, then it becomes very important to clarify just how economy and society interact, and in particular how extra-economic influences act to influence and change economic relationships. We shall return to a more detailed analysis of this problem in later chapters of this study.

A second aspect of the differentiation process involves *differentiation of cultural practices and perceptions.* There is a significant cultural difference, in particular between societies in which economic functions are embedded in wider social relations and those where economic functions are perceived as a clearly distinct aspect of social life, distinguishable from other aspects.

Wherever economies are embedded in wider social relationships, economic functions will be performed without any *strong* sense of the separability and distinctiveness of economic activity as such. Typically, such embedded economies depend, very largely, on the land – and in particular on hunting–gathering or agriculture. In such cases, economic functions are experienced as part of 'nature', and the natural and immutable order of things. In Aboriginal Australia, for example, this natural embeddedness is reflected in a special relationship with the land. Aboriginal people regard themselves as belonging to the land, rather than the land belonging to them. Land, in other words, is not conceived as part of an Aboriginal economy distinct from culture, religion and law. Land, on the contrary, is simultaneously a religious or spiritual source of identification, and a means to satisfy material wants.

It follows that where wholly embedded economies predominate, societies have yet to discover economic issues as a distinct aspect of human experience. Food, clothing and shelter remain important but they are not perceived as specifically economic problems. As a result, key modern ideas based on the differentiation of economy and society, such as economic growth or unemployment simply do not exist. Economic growth has no meaning to those whose cultural concerns are defined by the maintenance and integrity of religious and tribal tradition. Unemployment is an alien concept outside a system of labour markets, where access to work is dependent on the sale of labour-power or possession of capital. Exactly when the economy was discovered as a specific and autonomous aspect of social life is, however, a matter of some controversy. We shall pick up this historical issue later in this chapter.

Where economies are culturally perceived as differentiated from society, a keen awareness of the autonomy of the economy tends to arise, together with the existence of specifically economic issues and problems. One manifestation of this cultural pattern is the belief that those involved with the economy can in principle solve economic problems without the 'intervention' or 'interference' of those outside. What is entailed here is a strong sense of the capacity of economic systems to be self-regulating to a greater or lesser extent.

Another indicator of the perceived cultural differentiation of the economy from society is the view which sees economic life as an autonomous force for social change and shaper of human destinies – whether for better or worse. A classic statement of this viewpoint was provided in the middle of the nineteenth century in the observations of Marx and Engels on the differentiation of economic life from religion, the family and traditional forms of authority, honour and sentiment. In a much-quoted passage, Marx and Engels argue that

> The bourgeoisie, wherever it has got the upper hand has put an end to all feudal, patriarchal, idyllic relations. It has pitilessly torn asunder the motley feudal ties that bound man to his 'natural superiors', and has left remaining no other nexus between man and man than naked self-interest and cash payment. . . . It has [also] drowned the most heavenly ecstasies of religious fervour, of chivalrous enthusiasm, of philistine sentimentalism, in the icy waters of egoistical calculation . . . [and] . . . torn away from the family its sentimental veil . . . reducing the family relation to a mere money relation.
>
> (Marx and Engels 1962, p. 36)

This vision of cultural differentiation – shared by nineteenth-century conservatives and Romantics, as well as political radicals – is a powerful albeit pejorative interpretation of the negative features of cultural differentiation. It is to be contrasted with optimistic perceptions of the differentiation process as liberating or setting free expansive and beneficent economic forces from irrational, inefficient or despotic regulation.

This alternative, more optimistic scenario is not to be seen simply as a positive rational counter-myth to an essentially negative Romantic critique of capitalist civilisation. As Colin Campbell (1986) has recently pointed out, the differentiation of economy and society has generated positive as well as negative Romantic commentary. One example of a positive Romantic approach to differentiation is the idea of self-realisation through consumption. In this view, Romanticism in the form of dreams of individual fulfilment through purchase of consumer goods is as much a cultural dimension of the differentiation of economy and society as the spectre of a cold, calculating individualism.

A third dimension of the process of differentiation, of a more tangible kind, concerns the extension of *institutional differentiation*. A key development here is the increasing separation between personalised face-to-face institutions based on the kinship model, and impersonal institutions concerned essentially with the exchange of goods and services, and typified by market-based relations. In the latter case it is a matter of contingency rather than necessity whether the parties to exchange meet face-to-face, or whether they are known to each other. The sociologist, Ferdinand Toennies (1967) encapsulated the basis of this type of distinction in the twin concepts *Gemeinschaft* and *Gesellschaft*. Whereas *Gemeinschaft* referred to the 'natural' face-to-face communities of kinship, blood and closed villages, *Gesellschaft* referred to the secular individualistic and impersonal exchanges of a society of self-interested individuals. *Gesellschaft*, in German, doubles not only as a term for such a society, but also as a term for the public limited liability joint stock company.

A paramount mode of institutional differentiation is that between markets and money, on the one side, and personalised kinship relations on the other. While markets are compatible with many different types of economy, and may be embedded in forms of political or community control, their character and significance changes wherever market principles predominate. As differentiated institutions, markets serve merely as a means of impersonal exchange, and are thus unable to resolve problems of political order or cultural meaning. Markets serve rather to organise the exchange of commodities through the medium of money. A commodity is essentially a good or service which has a value in exchange, rather than an entity whose purpose is to cement social bonds or express the moral worth of its producer. Money, once measured in terms of physical objects with a use, such as sheep or shells, and more latterly with physical objects with an enduring value such as gold, has now increasingly become a purely abstract measure of exchange-value (Simmel

1978). Paper-currency has no intrinsic value, and bears no cultural messages about any potential bonds between its users, except for the obligation of money-issuers to redeem its face value.

Sketched out in its most general terms, the process of institutional differentiation involved profound changes in the organisation of human labour and its relationship to the household and division of labour between the sexes. The major process of differentiation here involved the separation of labour from a natural or subsistence relationship with the land, and the transformation of labour into a commodity. This shifted the context of labour from a face-to-face and personalised relationship, albeit an incredibly exploitative one, to an increasingly impersonalised one based on the labour market. In so doing it also shifted labour increasingly away from the household economy to separate places of paid employment or work. Whereas households once combined economic functions such as peasant farmwork or workshop production with social functions such as child socialisation and communal sociability, with institutional differentiation these processes became increasingly separated. This process is itself connected with a further aspect of differentiation between the sexes with males becoming primarily bread-winners and women home-makers.

Such processes of differentiation have, however, been immensely complex historical processes. In the first place, they have been and remain immensely dynamic. None of the patterns described here have proved immutable and all are constantly liable to further change including moves away from extreme forms of differentiation. Second, and following from this, such processes should not be seen as changes that happened overnight in some once-and-for-all short, sharp industrial revolution or Great Transformation. Hence the broad-sweep generalisations discussed here should not necessarily be confused with descriptions of the complexity of historical change. While this study is not primarily a work of history, we shall comment further on the dangers of not taking this complexity seriously later in this chapter.

Differentiation of social roles represents a fourth dimension of the differentiation process. On this dimension of differentiation we are concerned with distinctions between economic roles, such as occupations (teacher, bricklayer) or income-recipients (wage-earners, landlords), as distinct from other social roles such as those based on kinship (father, mother), or membership of a political, cultural organisation (citizen, voter, club secretary). Differentiation of social roles is clearly related to institutional differentiation because differentiated institutions supply the sets of positions available for individuals to fulfil.

One of the assumptions behind differentiation theory is that individuals gain multiple roles during the differentiation process. Whereas the denizens of embedded societies had an identity as tribal members defined in terms of kinship and perhaps area of residence, differentiation of roles has meant an increasing access, at least for some, to multiple affiliations such as father, worker, bricklayer, citizen and union official.

Nonetheless, differentiation does not necessarily mean that all members of society have tended to achieve multiple roles. Access depends very much on structures of power, and their degree of openness or closure towards particular groups. These considerations raise major concerns in the study of social stratification and social inequality, including gender relations, relations between ethnic groups and class relations (Parkin 1979; Crompton 1990).

The importance of power can be quickly appreciated if we try to imagine alternative combinations of multiple roles to the example of the male skilled worker given above. In terms of gender, for example, it is hard to conceive of a combination mother, housewife, worker, bricklayer, citizen and union official, except in cases of exceptional and heroic virtuosity, given various structural and cultural barriers to women as mothers and/or housewives taking up manual apprenticeships and representative positions in voluntary organisations. Indeed, the primary and differentiated relationship between public and work-centred roles for men, and domestic roles of women (e.g. housewife) persists through major segments of the social structure – even though increasing numbers of women have entered paid employment and higher education. We shall pick up such issues of power and differentiation again later in this study.

One further way of summing up the nature of the differentiation of economy from society is by means of a comparison between Polanyi's four types of economic exchange and integration. In Table 2.1 we compare key social relations within

Table 2.1 Differentiation of economy and society adapted from
Polanyi's concepts of economic exchange

Key relationship	Organisation within embedded economies	Organisation within differentiated economies
1 Economy and community	RECIPROCITY – economy embedded in intra-tribal relations focussed on community obligation. HOUSEHOLD – economy embedded in extended household community. REDISTRIBUTION – economy embedded in centralised political community.	MARKET – economy differentiated from the community through institutions such as private property and the market.
2 Economy and government	RECIPROCITY – economy embedded in governmental processes of the tribe enshrined in custom. HOUSEHOLD – economy embedded in governmental processes of the household based on patriarchy. REDISTRIBUTION – economy embedded in centralised political apparatus of states and empires constituted through geo-political control.	MARKET – economy differentiated from government through legal integrity of the individual and the corporation, and through freedom of market from political domination.
3 Economy and household	RECIPROCITY – both economy and household embedded in tribal community. HOUSEHOLD – the household is simultaneously the basic economic unit and the basic social institution. REDISTRIBUTION – both economy and household embedded in centralised political community.	MARKET – economy differentiated from the household in terms of separation of 'work' and 'home', 'employment' and 'leisure'.

the three embedded modes of economic exchange – reciprocity, household and redistribution – with the differentiated market mode of exchange.

Differentiation by function, cultural experience, institution or role represents four analytically distinct dimensions whereby the economy may be distinguished from the wider society.

Beyond this there is a further dimension to differentiation, namely *internal differentiation* within the economy. This process has many of the same kinds of elements, such as functional, institutional or role differentiation that we have observed in examining the differentiation between economy and society. In terms of functions, we may distinguish between key economic functions such as production and consumption or savings and investment. Alternatively, we may distinguish, as do Parsons and Smelser (see Chapter 1, pp. 20–1 above) between 'economic' (i.e. adaptive) features of the economy and those connected with political goal-setting or normative integration *within* the economy. Put another way, the economy has its own values, goals, power structures, norms and criteria of rationality, and is not merely constituted by the technical or organisational aspects of production and consumption or supply and demand.

Internal differentiation within the economy may also be applied to the institutional separation of finance and banking from manufacturing, and the separation of producers from consumers, or employers from employees. This type of differentiation is founded to a large degree on the existence of distinct and often competing interests, and the representation of interests in distinct institutions.

Finally, internal differentiation within the economy may be related to roles, through the development of an increasingly specialised division of labour. This relates not only to the structure of occupational roles which changes by expansion and contraction as technology, scale and economic conflicts or problems change, but also to the differentiation of property ownership roles from knowledge or competence based roles. The latter process is connected with the relative decline of owner-management and the family firm and the rise of managerial professionalism.

It is less difficult to outline the various dimensions of the differentiation process than to explain why differentiation has emerged. The most coherent type of explanation generally assumes some kind of evolutionary advantage for differentiated over non-differentiated systems (see for example Parsons 1964, 1966). The argument here is that differentiation permits the various social functions to be performed more adequately than where differentiation is absent. It is based on the advantages of specialisation. If society is differentiated in terms of functions, institutions and roles this permits each segment to concentrate on a specific set of objectives, thereby reducing complexity.

Applied to the economy, the argument states that differentiation of economy from society permits the better identification and realisation of economic goals such as greater efficiency and economic growth. This argument is usually connected with the further proposition that the differentiation of the market from political and social regulation permits a greater degree of economic efficiency, in terms of the production of commodities. Within modernisation theory, which became prominent in the USA in the 1950s and 1960s, it was assumed that markets were the most efficient means of delivering goods and services, and democratic political systems the best means of achieving participation and equality of opportunity (Lipset 1963; Parsons 1964, 1971). This argument located the major advances in achieving social differentiation of this kind within Western liberal democracies such as the USA.

This argument has a good deal of plausibility, especially in the light of the recent collapse of state socialist economic planning in Russia and Eastern Europe. While socialist societies of this type have attempted to embed these economies within a centralised political system aiming at public planning and social justice simultaneously with economic efficiency, their record in achieving such goals has not been good. Writing of the Soviet Union, David Lane (1985) points out that although the Soviet system succeeded in creating a low wage, full employment economy able to achieve economic growth over a long period, it failed to match Western levels of productivity growth, and failed to deliver high-quality consumer goods. Although part of this record might be explained by the lower stage of development of the Soviet as compared with Western economies, it is also clear that state socialist planning of the Soviet type has not proved a robust economic alternative to the market, as a means of generating high productivity economies responsive to consumer demand.

In spite of the plausibility of modernisation theory as applied to the differentiation of the market from the polity and culture, it should also be pointed out that the differentiation process has brought with it many serious problems. The foremost of these, as recognised by Marx and the classical sociologists such as Durkheim (1933) is the problem of integration. This problem may be put as follows, 'how can societies differentiated into different parts or segments hold together?' What will provide the new social cement, once economic life is freed from the integrative controls of tribal culture, religion and community?

Against the argument that social differentiation arose because it created an evolutionary advantage for societies in which markets were set free, writers like Marx and Durkheim, together with more recent analysts such as Polanyi, emphasised the problems, conflicts and crises associated with differentiation. In particular, they emphasise opposition to the growing predominance of institutions such as the market, especially in relation to the transformation of labour-power into a commodity, and the promotion of competitive and possessive individualism over community? Socialism – whether in Western European, Eastern European or Third World variations – emerged precisely as one response to the problems created by differentiation, and to the demands for a new means of social integration. In one sense, it could be said that socialism emerged as a means to save capitalism from the excessive differentiation of economy from society characteristic of market-based individualism and competition.

Marxists have typically argued that capitalist market institutions founded on private ownership of economic resources cannot solve the problem of integration. They have, however, been divided over the possibility that socialism might prove more economically dynamic if combined with markets, to form some kind of market socialism. Those Marxists who have promoted market socialism are in effect accepting a certain limited form of social differentiation between markets and society, as compared with those who wished to restore an embedded economy within a new integrated form of socialist political community. Since market socialism has itself failed in Eastern Europe however, some further credibility has been given to the argument that markets are more likely to provide an optimal solution to the performance of economic functions.

Nonetheless, this judgement has to be qualified by the point that markets do not necessarily operate in this efficient way. Markets may be inefficient in promoting productivity, they may also fail, creating economic depression. Beyond this, markets do not solve other social problems such as the achievement of legitimate government or of cultural meaning. As a result it is arguable that the differentiation of markets from society only confers an evolutionary advantage for societies if other forms of political and cultural differentiation are developed to solve wider problems of political authority and social integration. Put another way, economic efficiency is a great help to societies and may temporarily allow the buying off of discontent. It does not, however, guarantee political order or social peace over the long term. This was reflected in the explosion of political discontent in the mid-1960s in the USA, even at the height of the post-war boom.

The implication of this argument is that it is not differentiation *per se* that confers an evolutionary advantage. Indeed, differentiation may be a process fraught with conflict and disorder (Eisenstadt 1964; Alexander 1985). We may speak of modes of excessive or alienating differentiation, for example, wherever market autonomy creates economic crisis or social collapse. Evolutionary advantages may, on the other hand, accrue to societies which develop a pattern of differentiated institutions which simultaneously address economic, political and cultural functions. The mistakes of modernisation theory were two-fold. The first was to see differentiation as a relatively smooth evolutionary process. The second was to assume there was only one such pattern, that represented by post-war America, and the American combination of a market economy, political democracy and the rule of law.

Subsequent developments between 1960–90, indicate the viability of alternative patterns of differentiation, such as Scandinavian welfare capitalism (Stephens 1979; Korpi 1983; Esping-Andersen 1990). These typically involve higher levels of decommodification and political regulation of markets than is found in the USA. To some analysts they represent a modified version of the socialist project insofar as they remove significant elements of social life from the unilateral regulation of market forces.

We shall return to these contemporary issues and debates over the future of capitalism, socialism and democracy later in this study. For the moment, we may sum up the answer to the question 'Why differentiation of economy and society?' in the following set of propositions:

1 There are no net evolutionary advantages conveyed by differentiation as such, since the problems created may well exceed the benefits as judged by members of societies undergoing differentiation.
2 Some net advantage in terms of economic efficiency is associated with the differentiation of markets from society, but this advantage is not inevitable or automatic.
3 The advantages of differentiation of markets from society are generally only evident where excessive economic differentiation is avoided, and when political and/or cultural institutions and social movements emerge to address the problem of social integration.
4 There are therefore advantages to 'balanced' versions of differentiation where markets have a regulated autonomy from the remainder of society, but there is no one successful pattern by which such a balance may be achieved.

KARL POLANYI AND THE HISTORICAL DEVELOPMENT OF EMBEDDED AND DIFFERENTIATED ECONOMIES

The analysis of social differentiation of the economy and society is further complicated when we try to connect this overarching theory with actual processes of historical change. This problem of the historical development of differentiation has recently become a matter of acute controversy between the influential economic anthropology of Karl Polanyi and economists seeking to apply rational choice theory to a range of non-market institutions across history.

Polanyi's argument, as already indicated, is founded on the presumption that for most of human history economies have been embedded in, rather than differentiated from, the wider society.

It was not therefore until the Great Transformation process in late eighteenth- and nineteenth-century Europe that the economy really emerged as an autonomous element in the social structure, through the transformation of land and labour into commodities, linked with price-setting markets (Polanyi 1944).

Prior to that time, according to Polanyi, markets and commodification were never dominant social institutions. They were either absent, as in tribal societies based on reciprocity, or subordinated to political and administrative control as in the ancient empires of the Near East and Mediterranean. At such times, regulated markets existed in special enclaves controlled by political authorities, described as 'ports of trade' literally outside the gates of cities or in special sections or quarters (Pirenne 1925; Arnold 1957). Such markets, however, did not permit flexible price-setting capable of regulating patterns of supply and demand.

Two particular features of Polanyi's argument are noteworthy. First, there is an assumption of *discontinuity* between embedded economies (based either on reciprocity, redistribution or the household) and differentiated economies based on markets. Polanyi stresses, time and again, that the idea of self-regulating market transactions between private individuals is both a new and a very threatening proposition originating in the eighteenth and nineteenth centuries and not before. A second feature in Polanyi's argument is the *transitory* nature of differentiated and self-regulating market economies.

Although *laissez-faire* economies (literally meaning 'let private individuals do what they wish') and free markets had become powerful influences on economic affairs by the mid-nineteenth century, Polanyi maintained that they could not function successfully as completely self-sufficient institutions, free from political or cultural regulation. In the social legislation on working conditions enacted in nineteenth-century Britain, and even more in the twentieth-century welfare states he detected an equally powerful counter-trend to integrate the economy once more under wider social controls. Free markets and self-sufficient economies, therefore, are seen as transitory institutions, sandwiched, so to speak, between a long historical phase of economic embeddedness, and a recent historical phase of reintegration of economic into social arrangements once more.

This argument stressing the discontinuous and historically peculiar nature of market or capitalist economies has become influential throughout sociological and anthropological thought, including Marxist scholarship. The argument that market capitalism is not the inexorable fate of human society is also of course encouraging to political opponents of such systems, again testifying to the political relevance of theories of economy and society. And yet for all this, most economists and a minority of sociologists remain unconvinced, claiming that Polanyi's entire historical argument is misconceived.

Economists have found it necessary to tackle non-market economic systems for a number of reasons, most notably the contemporary challenges of economic under-development in Third World countries, and the robustness – at least until recently – of state socialist economies in many parts of the globe. The challenge for economists was to explain how non-market based systems actually worked. This problem tended to reduce to two sub-problems, namely 'How do peasant economies operate in the context of village and communal institutions?' and second 'How do states allocate and distribute resources in situations where a market is lacking?' These questions can of course be applied both in the contemporary setting and historically.

The reply to Polanyi and to other proponents of the embeddedness theory of economy and society is founded on the claim that the *discontinuity* and *transitoriness* theses simply do not stand up to systematic analysis. What is being claimed is first that there are plenty of examples of much earlier forms of economic differentiation than Polanyi accepts. This implies that differentiation is age-old rather than recent and transitory. A second even more powerful theoretical claim is that actual economic behaviour in non-market contexts can be explained with recourse to certain key concepts originally developed to apply to market economies. These include the concepts of rational choice, individualism and self-interest.

POLANYI: A HISTORICAL CRITIQUE

Polanyi's discontinuity thesis is one example of a more general approach which contrasts the shape of society before and after a fundamental transformation, whether this be thought of as the

Industrial Revolution, the take-off into self-sustained economic growth (Rostow 1960) or, as in Polanyi's case, a process actually called the Great Transformation. This type of reasoning, in which the key transformation phase is seen as a matter of decades rather than centuries has not stood up well to recent research in economic history and historical sociology.

The historical problem with Polanyi's account is that he underestimates the extent of social differentiation of economy and society before the eighteenth and nineteenth centuries. There is, of course, a considerable weight of empirical research by Polanyi and his associates in areas such as ancient Babylon (Polanyi 1957), ancient Mesopotamia (Oppenheim 1957), the African kingdom of Dahomey (Arnold 1957) and the Aztec and Mayan civilisations (Chapman 1957). It is certainly true that this body of work recognises limited instances of social differentiation prior to the Great Transformation. Of foremost importance here is the emergence of states as political entities gradually differentiated from tribal communities. Nonetheless, this example deals more with the differentiation of political and military power from the wider society, rather than the differentiation of economy and society.

Polanyi identifies the appearance of markets as late as seventh-century BC Greece, more especially with the commercial *agora* (or market place) of Athens. The *agora* represented the decline of reciprocity, and a rival to the self-sufficient household (*oikos*). However, Polanyi warns against exaggerating its autonomy, viewing it as fundamentally embedded with the redistributive *polis* of the city-state. Indeed, Athens is depicted as a '*polis* economy' (Polanyi 1977, p. 166).

From the ancient to the medieval period, Polanyi maintains that a profound continuity existed in the relations between economy and society. Thus up to the end of the Middle Ages (conventionally dated in the fifteenth century) 'markets played no important part in the economic system; other institutional patterns prevailed' (Polanyi 1944, p. 55). And although the volume of market transactions increased between the sixteenth and nineteenth centuries, Polanyi claims that market regulation increased rather than lessened until 'the sudden change-over to an utterly new type of economy in the nineteenth century' (1944, p. 55).

It may fairly be said that the focus of all this endeavour was not actually geared to emphasise historic aspects of social differentiation. The concern was rather to demonstrate the socially embedded character of economic relationships. Polanyi's assumption was that if cases of embeddedness could be demonstrated, then differentiation was either absent or extremely limited.

The empirical plausibility of Polanyi's economic anthropology is stronger for the earlier period of the ancient world than for the medieval and early modern period which neither he nor his immediate associates studied in any depth. Even for the ancient period, however, the argument about embeddedness and limited differentiation has been challenged, notably by Silver (1983) in a synthesis of recent research findings. There are a number of major gaps in the data on the ancient civilisations, and what data exists is often hard to interpret. Nonetheless, Silver assembled considerable evidence of autonomous markets with fluctuating prices, and limits to political regulation from both Middle Eastern and Mediterranean civilisations. In such cases the problem of securing social integration and social solidarity did not universally inhibit market autonomy or the search for private economic advantage. Periods of pervasive regulation were often interspersed with periods of relative freedom. In other words, the economy was neither totally embedded nor highly differentiated.

More systematic attempts to challenge Polanyi's embeddedness thesis have been attempted for late medieval Europe, notably by Douglas North and colleagues in the analysis of serfdom and manorialism (North and Thomas 1973; North 1977).

In some instances this reaction has gone too far in portraying highly differentiated institutions based on economic individualism and voluntary contract within the late medieval world of serfdom. North and Thomas' (1973) portrayal of serfdom as a 'contractual arrangement where labour services were exchanged for the public good of protection and justice' has been rightly criticised for abstracting serfdom out of its political and cultural context. Fenoaltea (1975) has pointed out that serfs did not necessarily receive protection from lords as part of a supposed contractual deal. Often the opposite was the case as serfdom operated as a form of extortion in which serfs were either obliged to work for lords, or required to flee elsewhere at the risk of entering equally servile conditions. The enthusiasm with which serfs attempted to liberate themselves by force of arms on many occasions belies any benign picture of a voluntary contract, and speaks instead of a culture of resistance.

This example indicates over-enthusiasm in depicting a highly differentiated set of economic relationships in a context in which serfdom still involved a significant degree of embeddedness in political regulation. This is not, however, to deny elements of individualism or market autonomy, especially where lords and serfs could come to voluntary agreement, as they often could, for example in buying themselves out of serfdom to become rent-paying farmers. While servile forms of political regulation could be overcome, so too could customary limitations on private initiative and self-interest.

More successful attempts to undermine Polanyi's embeddedness model have depended on a more careful and muted analysis of peasant economies in late medieval and early modern Europe. Until quite recently peasant economies have been conceived as a moral economy (Thompson 1971; Scott 1976), based on the primacy of values such as community cohesion and mutual aid. While Polanyi himself wrote more about the ancient empires or city-states than the peasantry, this type of analysis is very much in the spirit of his theory of embeddedness. And as far as social change is concerned the moral economy view, like Polanyi's own approach, emphasises change only through discontinuity. This is because peasant society is regarded as being unable to generate change from within in a gradual piecemeal fashion. The transformation of peasant-based societies into modern societies is therefore conceived of as a traumatic clash of two different worlds.

This whole approach has been challenged in a number of studies. The English historical sociologist Alan Macfarlane (1978), for example, has demonstrated the existence of significantly differentiated peasant societies in medieval England. These are characterised by high levels of private rather than exclusively communal relationships, and by market responsiveness. The peasant community is, therefore, an attenuated phenomena or, put another way, the phenomenon of unitary embeddedness has been overtaken but not obliterated by the advance of differentiation by private household.

41

While Macfarlane tends to regard this research as evidence of a peculiarly precocious 'English' phenomenon of individualism, linked to the inheritance of Germanic peasant life, other scholars writing in different contexts have come up with similar criticisms of the peasant moral economy or embeddedness approach. Some like Samuel Popkin's work on the Vietnamese peasantry (1979), argues that 'far more attention must be paid to motivations for personal gain among the peasantry', and that peasant communities are typically fractured by conflicts between individual or household interests and the group. Here again a high degree of differentiation is found, while relatively limited forms of embeddedness still remain.

At the most general level, therefore, Polanyi's theory of economic embeddedness prior to the Great Transformation is liable to historical critique simply because it does underplay the gradual process of differentiation of economy and society over the course of history. To portray this process as gradual should not be taken to imply that it was an inexorable or inevitable process of change in one direction – year by year or region by region. To claim this is to smooth out the complexities, the ebbs and flows, the rapid expansion and crisis or depression patterns, the wars and migrations of pre-eighteenth-century world history. Change may not happen at all, or it may falter and collapse. And if it does happen it may involve very different causal agents and lead in different directions. As Barrington Moore (1966) points out, British, French, German, Russian, Japanese and Chinese processes of industrialisation and modernisation have taken remarkably different forms. Some were stimulated centrally from above and others in a decentralised manner from below. Some led to differentiated democracies and market systems, others to totalitarian dictatorships and command economies.

If we do speak of continuity and gradual change as much as radical discontinuity, this brings into sharper focus the long and complex processes of institutional and role differentiation associated with the long historical trajectory of differentiation. To take, as one example, the history of trade and trading organisation, there is far more to be said about this than is implied in Polanyi's emphasis on the embedded character of markets prior to the Great Transformation. While Polanyi focusses almost exclusively on the fact that markets prior to the

Great Transformation tended to be regulated and lacking in flexibility, he fails to point out just how far trading organisation had become differentiated from the community prior to the modern epoch. As Max Weber (1924, 1927) realised, the differentiation of trading business from the household and the development of autonomous trading law and new accounting and contractual arrangements had already gone a long way in Europe by the fifteenth and sixteenth centuries. Abu-Lughod (1989) has traced a number of parallel developments in Asian and Middle-Eastern economies of the same period.

Polanyi's theory of economic embeddedness is liable not only to historical criticism of this kind, but also to theoretical challenge. The foremost challenge to date has come from economists and other social scientists who believe, as already indicated, that non-market economies, including that of the peasant village or the ancient empires, are subject to the same analytical rational choice framework as the market. It is claimed, in other words, that economies have *always* been differentiated to a significant extent in the sense that individuals and organisations seek to maximise their private as against some community advantage. Even where collective action is undertaken, this school of thought sees ways of interpreting it as the result of prior individual or private calculation. For example, collective action by communities may arise if it is the only effective way of enforcing compliance on individuals who refuse to accept the rules of the game which the majority of individuals accept. This applies especially to collective goods such as common land or community defence which require co-operation and fiscal support. Here community norms and sanctions to secure co-operation are typically interpreted by adherents of this approach as ways of solving the so-called free-rider problem. By this is meant the problem of individuals getting the benefit of collective goods without co-operating or sharing the burdens with others.

We thus have a situation in which Polanyi is, so to speak, turned on his head. Whereas the theory of embeddedness sees individual self-interest and the differentiation of economy and society as a peculiar, historically atypical social institution, the rational choice theorists take the differentiation of private self-interested individuals from society and community as a basic feature of social life whether in the past or the present. We shall

43

consider the theoretical structure and assumptions of rational choice theory in more detail in Chapter 4.

Two major and related points need to be emphasised in the evaluation of Polanyi. The first is that Polanyi and his associates have over-exaggerated the scale of embeddedness and under-played the extent of differentiation between economy and society prior to the Great Transformation. The research evidence to this effect is compelling. Various forms of differentiation are evident well before the eighteenth and nineteenth centuries, and the process of change, therefore, is not to be associated with some kind of cataclysmic 'Great Transformation'.

In the second place, however, there are good grounds for believing that many opponents of Polanyi have grossly exaggerated the predominance of economic differentiation, self-interest and private advantage prior to the modern epoch. This exaggeration has arisen because individualism and private self-interest have often been *assumed* as methodological principles rather than demonstrated in each case as social institutions which exist. The procedure all too often has been to work out how it would be logical for individuals to act, if they were motivated by self-interest and cost–benefit calculation, and then to see if the historical outcomes match the hypothesised behaviour.

It is of course interesting when this type of match occurs, and, in such cases, there is certainly prima facie evidence of the *plausibility* of the approach. However explanations, where based on such procedures, are neither exhaustive nor conclusive. There is no privilege for economistic explanations over other potential explanations, even where a prima facie plausibility is demonstrated. Other possibilities must be considered, including the possibility that community norms exist and are supported for cultural and expressive reasons as much as calculative instrumental ones. Unless this stage of analysis is included, the 'logic of the rational choice' approach is methodologically flawed because it fails to provide an account that engages with the meaning of action for the participants concerned.

CONCLUSIONS

The conclusion reached here is very similar to that reached by Mark Granovetter (1985) in an important paper on the problem of embeddedness. Granovetter's position is that both Polanyi and the rational choice advocates are in error. Whereas Polanyi exaggerates the level of embeddedness in non-market or pre-Great Transformation societies, the rational choice theorists under-estimate the importance of embeddedness in such contexts. They do this, I would add, by simply ignoring the problem.

It follows from this that embeddedness and differentiation are not to be regarded as mutually exclusive options. Any notion that embedded economies are essentially dominated by cultural forces, while differentiated ones are dominated by economic forces, is also rejected. The alternative proposed here is that embeddedness and differentiation are omni-present features of most if not all societies – even though the scale of each may vary. This proposition may be linked in a more theoretical way with a model of a simple two-dimensional society, faced with two functional exigencies namely differentiation and integration. The first seeks to provide the advantages of specialization and a division of labour, while the second tries to achieve coherence and cohesion.

Another implication of this argument is that we do not need to deploy discontinuous notions of a Great Transformation or Industrial Revolution to understand social change and world history. Even if the recent pace of change has increased, and even if the extent of differentiation has increased too, especially in nineteenth-century Britain, this need not amount to a 'big-bang' theory of social transformation. The argument is that differentiation and embeddedness or integration have continued to coexist alongside each other in complex configurations right through the last few thousand years of human history. This has been obscured, however, by the two powerful myths. The first is Polanyi's myth of the loss of embeddedness and the challenge of differentiation. The second is the rational choice myth of Economic Man bent on individual acquisition, and the evasion, where possible, of social control. For many social scientists it seems that these myths function as secularised deities, prowling around theoretical and historical scholarship. Neither myth approximates very closely to reality in any general trans-contextual sense, though each may prove fruitful ways of understanding particular case-studies.

45

In order to pursue the argument of the co-existence of embeddedness (integration) and differentiation further, this approach requires evaluation against the record of economic activity in the modern world. Just because it can be applied to historical record, this does not mean that it continues to apply today. There are indeed many who see the modern epoch in terms of the triumph of excessive differentiation over the coherent integration of economy and society.

Having established the crucial importance of a historical dimension to the theory of economy and society in this chapter, we now turn to a more contemporary analysis in the remainder of the study. This proceeds by way of the identification of three major theoretical traditions in the analysis of economy and society, namely economic liberalism, political economy and economic sociology.

Part II

INTRODUCTION

What are the main theories of economic life and the relationship between economy and society? Not surprisingly this is a very difficult question to answer. There are many varied contributions to this topic, ranged, as we have already noted in the past two chapters, across a number of intellectual disciplines. While some contributions are oriented quite explicitly to some general theory of economy and society, others focus on delimited middle-range theories, often pursued through detailed case-studies. Analytical literature on economic life has often been quite pragmatic or eclectic in its theoretical orientation. This is especially true of the diffuse approach known as institutionalism, whose proponents have included scholars such as J.R. Commons and J.K. Galbraith. In work of this kind the primary focus is on establishing how institutions such as governments or trade unions actually work in constituting economic relations, with little overt attention to grand theory.

There is in fact no consensus as to the best way of proceeding, and many analysts deliberately ignore general theory-building exercises, seeing them as irresolvable and thus fruitless exercises in intellectual vanity. An alternative procedure is to discern the theoretical bearing of case-study material in a more cautious manner, alert to contextual variation and complexity.

Within the complex mass of research and analytical literature bearing on economic life and the relations between economy and society, certain recurrent theoretical frameworks are nonetheless evident. As a first approximation three major frameworks of this kind are identified, namely economic liberalism, political economy and economic sociology.

Since these three frameworks tend to recur in one shape or form over time, they may be usefully regarded as theoretical *traditions*. By a theoretical tradition is meant a set of intellectual assumptions, key questions and fundamental concepts which generate a common set of reference points for social analysis over an extended period of time. It is not necessary for exponents of the same tradition to agree in all respects with each other, but it is necessary that the core elements of the tradition be shared, and reproduced across several generations of scholarship. Over time, such traditions may be followed not so much because of any intrinsic explanatory superiority, but because they are inherited from the past and are reinforced by organisational power. Nonetheless, as Alexander and Colomy (1990) point out, these considerations do not mitigate the rational aspirations of social science . . . .

The bare outlines of the three traditions are provided in Table 3.1. What is contained here is a sketch of the key points of reference which define the traditions involved. Each tradition is historically robust in the sense that its core components have been articulated in differing ways across the last two hundred years of intellectual scholarship. Each tradition has, in some sense, stood the test of time.

As first approximations, the traditions are regarded as different general options for theorising the nature of economic life and the relationship between economy and society. At this stage it remains an open question as to how far the traditions are mutually incompatible with each other, and how far they may be combined together in the process of analysis. A similarly open question involves the possibility of individual theorists combining elements from more than one tradition. It would be surprising if a significant component of synthesis were not present, since much theorising takes as its starting-point the strengths and weaknesses of previous approaches. Notwithstanding complexities of this kind I want to foreshadow a more specific argument to be advanced in the next three chapters of this study concerning the explanatory power of the three traditions. The argument is that economic liberalism and political economy represent insightful yet incomplete accounts of economic life, while economic sociology represents a new synthesis capable of redressing these problems in a more comprehensive

Table 3.1 Three traditions in the theory of economy and society

Economic liberalism	*Political economy*	*Economic sociology*
Basic focus		
Private economic interests and market freedom	Power relations in economic life	Markets, power and culture
Prominent individuals and movements		
Adam Smith	Ricardo and Marx	The Scottish
Neo-classical economics	Class theory	Enlightenment
	World-system theory	Weber and
Milton Friedman	Labour-process theory	Durkheim
Public choice theory		Parsons
		Polanyi (economic anthropology)
		Habermas
Some key concepts		
Individual sovereignty	Mode of production	Modes of social integration of economy and society
Self-interest	Social relations of production and exchange	
Rationality		
The self-regulating market	Property rights	Embeddedness and differentiation
	Capitalism	
	Commodification an decommodification	Rationalisation

way. Put another way while economic liberalism and political economy are dealing respectively with market freedom and power relations, and offer one-dimensional insights, economic sociology offers a multi-dimensional synthesis of markets, power and culture. This synthesis draws on the insights of the other two, but extends and augments these insights within a wider set of theoretical perspectives.

This argument is merely foreshadowed at this point. It will now be elaborated in more depth.

3

ECONOMIC LIBERALISM AND THE THEORY OF THE MARKET

Economic liberalism represents one of the most enduring traditions seeking to explain the nature and dynamics of economic life. Its roots lie in European liberalism which developed in the seventeenth and eighteenth centuries as a social and political movement, critical of institutions such as the absolute monarchy, feudalism, aristocratic privilege and religious faith. Liberalism took as its major political and intellectual premise the sovereignty of the individual. The argument was that individuals had the capacity to reason and were therefore best able to express and pursue their own interests without the intervention of absolute monarchs, aristocrats or priests. The goal of liberalism was a society of autonomous, free-standing individuals, able to make free and rational choices according to their personal dispositions and conscience.

Liberalism as a historical movement, therefore, was associated with a range of social issues. These included the increased democratisation of political institutions (through developments such as constitutional monarchism or republicanism), expansion of freedom of thought and worship (including challenges to censorship, and tolerance for religious minorities), the expansion of educational and scientific institutions through which reason might become more highly developed, and a challenge to economic regulation by state and community in the name of economic individualism and market freedom.

Such issues surfaced in a range of momentous political events, such as the English Revolution of the mid-seventeenth century, and the French Revolution beginning in 1789, as well as in a range of less spectacular social and political initiatives such as the movements for free trade or the abolition of slavery. Needless to say, the broad goals of liberalism were only imperfectly realised, even in the nineteenth century, given the continued vitality of political conservatism, and a tension within liberalism between a perceived need for radical social change on the one hand, and a perceived need for political order and stability on the other. Liberalism found itself challenged not only by political conservatism from above, but also by popular radicalism and socialism from below.

What started out as a movement aiming at greater liberty, freedom and democracy had, by the end of the nineteenth century, no exclusive monopoly on these values. Liberalism at times found it expedient to compromise with conservatism and traditionalism, rather than remaining constantly at the head of movements aiming at radical social change.

Liberals also varied in the comprehensiveness of their liberalism, focussing on some areas and neglecting others. This is evident in the discussion of women in society. While liberalism provided a pioneering opportunity for the application of the principles of individual sovereignty and the capacity for reason to women as well as men, only a minority of liberals were to take this universalistic step prior to the twentieth-century development of liberal feminism.

It is within this general historical context that the intellectual characteristics of economic liberalism can be most faithfully understood. Two major points require emphasis here. The first is that economic liberalism emerged as one part of a more general development of liberalism. It was not therefore simply a movement concerned with narrowly circumscribed economic issues. The second is that the political implications of liberalism were ambivalent – radical in the face of absolutism, aristocratic privilege and religious tradition, conservative in the face of socialism.

This study is not primarily a history of ideas about the economy. Hence the discussions of the three major traditions will not be organised in a chronological manner, but will focus on major themes of theoretical significance. In the case of economic liberalism for example, as the first of the major traditions to be analysed, the focus will not be on the development of ideas from pioneers such as Adam Smith through major theorists such as Alfred Marshall to modern exponents such as Milton Friedman.

A chronological focus is available elsewhere in key works such as those of Schumpeter (1954) or Clarke (1982). The alternative thematic approach, while mindful of the broader historical context of the development of liberalism, is concerned primarily with core concepts and key ideas shared to a greater or lesser extent by theorists working within the liberal tradition.

Another preliminary point requiring emphasis, is that each of the three traditions, economic liberalism included, is by no means homogeneous. While we may speak of core components, equally it has to be recognised that certain internal variations are evident within this broad framework. It is also apparent that certain key theorists may span different traditions; they cannot be neatly categorised in one or other theoretical box. Attention will be drawn to such complexities where relevant.

THE CORE COMPONENTS OF ECONOMIC LIBERALISM

The core components of economic liberalism as outlined here, represent an amalgam of ideas taken from a range of sources. These include the eighteenth-century theorist Adam Smith, the neo-classical school of economic thought which emerged in the late nineteenth and early twentieth century, and more recent post-war theorists such as Milton Friedman of the Chicago school of economics.

The key concepts of this tradition include the following:

Individual sovereignty
Self-interest
Rationality
Private property rights
Self-regulating market
Spontaneous order

Individual sovereignty

Economic liberalism draws from the general stock of liberal ideas an emphasis on the sovereignty of the individual. This entails the proposition that the individual is the final arbiter of decisions or choices about individual welfare and the actions required to achieve it. The proposition is both moral and sociological, in the sense that liberals believe both that individuals *ought* to be free to make their own choices, and that individuals in the real world have progressively secured a freedom of action to act in a sovereign manner once reserved for kings and powerful elites.

Propositions about individual sovereignty are not simply moral or sociological, however, since economic liberals usually take it as axiomatic that the capacity to exercise individual sovereignty is part of human nature. Economic liberalism does not first conduct a survey to determine if individuals are in fact exercising sovereign choices over their lives. Rather they presume that this is how people will and do act, unless coerced or restrained by some other force. Thus they believe that it is 'natural' to be a sovereign individual, but arbitrary to act in some other manner. If some external body such as the government or the community exercises an all-embracing sovereignty over individuals then this is regarded as interference with human nature, unnatural, and thus interference with human liberty. We may sum this discussion up by saying that economic liberalism starts out from an abstract concept of what individuals are like, rather than observation of what they are actually like. This concept treats the individual as pre-social, in the sense that the capacity for individual sovereignty is inscribed in the individual in a natural state, prior to any involvement with other individuals in human society. This construction of the pre-social individual is to be founded in Adam Smith's reference to the capacity of individuals 'to truck, barter and exchange', in order to realise their individual objectives.

Another way of describing this concept of a world of individuals with pre-socially formed characteristics is through the notion of *atomism*. Individuals represent self-contained atoms, whose objectives and strategies for action are formed without any necessary interaction with others. Needless to say this approach has been subjected to many criticisms for the lack of reality of its atomistic picture of human affairs. We shall review these criticisms below. For the moment it is important to note that many recent adherents to the tradition of economic liberalism have abandoned a strictly atomistic approach by acknowledging that the setting of individual objectives and decisions about strategies of action does impact on others. In particular, a number of writers in this tradition have had recourse to game

55

theory to analyse the actions of individuals in group settings (Hilderbrand and Kirman 1976; M. Friedman 1977).

Self-interest

The concept of individual sovereignty in liberal economics is closely linked with the concept of self-interest. The argument here is that the pre-social individual is not only equipped with capacity to exercise individual sovereignty, but is also motivated to do so by self-interest. Prior to interaction with others, individuals articulate a sense of their own objectives and a commitment to secure those objectives as best they can. Their interests in so doing are therefore peculiar to themselves. These are typically regarded by economists as 'tastes', that is dispositions or preferences analogous to the natural peculiarly personal requirements of the biological organism for specific types of food. In the economic sphere, therefore, just as individuals may have tastes for whisky rather than wine, so also may they have tastes for hiring men rather than women, or whites rather than blacks. For those economists who reason in this way, tastes involved are believed to be of the same order. The taste for alcohol is in no sense different from the taste for discrimination.

There remains great controversy, however, as to the place of self-interest in the total pattern of motivation affecting individuals. Are economic liberals claiming that self-interest is merely one of several aspects of human motivation? Can self-interest be accompanied by and mollified by altruism, or is altruism a form of self-interest, so to speak, a taste for moral behaviour? Or is self-interest an analytical assumption rather than a generalisation about actual individuals – an assumption which takes the form 'Insofar as individuals behave purely from self-interest, this is how they would behave in this situation?' Such an assumption can be seen as a yardstick against which to measure the extent to which self-interest is actually present in any particular case. We shall pursue these questions below when we come to evaluate the core assumptions of economic liberalism.

Rationality

Another component of the liberal approach concerns self-knowledge. Only individuals are in a position to know best what their interests really are, since such interests are generated within the pre-social self rather than in interaction with others. This doesn't mean that individuals never make mistakes or change their minds on the basis of experience. However it is typically associated with a further component of the liberal world-view, namely the assumption of individual rationality.

There is a considerable literature on the meaning and analytical usefulness of the notion of rationality. (See for example Weber 1978; Harrison 1979; Simon 1982; Brubaker 1984; Habermas 1984; Hindess 1988.) Analysts have used rationality in many different and often contrasting senses. To act 'rationally' may sometimes refer to actions that are technically effective in securing actors' self-interested objectives given the choices open to them. Typical examples are as follows: 'Given an increasing price for oil, it is only rational for consumers to look for a cheaper source of energy' or alternatively 'Given a decreasing price for oil, it is only rational for producers to delay the costly search for new oilfields until prices revive.'

To act 'rationally', may by contrast, simply mean that actors can give a plausible reason why they acted as they did, whether this involves technical efficiency or some quite different consideration. Typical examples are as follows: 'Given commitment to an ecologically responsible use of energy, it is only rational to invest in pollution-free sources of energy such as solar or wind power', or alternatively 'Given that her family for three generations used gas for cooking and heating, it is only rational that she wants gas installed in her new house.' Whereas the first set of examples associates rationality with technically efficient solutions to questions of how best to secure self-interest, the second set of examples associates rationality respectively with environmental values and with tradition.

In the case of economic liberalism, rationality is defined in terms of the former rather than the latter. In other words, it is rational to seek the best deal measured in terms of the balance of benefits over costs. From this viewpoint it is rational to buy cheap and sell dear because this maximises profits and incomes. It is quite irrational to buy dear and sell cheap, or to let other considerations of values, emotions or customs to enter into the calculation. Economic liberalism is therefore committed to an instrumental view of rationality, where rational action is regarded as a characteristic of the way we choose means to reach a given end. Values or emotions in this respect are not in themselves rational. This position contrasts with the sociological discussion of rationality by Max Weber (1978), in which no privilege is given to instrumental rationality as being any more rational than value rationality or custom-based rationality. For Weber, actions can only be said to be rational with reference to a particular standpoint. The search for efficient cost–benefit solutions is only one possible standpoint.

The instrumental way of deploying the term 'rationality' looks, at first sight, to be scientific rather than moral. This appearance is deceptive, however, because technical or instrumental rationality may become an end in itself. Hollis (1979) has pointed out that economic liberals typically smuggle into their analyses the assumption that what the rational person would do in any set of circumstances, the ordinary person *should* do. In other words it is not merely efficient to be rational, but desirable too. And this leads to the further proposition that it is undesirable to be irrational, in the sense of rejecting or giving a low priority to technical efficiency. Opponents of this type of calculative rationality may then be branded as 'irrational' simply because their values differ. This pejorative sense of the term 'irrational' is nonetheless typically used as if it were a clear-cut scientific term without moral overtones. Such considerations remind us once again that economic liberalism, like the other two major traditions of political economy and economic sociology, is as much a moral standpoint as it is a social scientific world-view.

Having started off with the pre-social individual already equipped with the capacity to act in a sovereign fashion, guided by rationality and in pursuit of self-interest, economic liberals typically make a bridge between pre-social attributes and social life through the key institutions of private property rights and the self-regulating market.

Private property rights

Private property rights are the principal means whereby sovereign individuals secure command over economic resources in order to satisfy their wants. Private here stands in opposition to public communal rights over resources. The essential point about private rights is that they enable individuals to assert their own self-interest in pursuing their own objectives without the necessity of accounting for their actions to others. Under a system of private rights individuals have the right to do what they like with their own. Under common rights, the community has this right, which takes precedence over the personal objectives of individuals.

In its earliest days in the late seventeenth century, liberalism focussed on the rights of individuals over their own labour, including the fruits of that labour, as the starting point for the analysis of private property rights. The argument, as stated by the liberal philosopher John Locke, was that individuals had private rights over the resources they had utilised in their own labour, together with the goods arising. The primary example here was the private property rights of farmers over land upon which they had laboured. Such private rights were justified provided sufficient land was available for others to do likewise. Whether such free access has been easily available at most points in history is of course debatable. However, the assumption made more sense in late seventeenth-century England and the North American white settler colonies, with the breakdown and erosion of previous communal rights releasing land for private use, than it does in the late twentieth century, when most land is already in private hands.

Deriving from this early liberal legacy is a belief that land-ownership represents the bedrock of individual freedom and liberty. This belief has, however, become transformed with subsequent changes in economic history with the shift of populations from the land to urban-industrial employment. In this context the key economic resource is capital, which may be deployed for profit, rather than land which represents only one vehicle for capital investment. In this context Locke's original liberal justification of private property rights only applies in strict form if capital accumulation represents the embodied labour of the owner of capital. This may be true in small business, self-employment and the professions, but is less applicable to large-scale bureaucratic corporations and industrial monopolies that can control access to capital.

Most recent liberal economists have therefore been less

concerned with justifying private property rights in terms of Locke's labour theory of value. What they have been more concerned with demonstrating is that private property rights maximise the capacity of economic systems to satisfy human wants in a flexible and technically efficient manner. Such rights, it is claimed, do so by permitting individuals to articulate their wants, and by motivating individuals to pursue their objectives in a self-interested manner through the personal self-interested stake they have in efficiency and optimal use of resources where private property rights exist. The claim is also made that communal rights discourage personal effort, because this stake is missing. The implication is that under communal rights, no-one has a stake in the effective management of resources, while under private property rights, every individual owner has.

This argument is also linked with discussion of the so-called 'tragedy of the commons' (Hardin 1968). The 'tragedy', as perceived by liberal economic theory, stems from the inability of communal property rights in land to produce an efficient and viable basis for the long-term use of common resources. Under common rights each villager or peasant is assumed to maximise their personal usage of the commons, yet if all do so the commons will become over-exploited and the land exhausted, to the loss of all. In such situations it is believed to be impossible to enforce optimal use of resources, except through private property rights. Private rights allow policing, and simultaneously allocate clear responsibilities to individuals to take account of the consequences of their actions. The main difficulty with this argument, as it stands, is its failure to explain the many private examples of environmental degradation wherever private interests succeed in freeing themselves from communal obligation.

Liberal arguments about economic efficiency and wealth maximisation are pursued further by linking private property rights with self-regulating markets.

The self-regulating market

The analysis of the self-regulating market, pioneered by eighteenth-century writers such as Adam Smith saw the market not simply as a means of economic exchange, but also as a system permitting human freedom and liberty. This reminds us once more of the philosophical and moral, as well as scientific and technical side of liberalism. Smith spoke of the market operating as if by the action of an 'invisible hand'. Instead of the conscious design and purpose of the state, community or tribe, the market more or less regulated itself, relying only on a minimum of state support to secure a stable legal framework, backed up by coercion where necessary and by social support for those unable to participate in the market such as the infirm.

The mechanism by which markets regulated themselves is seen in this tradition as the price mechanism. The analysis of price determination within market relationships was developed to a high degree of technical sophistication by the late nineteenth- and early twentieth-century school of neo-classical economics. This legacy has been further developed more recently by economists such as Milton Friedman (see for example M. Friedman and R. Friedman 1980).

The essential feature of the price mechanism is its capacity to regulate and bring into equilibrium the demand for and the supply of commodities. The behaviour of prices, whether they are rising or falling, gives both information and incentives to producers and consumers. Producers will be guided in their decisions about what to produce and how much to produce by the demand for commodities as expressed through the price mechanism. Similarly, consumers will be guided by decisions about what to consume and how much they can afford to consume through the price mechanism. What matters in this analysis is the relative cost and benefit involved in different courses of action as expressed through the relative prices of different commodities.

The structure of incentives follows the information provided by market signals. If the demand for a particular commodity is considerable but the supply highly limited, then prices will tend to be high relative to other commodities. Such a situation gives producers an incentive to seek cost reductions in order to lower prices and secure greater profits from the ensuing switch by consumers to cheaper versions of the same product. Alternatively, the same initial situation gives consumers the incentive to look for substitutes for the original expensive commodity. If a cheaper substitute can be found, the lower price gives consumers an incentive to switch to the alternative product.

Underlying this approach is the assumption that the price system permits a high degree of self-regulation within market relationships. Prices are free to respond to changes in supply and demand and require no regulation from institutions outside the market. The only major qualification brought into the discussion is where producer monopolies exist within the market. In this special case producers will have a greater control over price-fixing. However, in all other cases where the market approximates to free or perfect competition, market prices will be influenced by consumers as much as producers. Perfect competition is taken as the norm, at least for analytical purposes, rather than the limiting case or exception.

A further assumption in the economic liberal model of market exchange is that each equilibrium price balancing current supply and demand will be set more or less instantaneously. Behind this is the view that markets will tend to clear (i.e. all goods will be sold) at any given moment in time. The neo-classical economist Leon Walras likened this process to an auction (without reserve prices) in which all commodities for sale will be sold at some price. For analytical purposes then the dimension of 'time' or 'history' is not necessary in this model. Not all economic liberals accept this proposition, however, and we shall examine their modifications of it below.

A final characteristic of this approach is the association of the market with efficiency – in the sense of technical efficiency in finding least-cost solutions to economic choices or problems. Given rationality and self-interest, it is claimed that the market provides both the information and the incentive to seek out efficiency and hence higher productivity. This in turn is linked with arguments about the high growth potential of market economies, and hence their evolutionary robustness and resilience in comparison with other types of regulated economic systems, notably command or socialist economic systems.

Spontaneous order, private morality and small government

While economic liberalism has functioned primarily as a theory of economic life, and more especially economic exchange, it has also given some attention to the articulation of the economy with the wider society. This concern is perhaps less evident among the mass of working economists with market transactions than with the major theorists of economic liberalism such as Adam Smith or, in the more recent period, the Austrian School economist Friedrich Hayek and the American public choice theorist James Buchanan.

The idea of the self-regulating market is of course the most striking example of a theory of spontaneous order. That is to say, the self-regulating market is seen as holding together not by conscious intention or planning, but as a result of the unintended order-generating effect of the actions of self-interested individuals. This idea can be encapsulated in the formula 'private interest: social order'. Economic liberals typically explain the historic origins of key economic institutions such as money or the division of labour as a result of such processes, in the sense that no individual or political agency until the last hundred and fifty years as consciously aimed at creating new economic institutions.

The next question that arises in the course of this emphasis on market self-regulation and spontaneous order, is 'What connection if any is to be found between the market and other potential order-generating institutions such as morality and government?'

In the case of Adam Smith, it is quite clear that he did not regard the market as capable of being completely self-subsistent. In this sense, a *laissez-faire* society is as such impossible. However, Smith did posit significant relationships between the market economy and other order-generating institutions. Such relationships, however, implicated government more than morality.

Although Smith wrote a treatise on 'moral sentiments', it appears he regarded the passion of self-interest as an even more critical aspect of contemporary society. He therefore said comparatively little either about the effect of changing values on the emergence of the market, or on the significance, if any, of values for the effective operation of a market economy. This position is summarised in the famous aphorism that 'It is not from the altruism of the butcher or baker that we obtain our dinner, but for their regard for their own self-interest.'

Smith looked rather to government as a key support for the market economy. Interestingly, he did not argue for a night-watchman state or for minimal government, concepts which emerged rather later in the development of nineteenth- and twentieth-century liberalism. Rather he specified a limited but important set of valid state functions including national defence and the social protection of those unable to secure their own welfare from the market. It is somewhat ironic that these have been two of the largest categories of public expenditure in the dramatic expansion of government in the two hundred years since Smith died.

Economic liberalism has indeed had some difficulty in responding to this expansion of government. Outside Britain and the USA, the impact of liberalism on intellectual opinion and government policy-making in the last two hundred years has generally been far less than nationalism and various types of conservative or radical demands for social protection from adverse consequences of the market. Although radical forms of state socialism have not turned out to generate long-term economic growth and social security, witness the collapse of Russian and East European socialist economies, the large scale of governmental activity within the Western world remains difficult for strict economic liberals to explain. Why, even in the face of an increasingly robust market system since the Second World War, has the scale of government activity grown so considerably?

One type of answer developed by recent schools of economic liberalism is that the expansion of government reflects the dominance of self-interested political alliances over public expenditure. Public choice theory, developed by James Buchanan and his associates during the last thirty years, seeks to extend the analytical framework of economic liberalism to the political process through notions such as the 'economic theory of democracy' and the 'post-constitutional contract' (see for example Buchanan and Tullock 1962; Buchanan 1975, 1986).

Buchanan's work offers a striking confirmation of the aspirations of economic liberalism to address both issues of economic analysis and moral philosophy. He and his colleagues are concerned even more with maximising human freedom and liberty than with maximising economic efficiency and profit. In *The Calculus of Consent* (1962), Buchanan and Tullock drew on the previous work of Downs (1957) to argue that politics and the non-market activities of government could be analysed in a manner similar to the liberal economic analysis of the market.

Politics involves public choices and these are subject to the same logic of self-interested exchange between actors as are markets. The problem this creates, however, is that the multiple-person exchanges characteristic of politics under conditions of democracy are less easily regulated, in their view, than the smaller-scale exchanges of the market, many of which involve two-person relationships. While they applied the 'economic man' postulate to politics, Buchanan and Tullock were therefore aware that the multiple-person exchanges of politics were liable to result in political alliances and coalitions in which power took precedence over individual sovereignty.

Two sets of arguments follow from this. The first, more empirical argument attempts an explanation of government expansion. This is conducted in terms of the market-like characteristics of democratic politics, in which politicians are seen as competing for votes to stay in power by buying voter support in the form of public expenditure give-aways. These mechanisms appear more directed at domestic political claims on spending (e.g. government contracts for business or welfare spending) than international sources of claims e.g. for defence. Such domestic voter coalitions are regarded by Buchanan as predatory influences on government, tending to raise taxes and constrain individual freedom. The implication here is that much public spending takes the form of getting others to pay for the satisfaction of one's own interests.

In later work, more attention was given to establishing why it is that not all government spending or government activity takes this form. Buchanan (1975) specifies two types of role that remain necessary to the articulation of economy and society. First there is the 'protective role' in which the state exists to enforce rules, including the legal enforcement of contract and the protection of other property rights. Second, there is the 'productive role' in which the state carries out activities that it would be inappropriate for private individuals to conduct. Such activities include those which require maximum participation of society's members, and those which private interests cannot control by excluding others.

The second, moral and philosophical argument examines changes in political arrangements that would be required in order to subject predatory political alliances to regulation, so as to maximise what counts as individual liberty and freedom in the liberal public choice world-view. In this discussion Buchanan and Tullock revive liberal social contract theory, developed initially in the seventeenth and eighteenth centuries to harmonise liberal emphases on individual sovereignty with the need for government. Such early theories focussed on contracts between individuals and government, simultaneously able to protect the individual while at the same time continuing to guarantee individual freedom.

Buchanan and Tullock attempt a redefinition of the constitutional contract appropriate for the epoch of large-scale government, yet able to secure an orderly balance between political despotism and individual anarchy. They develop this argument through the notion of rules regulating the procedural processes of democratic decision-making. These rules are designed to avoid specifying substantive social objectives, such as specific welfare outcomes. They are also designed to prevent political power consolidating in the hands of a small group who dictate what the public interest should be. What they do set out to do is to reform the procedural rules of the political game. One example of this line of thinking is support for constitutional limits on government public expenditure and taxation levels, requiring express plebiscitary support before than can be changed. Many such limits have been instituted within state-level jurisdictions in the USA.

Some emphasis has been given to public choice theory as a recent and highly influential application of economic liberalism to economy and society. What is noteworthy in this theory is not only the application of liberalism to politics, but also, in Buchanan's more recent work, a concern with moral as against political aspects of order.

Conventionally, liberal contract theory invoked the pre-social, self-interested individual as the base unit of action implicated in the construction of a contract between individual and government. This pre-social individual is entirely analogous to the base unit of action in the market, as already analysed. In his more recent work, Buchanan has raised problems with this pre-social assumption in pursuit of the question 'Where do individual rights come from?' and 'How are individual rights secured?' While such rights can simply be asserted within liberal moral philosophy, Buchanan now seeks a more socialised explanation of their origins and determination. This is clearly influenced by difficulties in securing such rights by exclusively political means, and by perceptions on his part that modern societies are becoming ungovernable through increasing moral anarchy.

Influenced by Hayek, Buchanan examines the significance of moral order to individual sovereignty in a manner that transcends the conventional 'economic man' assumptions of liberalism. These assumptions take no account of obligations to others, merely the pursuit of self-interest. Following Hayek (1949, 1973), Buchanan (1986) now wants to extend the liberal notion of spontaneous order to the normative arena of social life, rather than restricting it to the realm of exchange. He pursues this means of a distinction between moral community in which individuals identify with obligations to a collectivity, and a moral order in which 'participants in social interaction treat each other as moral reciprocals, but do so without any sense of shared loyalties to a group or community' (1986, p. 109). Buchanan believes the looser framework of moral order is more appropriate to modern societies, but compares what he sees as the current erosion of moral order in the USA unfavourably with the more impressive moral order of contemporary Japan. Such comments are interesting but scarcely amount to a systematic treatment of the problem of moral order and economic life. Buchanan points to the need for such a treatment, but economic liberalism has yet to provide it.

For the moment it is not intended to evaluate all the claims made in Buchanan's impressive intellectual journey. What is worthy of emphasis in this discussion is his demonstration of the breadth and continuing dynamism of liberal theories of economy and society. Liberalism has not stood still. Even more important, the theory of market exchange and self-regulation and the old liberal social contract theory have not proved sufficiently comprehensive to encompass the complexity of contemporary relationships between the economy, government and culture. It is important to stress this point to avoid the superficial caricaturing of liberalism as a narrow economistic and outmoded tradition. It is equally important to emphasise the moral philosophical dimensions of liberalism to avoid another conventional caricature, namely that liberalism is merely a conservative apologia for market-based inequalities.

CONCLUSION

Taken overall then, the discussion of markets completes the chain of core propositions involved in the tradition of economic liberalism. Starting out from pre-social attributes of the individual including self-interest and rationality, the tradition links these to social institutions, notably private property rights and the market. An underlying theme throughout is that of self-regulation through an invisible hand expressed in terms of the process of price formation. Key institutions such as private property or the market have not emerged through history through conscious design – not at least until the last hundred years or so. They have emerged in a mostly unplanned and unintended way in accord with what most economic liberals regard as 'natural' or essential features of human personality and motivation. There is therefore a paradox at the heart of the theory of the market, namely that a set of relationships which no one initially planned is nonetheless capable of producing an inner order through self-regulation.

This unplanned spontaneous characteristic of market emergence has of course now become consciously theorised and expressed in public policy, most notably in policies of 'free' market deregulation. The invisible hand, it seems, requires some assistance from more visible political sources through legislative deregulation to achieve coherent market regulation. The ideal of market self-regulation remains nonetheless a powerful one, not only politically and ideologically, but also among those who associate the ideal with individual freedom, personal responsibility and social progress.

What is striking about this argument is not only the conflation of scientific analysis about 'what is', with convictions about 'what ought to be', but also the belief of its adherents that economic liberalism is radical and progressive rather than conservative. It is certainly important that a distinction be made between liberalism and conservatism. From a historical viewpoint liberalism undoubtedly had a corrosive effect on conservative practices of arbitrary government, aristocratic privilege and economic traditionalism. Such distinctions have unfortunately been blurred by those who prefer sharp binary oppositions between conservatism and radicalism, capitalism and socialism, and right and left. This has led many critics of economic liberalism to see it as an intrinsically conservative tradition, rather than a genuine agent of radical change. These claims require further scrutiny. We shall therefore investigate criticisms that liberalism is a form of conservatism, together with alternative claims that liberalism has continued into the present-day as an authentic agent of change and modernisation.

4

AN EVALUATION OF THE TRADITION OF ECONOMIC LIBERALISM

We shall evaluate economic liberalism through a number of discussion points many of which have already surfaced in the outline of the liberal position:

1 The problem of pre-social attributes claimed for Economic Man.
2 The assumption of self-interest.
3 The problem of action through time.
4 Individualism and the place of organisation.
5 Power and the market: civilising and liberating or controlling and self-destructive.
6 Markets and the problem of a moral framework.

We shall consider each of these points in turn.

THE PROBLEM OF PRE-SOCIAL ATTRIBUTES CLAIMED FOR ECONOMIC MAN

It is conventional to describe the portrayal of the individual in economic liberalism as an essentially Economic Man (or *Homo Oeconomicus*). By this is meant a person dominated by economic concerns and by the pursuit of rationally calculated self-interest. One of the most striking features of Economic Man is the considerable degree to which his wants and basic personality structure are taken as 'given' elements which exist prior to entry into society. This pre-social emphasis is typified in the assumption that individual wants are arrived at independent of social interaction, and that such wants represent choices freely made by individuals. In this view the only real constraints are set once individuals enter society to deploy various means of satisfying wants. The implication is that means are socially formed and hence scarce given the infinite multiplicity of pre-social wants.

Over the last two hundred years, economic liberals have become more guarded about the pre-social character of individuals. For much of the nineteenth century it was assumed that wants had some kind of physical or psycho-physical basis. This belief was associated by many with the doctrine of hedonism, whereby individuals seek to maximise pleasure over pain. This doctrine, it was thought, could be linked both to the existence and the intensity of human wants, such wants reflecting the differing measures of pleasure over pain involved in consuming different goods. Each good, it was thought, had a different utility as measured in hedonistic terms.

This whole approach has been modified in the present century, mainly because of the problems associated with locating the precise mechanisms of hedonistic behaviour. Certainly no basic psycho-physical hedonistic law, with observable causal mechanisms, has been located. Beyond this, many modern economists have argued that the quest for the origins of wants is unnecessary and perhaps irrelevant. Wherever they may come from, liberal economics needs only to take them for granted as the given data on which choices are made.

As a result, liberal economists have switched from talking about hedonism or utility, and talk instead of revealed preferences. Whatever goes on in the private world of individual biology, psychology or mental reflection, it is assumed that all that matters is the wants or preferences that individuals reveal. This of course begs the question about how far such preferences are in fact pre-social or given. For analytical purposes then economic liberals simply assume (1) that individuals have a set of revealed preferences (2) that these preferences can be arranged in rank order of priority and (3) that individuals will substitute different amounts of particular goods for each other in an orderly way as the relative price of each changes. Where then does this leave the issue of pre-social characteristics?

How this question is answered depends very largely on the extent to which individual actions are regarded as socially determined, rather than biologically or physically determined. It

71

is a reasonable generalisation to say that economic liberals tend to regard individuals as less completely determined by social causation than do sociologists. Another way of putting this is to say that liberal economics tends to operate with an under-socialised view of humankind, whereas political economy and economic sociology tend to operate with an over-socialised view. In the former case, it is held *either* that many economically relevant aspects of action are in fact caused by non-social (e.g. biological) factors, or that we cannot know what causes them because they appear to be random. In either argument, a social cause cannot be found. In the latter case, by contrast, it is assumed according to the dictum of the French sociologist Emile Durkheim (1938) that every social fact has a social cause or causes. It is therefore necessary to seek out a social explanation in order to understand why individuals act in the way that they do.

It is difficult to resolve this debate because no conclusive evidence has or can be found to adjudicate between the different views. Each argument ultimately rests on some kind of faith in the preferred explanatory strategy. This applies especially to those asserting the reducibility of all wants to either physical or social sources. In the case of those who believe in randomness of wants, that is wants outside any kind of patterned determination, however, a significant dilemma identified by the American sociologist Talcott Parsons (1937) arises. Either we accept randomness, in which case it is hard to explain how any kind of patterned social arrangements are possible for chaos would always predominate over order. Or, alternatively, if we deny randomness and assert social determination, it is difficult to see how the postulate of individual freedom can be maintained. In other words one route defends individual freedom but denies society, while the other defends social determination at the expense of individual freedom.

One of the main reasons economic liberals produce an under-socialised conception of humankind is the prior wish to promote individual freedom on the ideal of the self-regulating market as one of the highest human values. The fear is that social determination is incompatible with individual free will and with economic choice. Hence Mrs Thatcher's celebrated maxim, 'There is no such thing as society, only individuals'. The whole structure of analysis is therefore geared not so much to assertion of non-social determination, as to defence of a moral philosophy of human freedom. This defence is also associated with the fear that social knowledge about individuals will lead to tighter social control and to invasive and repressive forms of social engineering.

This perspective may justly be criticised for its arbitrary assumption that 'society' represents constraint and control over individuals. The liberal position had merit, nonetheless, in laying bare some characteristic features of modern society. These centre on the dominance of a possessive form of individualism, much freer from social controls than at any previous point in human history. This is not to say that individualism begins only with the advent of the modern market-based economic systems. Abercrombie et al. (1986) demonstrate quite clearly a much longer pedigree. This is linked as much with legal and religious traditions going back to Graeco-Roman and Christian thought, as with recent secular and economic doctrines. Nonetheless, in spite of this historical complexity, it is also the case that possessive as opposed to spiritual or legal forms of individualism have been massively advanced through the looser-knit pluralistic and impersonal networks of market relations. Put another way, the extreme differentiation of individual from strong social bonds of religious community and kinship is a comparatively recent phenomena as far as the mass of the people is concerned.

The major problem for economic liberalism is the failure to appreciate individualism as a social product rather than a pre-social or random phenomenon.

Economic liberals have been resistant to this line of argument in part because of a pragmatic delimitation of their analysis to the means of want-satisfaction, rather than the origins of wants. This is not, however, the only reason for resistance. Another reason is scepticism about the over-socialised explanations that sociologists have produced. These have sometimes produced mechanistic caricatures of human action in which the wants of a mass of heterogeneous individuals are somehow reduced to one simple variable such as class background. Mary Douglas and Baron Isherwood (1978) have pointed to an explanatory vacuum amongst social scientists in response to the question 'Why do people want what they do?' In this regard the scepticism of economic liberals may be interpreted as a valid reaction against bad sociology as such, rather than a rejection in principle of the possibility of an adequate sociology. To put it simply, the onus is now on those who tend to a highly socialised view of human society to come up with better models of the socialisation process consistent with high levels of individualism, rather than on economic liberals to abandon their scepticism. Whether political economy or economic sociology have succeeded in meeting this challenge will be analysed later in this study.

In the meantime, there is one further dimension to the problem of pre-social attributes which is less easy to resolve. This centres on the capacity of social theory to produce explanations of every nuance of individual variation. We live in highly differentiated societies where the uniformities of tribe, caste, religion and geographical community have increasingly broken down, and where access to global cultural variations has been magnified through the mass communications media. Given the legitimacy of individualism and the access to multiple variations in consumption possibilities, it seems impossible that sociology could produce fine-net analysis of why discrete individuals want what they want. The best that may be possible is an analysis of patterns more or less present in different groups that vary by class, sex, age, ethnicity and so forth. The possibility of a sociology of want-formation at the level of individuals seems to be a fruitless dream. Neglect of this limitation on social scientific understanding has tended to create an authoritarian disregard for individual choices, often instituted in the substitution of centralised state-sponsored want-determination for individual choice. There is a temptation for sociologists to play philosopher-king in such situations, asserting what wants 'really' are or would be if it were not for 'ignorance' or 'false consciousness'. This reminds us that many opponents of economic liberalism have a moral as well as intellectual stake in these debates, just as economic liberals do. The economy is a morally charged terrain in which human values clash just as in any other part of society.

Where then does all this leave the problem of pre-social attributes? Several generalisations may now be made in the light of the preceding discussion.

First there is no plausible case for reducing the origins of wants or rationality to exclusively physical, biological or psychological factors. Second, economic liberalism is not necessarily committed to an extra-social explanation of wants or rationality, even though many of its adherents do think in this way. Third, a plausible social analysis of want-formation and the development of rationality must be capable of coping with the problem of individualism and pluralities of choice, before the credentials of the social explanation can be accepted as convincing. Such an explanation would need to address the problem of over-socialised accounts of human action.

A final, difficult consideration in this discussion is the role of simple axioms about human nature in any kind of theory construction. While economic liberals have been criticised for the use of pre-social assumptions about individuals, it has to be asked whether any social theory is possible without the use of some kind of pre-social assumptions about human nature? Are not certain 'given' attributes or capacities, such as the capacity to learn, to classify or to evaluate, necessary in the constitution of any theory?

The main sociological response to this is that the substance of what is learned, what classifications are used, or what evaluations are made, varies in different societies. In terms of evaluation, for example, what counts as good or bad, beautiful or ugly varies depending on the type of society involved, the nature of religious and moral values, ideals of beauty and so forth. When faced with the notion of economic man, or *homo oeconomicus*, this line of argument claims this not as a universal feature of human nature, but a particular personality type whose self-interested instrumental rationality is largely confined to modern societies where the economy is differentiated from the wider society.

The challenge to the use of pre-social assumptions does not necessarily deny the existence of human nature, as evidenced in certain generic capacities all human beings have. The argument, however, is that such capacities are formed in society rather than outside of it. Such capacities depend on the interactive nature of social life in which individuals must interact with others from birth. It is from this interaction that learning, classification evaluation and specifically economic activities such as production and consumption emerge. The physical environment around us, and our physical embodiment in a biological organism with limited physical and biochemical capacities are the only non-social 'givens' which constrain social life. It is only in this sense of a given limiting framework that pre-social assumptions or axioms about human nature are valid.

As far as economic life is concerned, most liberal economists have now abandoned strict hedonistic assumptions. Most of the major areas of debate now concern conflicts or tensions over different social assumptions about human nature, rather than being over pre-social versuus social assumptions. The conflict between views of human nature as privatised, self-interested and possessive as opposed to communal and morally sensitive is perhaps the foremost of these. We now turn to this debate.

THE ASSUMPTION OF SELF-INTEREST

It is possible to make two different kind of *social* assumptions about human beings. One type of assumption is so highly generalised and fundamental as to be an axiom we simply take for granted rather than a hypothesis whose existence we need to prove. An example is the axiom that all action has a meaning to the individual undertaking it. The other type of assumption is based more closely on empirical investigation and observation and takes the form of a hypothesis or an interrelated set of hypotheses which require to be demonstrated. An example is the hypothesis that secular meanings to action have overtaken religious meanings. It is very hard to conduct any kind of analysis without taking some social assumptions as given axioms, but where such assumptions are made it is as well to be aware that they are assumptions or axioms and not necessarily well-researched or based on documented empirical findings.

Sometimes it becomes necessary to cease treating assumptions as 'givens', and start testing out whether they are really true and accurate. This often happens when the commonsense obvious-ness of the axiom is challenged in a fundamental way by contrary findings, or whether hypotheses formulated on the basis of another axiom prove to have more explanatory value.

We can express this argument, diagrammatically, as in Table 4.1. Here a *hypothetical* research progress is conducted over three stages, starting with rival sets of axioms and hypothesis. During Stage 2, the plausibility of Hypotheses A1 and A2 is shaken,

Table 4.1 Axioms and hypotheses in the research process: a simple model

STAGE 1	AXIOM A	All human action is exclusively self-interested.	Hypothesis A1	Workers seek the highest wages for the least effort.
			Hypothesis A2	Producers buy cheap and sell dear to maximise profits.
	AXIOM B	All human action is morally-sensitive, at least in part.	Hypothesis B1	Workers will refrain from pushing for the highest wages where some moral principle (e.g. dedicated service to the public intervenes).
			Hypothesis B2	Producers may not seek to maximise profits if doing so violates some moral principle (e.g. prevention of death or injury to the workforce).

STAGE 2 Hypotheses B1 and B2 are supported empirically, while A1 and A2 are not.

STAGE 3 AXIOM A is converted from an axiom to Hypothesis A3, and reformulated as a question 'How far is all human action self-interested?'

Meanwhile the status of AXIOM B is enhanced and becomes increasingly regarded as commonsense unless challenged at a later stage.

leading in Stage 3 to the conversion of Axiom A into Hypothesis A3. At this stage the point of Table 4.1 (which could be repeated with many other axioms and hypotheses) is to demonstrate a general methodological approach, rather than advance the actual substance of the argument described.

If we now return to economic liberalism and the assumption of self-interest, we find that an erosion of confidence in the assumption has in fact taken place in the last decades.

The starting-point here is some comments by Amartya Sen, on the key notion of self-interested economic man (1976, p. 235). He has pointed out that if the assumption of self-interest was put to a poll among economists, considerable disarray would be indicated. This would centre on three alternative propositions:

(a) that the assumption cannot be falsified by evidence since it is true by definition
(b) that the assumption is capable of empirical falsification and so far has stood up quite well, and
(c) that the assumption is capable of empirical falsifrcation and has in fact been falsified.

The first of these responses – response (a) requires some further elaboration. The argument here is essentially that all individuals are self-interested because they can be nothing else. Put another way, whatever the self desires, whether it be a luxury car, love or altruistic behaviour in helping others, all of these arise from self-interest. Even altruism, in this approach, can be regarded as an assertion of the self. Whereas some people may have exclusively material wants others, so the argument goes, have tastes for altruism. Material and altruistic wants are thereby put on a par with each other. Just as an individual may get greater self-interested satisfaction from trading up a Ford for a Ferrari, so the argument goes, a similar increase in satisfaction may be gained from altruistic behaviour such as giving to a charity.

If this approach is followed strictly then self-interest becomes a truism. If anything we want is described as the exercise of self-interest simply because all action involves an element of human volition, then all behaviour is by definition self-interested. This logical tautology, however, is of very limited usefulness as an account of actual human behaviour because it ignores and cannot explain the complex variations in human motivation and social psychology. It is, so to speak, empty of content, and cannot therefore tell us which track this logically necessary self-interest will take in a given situation.

Even greater problems have emerged however, when the tautology is mistaken for or conflated with actual behaviour, or used as a complete explanation to the exclusion of all alternative explanations. It is on this terrain that most recent controversies have taken place.

One problem with using the self-interest assumption in combination with assumptions about wants and preferences is that not all preferences are of the same type nor can they be easily assimilated to the notion of self-interest. For one thing, to treat all preferences as potentially equivalent and transferable is to neglect a distinction between simple material wants for more of this or that commodity, e.g. the 'taste' for steak or hamburgers, as compared with other more complex kinds of wants, e.g. the desire for a peaceful world.

Both Sen and others concerned with this problem such as Albert Hirschman (1984), advise a distinction between preferences and meta-preferences. They argue that economists have conventionally dealt with direct preferences as revealed in the purchase of goods and services. This is all very well, but it does not embrace another category of preferences, namely those that arise when individuals stand back for a moment, reflect on their preferences and evaluate them. This process of reflection involves asking questions as to whether we really want the kind of things we habitually buy. Hirschman implies that this standing-back process generates meta-preferences which guide us between different sets of preferences.

Two implications of this analysis are noteworthy. In the first place it suggests that all preferences are not of the same order and not easily substituted for one another in terms of cost and benefit. The 'taste' for sausages, may not be of the same order as the 'taste' for peace, in the sense that the latter is not reducible to cost–benefit analysis. It is not so much as taste or preference as a meta-preference which may guide other preferences.

Second, such meta-preferences may not only guide but also change our tastes or preferences. In buying presents for children for example, choices between different toys on the basis of cost and durability may become influenced by a meta-preference to

79

boycott war-games or those that encourage aggressive behaviour. Whether or not such games really encourage war or aggression is here a separate issue. What matters in terms of consumption preferences is that a reflective stage of concern has intervened to change preferences through assertion of a value judgement rather than a purely cost–benefit calculation. If we intend to retain the notion of self-interest, it is as well to amend the conventional account of preferences in this more satisfying way.

Another major issue in the discussion of self-interest and human wants involves that category of wants that arise in interaction with other people. Hirschman's discussion of preferences and meta-preferences is directed in the main at debate and reflection by individuals, so to speak arguing with themselves about what they really want. A further major dimension to the discussion is introduced when we come to consider action arising in interaction with others, where the welfare of others is taken into account by individuals in determining their own course of action.

Concern for others may of course involve some element of increased personal satisfaction for the altruist. Sen has argued that, in some instances, concern for others may indeed directly affect one's own welfare and hence be reducible to a form of self-interest. However, in many other cases concern for others may not arise from attention to one's self-interest, but from a belief that some actions are right and others wrong, and that one must do right even at the cost of personal welfare. He calls the first type of action 'sympathies' and the second type 'commitments'. Sympathies are connected with a positive sense of psychological well-being among individuals, commitments on the other hand apply even at the cost of well-being. Commitments, in other words, are not self-interested. Sen therefore believes that responses (b) and (c) to the hypothetical poll of economists are too simplistic because they fail to allow for a combination of 'sympathies' and 'commitments' in our dealings with others.

Amitai Etzioni in his recent study *The Moral Dimension: Toward A New Economics* (1988), has gone much further than Sen in developing a more systematic understanding of the wide range of motivations involved in human action. This starts off from the premise that pleasure (linked to self-interest) and morality (linked to normative evaluation) are two irreducible features of human behaviour. We cannot explain the existence of one in terms of the other. Morality for Etzioni is an irreducible feature of human interaction and inter-personal responsiveness. It is not, therefore, located in some basic human psychology but arises as a property of social life embracing individuals.

Following Max Weber (1978) Etzioni assumes that human behaviour is multi-faceted rather than one-dimensional. Motivation involves emotion and moral evaluation as well as self-interested calculation. The economists' self-interest assumption is not unhelpful as an empirical account of behaviour, the problem is rather that it is hopelessly incomplete. Action such as consumer behaviour is not simply a matter of articulating preferences and calculating the relative costs and benefits of particular mixes of purchases. It also involves pride, euphoria, guilt and shame and may involve sharing with others or public display as much as privatised consumption. Etzioni's point is not that economists are unaware of this, but rather that they ignore it for purposes of analysis. This neglect is untenable because such complex motivations *enter into the constitution of preferences or wants* rather than being ephemeral side effects. More fundamentally, where moral behaviour is concerned this functions to 'affirm or express a commitment' rather than as one of a number of preferences of the same type. We cannot equate cheese with community, therefore, or sausages with solidarity. Moral behaviour is concerned with life processes, rather than one-off outcomes such as the consumption of foods. As such, moral factors exert constraints on action, as well as influencing the nature and content of wants – it is simply untenable to lump these very different activities together.

While some liberal economists accept the force of this argument, many remain unconvinced. This is reflected in the popularity of rational choice theory based on self-interested presuppositions. A key point of reference in this theory is the so-called 'free rider' problem. This problem centres on the perceived preference of individuals to want the benefits of goods, while trying if at all possible to avoid the costs associated with their production. The 'free rider' is the person who participates with others in enjoying a 'good' which others have paid for directly or through taxes, without paying himself.

81

Many economists retain an obsession with cheating, faking and other forms of self-interested behaviour. This is evident in the work of writers who use game theory as a means of understanding human behaviour. The use of game theory in the social sciences has been directed towards laying bare the essential logic of human action. In so doing it has focussed in part on dilemmas in which individual self-interest may be in conflict with collective interest. One such example is the Prisoner's Dilemma game. The challenge here is set by the attempt by a set of individual prisoners to escape from gaol. The dilemma arises because each needs the assistance of the others, but each equally wants to escape at the earliest moment irrespective of the welfare of others. Underlying the dilemma is a lack of trust in other people sufficient to secure an orderly escape for all. This dilemma may be applied to other situations, such as panic in a burning theatre, where all try to stampede to the door making it difficult for any single person to escape. This panic behaviour arises because no one has sufficient trust that anyone else will walk out quickly and calmly given the high risk. Mark Granovetter (1985), in commenting on this example, makes the point that inter-personal trust is not necessarily absent from all situations, and hence the prisoner's dilemma may not always be a dilemma. He cites, first of all, the counter-example of a family trying to escape from a burning house where a tendency is not to stampede, but to trust and assist each other. In this situation others can be counted on. This type of example can also be extended to economic life, where informal networks of trust may be evident.

Granovetter accepts that distrust and opportunism will be prevalent wherever self-interest is found. However he also sees trust as a solution to problems of distrust and business instability thus 'prisoners' dilemmas are often obviated by the strength of personal relations. Standard economic analysis neglects the identity and past relations of individual transactors ... [transactors however] are interested in whether a particular other may be expected to deal honestly with *them*' (1985, p. 491). This in turn depends on whether these are existing inter-personal contacts based on a sense of obligation to accept norms of honesty and trust. Trust can of course be broken, to the advantage of the maleficent. However if trust never worked no-one would be inclined to operate it. Fortunately there is a good deal of research to indicate that while self-interest is a powerful motivation, people do not universally cheat when they can get away with it (Marwell and Ames 1981; Marwell 1982; Rapoport 1985). Etzioni's conclusions are worth citing for their boldness. 'Public choice is but an extreme example of a neo-classical economic theory that finds little support in the facts and is widely contradicted because it does not tolerate moral factors as a significant distinct explanatory factor'(1988, p. 63). Put another way, moral behaviour is not dead, nor is there any reason to prefer a self-interested to a moral explanation, unless it fits the facts better. What is important, however, is the need to expand our conception of moral behaviour to include low-key items like trust alongside full-blown items such as altruism.

One of the reasons many liberal economists have persisted with the self-interest assumptions is their belief that it could only be dispensed with or revised if altruism could be demonstrated to be widespread. This test, however, is overly narrow and restrictive since less wide-ranging or self-denying forms of inter-personal obligation, such as trust, must also be taken into account as limits on self-interest.

Summing up this section so far, it may justly be claimed that the self-interest assumption behind liberal economics has not stood up well to theoretical and empirical interrogation. It either functions as a tautology about human behaviour of little explanatory use, or as an empirical generalisation which is only of limited explanatory use. The attempt to found an exhaustive account of human behaviour on the basis of self-interests fails. The continuing insistence of many economic liberals on its usefulness is puzzling given the weight of counter-argument. Some of this insistence appears to arise because of the preference of economists for a unitary or one-dimensional theory of behaviour that can be portrayed as human nature. Insistence on this preference is simplistic and ahistorical.

Having said this, it remains highly important to investigate the empirical applicability of the self-interest assumption, and to establish the relationship between self-interest and other specific types of behaviour, not simply moral behaviour. One productive way that this more empirically sensitive research has proceeded is in modifying the conventional association of self-interest with the idea of maximisation. Many formulations assumed that self-interest would inexorably take the form of wanting more rather than less, or the same with less effort. Companies would seek maximum profits, while workers would seek maximum wages. There is more than a grain of truth in this presumption.

Research on what economic actors actually do is now extensive and much of it significantly modifies the picture of maximisation. Max Weber (1927) pointed long ago to evidence that workers would not necessarily work longer to maximise incomes. At some point the preference for leisure or conventions about the working day would prove stronger. This example is not necessarily corrosive of economic liberalism in that it can be portrayed as a trade-off between two wants, 'income' and 'leisure'. We may try to balance the two to maximise overall welfare. Another attempted corrective to the maximisation assumption is provided by Herbert Simon, the American management theorist and political scientist. He argued that firms seek not to maximise profits or growth but to achieve satisfactory returns – a form of behaviour known as satisficing (Simon 1959, 1979). This emphasis on satisficing leaves open the reasons why particular levels of performance are sought for or set as goals. The simple nexus between self-interest and maximisation is broken because a wide range of motivational and organisational factors may be involved.

Underlying the analysis of human behaviour is of course a relationship between the context or environment in which action takes place and the structures and motivations that arise among human actors. Economic liberals, as we have seen, emphasise the context of scarcity of means with which to satisfy wants. Self-interest is thereby constrained by conditions of action. But what exactly are the main conditioning factors likely to be involved?

One of the problems with early versions of economic liberalism was the assumption that individuals could, if they acted rationally, gain perfect information of the environment in which they operated. Such information would include the prices and availability of goods able to satisfy wants. Later theorists, however, have recognised that perfect information of this kind is unlikely to be available, and that the search for information is itself a cost to measure against benefits. Herbert Simon's conception of satisficing behaviour was designed in part to illuminate the *grounded* nature of the information available to individuals. Since we cannot know everything the search for the best course of action depends on bounded or imperfect information, and on a pragmatic setting of aspirations. Such contingencies militate against maximisation, but not necessarily against the pursuit of self-interest. A more radical challenge to the self-interest–maximisation nexus has been suggested by Charles Perrow (1986).

While Simon demonstrates that the operation of self-interest in conditions of imperfect information need not produce maximisation, Perrow argues that different contextual settings may stimulate or retard self-interest itself. The key to this for Perrow is the organisational setting in which individuals operate. In the analysis which follows Perrow demonstrates the merits of treating self-interest as a research hypothesis to be tested rather than an axiom that is assured irrespective of the evidence. As such Perrow bring us closer to the real world of firms, assembly lines, managerial hierarchies, migration in search of work and family ties, rather than free-floating, self-interested individuals with preferences. He assumes that people will adopt behaviour to fit in with the larger structures they encounter, rather than going for self-interest irrespective of its relevance. Perrow identifies six organisational contexts in which self-interested behaviour is encouraged. I have reformulated his analysis diagrammatically in Table 4.2, in terms of six dimensions along which encouragement or discouragement of self-interest is represented. Here we can see the formulation of a very complex set of hypothesis centred on six organisational variables which tend to influence the presence of self-interest.

This is not the place to review the vast range of evidence bearing on this argument. Suffice it to say there is considerable support for the proposition that many organisations – both private and public – do contain elements which discourage undiluted self-interest. One of the most graphic examples is drawn from Japanese corporations in which managerial hierarchies and industrial relations involve differing team-based patterns of interaction, reward and authority than those more individualistic patterns often found in the United States and Britain (Dore 1973).

Table 4.2 Encouragement or discouragement of self-interest

Variable	Encourages self-interest	Discourages self-interest
Patterns of interaction	Minimal interactions with others e.g. fluid labour markets based on single migrant workers, temporary or high turnover labour; occupations with a heavy emphasis on individual promotion.	Close interactions with others e.g. occupational communities where workplace and residence are stable and coincide for most of the workforce; occupations with group job rotation.
Basis of rewards	Rewards accrue to individuals e.g. steep salary structure reinforced by individually assessed tax structure.	Rewards accrue to group e.g. co-operative, teamwork-based labour.
Measurement of effort	Effort of individuals can be measured e.g. piece rates, personal evaluations.	Effort of individuals cannot be measured e.g. large indivisible projects based on teamwork and job transferability.
Work design	Minimise inter-dependence e.g. Taylorist breakdown of work-tasks; surveillance of individual worker.	Maximise inter-dependence e.g. co-operative effort; activity defying precise contractual specification.
Leadership and authority	Preference for stable leadership e.g. individual leaders taken to be omni-competent and positions held continuously.	Rotating leadership e.g. all regarded as potential leaders, and hence skills develop in group context.
Hierarchy	Tall hierarchy e.g. rewards un-equally distributed such that access to better rewards requires pursuit of self-interest.	Flat hierarchy e.g. greater participation and less inequality puts less premium on self-interest to advance.

Overall then we may say that the assumption of self-interest is better regarded as an empirical hypothesis of varying significance in economic life, than a clearly-supported axiom without which economic action would be incoherent and impossible to fathom. While economic liberalism is right to emphasise the importance of individualism and self-interest, especially in modern differentiated economies, it is wrong to see this as the sole foundation of economic behaviour. Similarly, while its critics would be wrong to deny the profound importance of secular individualism, privatism and the collapse of strong, all-encompassing moral bonds, they are right to dispute the proposition that self-interest is the foundation of human behaviour.

THE PROBLEM OF ACTION THROUGH TIME

We have already noted that the neo-classical picture of economic action within the self-regulating market focussed on the effectively instantaneous adjustment of supply and demand to reach an equilibrium price. Following writers like Walras, economic life could be regarded as a series of auctions in which new equilibria would be set if the factors affecting supply and demand changed. The failure of the harvest, for example, would reduce supply and in the absence of alternatives, prices would rise to a new level. In this approach, the economy proceeds as a series of instantaneous readjustments, changing as underlying patterns change.

One problem with the approach is how to account for economic development over time, including structural changes in economic life embodied in processes like industrialisation. One option is to regard the underlying basis of change as outside or exogenous to the market. Technological innovation, for example, might be regarded as exogenous insofar as it emerged randomly from heroic acts of genius or discovery rather than being market-led. If such assumptions were made, economic change could be regarded as a matter for historical analysis, distinct from the rational self-interested model adopted to explain market behaviour.

Another option has been to try to assimilate change to the core assumptions of economic liberalism itself. This was the original approach of Adam Smith, who was rather more historically-minded than latter-day followers (1976). Although Smith asserted a natural tendency to rationality and to truck, barter and exchange, he was also sensitive to the historical changes that accompanied the eighteenth-century expansion of markets – what he referred to as commercial society. One major theme for Smith was the importance of political liberalism, nurtured in the cities of early modern Europe, to the struggle to free economic life of arbitrary controls. The implication was that it would not free itself spontaneously. But once freed, of course, the temptation for latterday liberals is to assume that the market economy is both self-regulating and in Rostow's (1960) terms 'self-sustaining'. Political vigilance is only required to maintain market autonomy; left to its own devices the efficiency of the market will guarantee growth. In extreme versions of economic liberalism, history is 'dead' because liberalism has defeated all its rivals (Fukayama 1989).

There are numerous attempts to assimilate economic change to the key concepts of economic liberalism, such as self-interest and instrumental rationality, as in Adam Smith. All such attempts generally have recourse to additional supporting propositions not derivable from the theory itself. This is because economic liberalism is better at explaining how markets operate once they exist and the extent to which they are self-regulating, rather than how they came to exist. One of the central supporting hypotheses is the idea of the institutionalisation of private property rights, giving individuals or organisations effective control over economic resources (North and Thomas 1973). Such rights do not emerge spontaneously but usually require political and sometimes cultural support too. Nonetheless the failure of communal property rights, unconducive to private individualism, is assumed to flow from their incapacity to satisfy underlying Smithian tendencies to self-interested behaviour. This assumption is rarely justified against rival explanations of market emergence (Holton 1985).

There are, however, two main intellectual reasons for the rethink by economists of the assumption that economic action takes place instantaneously without a chronological dimension. While the first is the problem of explaining the historical emergence of markets, the second is more philosophical. It concerns the epistemological basis of human action.

Epistemology is the systematic study of knowledge, of how and with what degree of certainty we claim to know what we do. As we have already seen, the original epistemological assumption of economic liberalism was that of the possibility of perfect knowledge. This has often been labelled positivism. Positivism has different meanings in a technical philosophical, as compared with broad sociological, usage. In the latter case it refers to the possibility of objective knowledge achieved through scientific methodology, and founded on the distinction between facts and values. Under economic liberalism Economic Man was positivistic in that he could rationally obtain the factual knowledge necessary to make rational choices.

This confident positivism, however, has been seriously revised in twentieth-century economic theory. Perfect knowledge is a chimera. The best we can hope for is imperfect information. Even in the late nineteenth century the Austrian wing of neo-classical theory had already pointed out that positivistic assumptions were unrealistic (for further discussion see Holton and Turner 1989). In fact economic action takes place under conditions of uncertainty about outcomes (Hayek 1937). Faith in rationality as a certain source of knowledge is misplaced. Under this warning economists have reformulated their assumptions. They now speak of 'expectations' about future outcomes arrived at after limited searches for information, rather than rational cost–benefit calculations about different courses of action. Stable equilibria may never be reached.

How then does all this affect the approach to change through time? Above all else it requires an abandonment of the metaphor of the auction clearing markets virtually instantaneously at an equilibrium price. Instead action must be thought of as a process that takes place through time in which individuals choose options on the basis of expectations about the future. How well these expectations work out cannot be known in advance, and deviations from expected outcomes will need to be taken into account in modifying behaviour through time.

A typical example of this approach applied to economic life is in the functioning of interest rates. These may be interpreted as measuring the terms upon which individuals may forego current consumption expected for future returns. High interest rates reflect high levels of uncertainty, reflected in uncertainty as to the value of money. Interest rates reflect expectations about the future under conditions of imperfect information.

This epistemological revision in economic liberalism certainly extends the scope of the conventional analytical framework, including a time dimension within economic action. As such it does not provide an historical account of the emergence of market institutions in any direct manner. It is, however, of considerable relevance to the organisational framework of economic life, to which we now turn.

INDIVIDUALISM AND THE PLACE OF ORGANISATION

One of the major features of economic liberalism in the seventeenth and eighteenth centuries was its emphasis on the free-standing, sovereign individual as the centre-point of economic exchange in the market. In this approach, the individual is conceived as master of his or her own destiny, equipped with the rationality to pursue strategies of individual self-interest. For both John Locke and Adam Smith, market exchange was connected with individuals, individual liberty and private property, in contra-distinction to the collective sphere of government and community.

This focus developed, of course, in an era when the economy was organised in small-scale units of production, notably individually-owned or family-owned businesses. Economic organisation was typically personal and small scale, rather than impersonal and large scale or bureaucratic. In this context the association of economic behaviour with individual action made a great deal of sociological and historical sense.

In the nineteenth and twentieth centuries by contrast, economic organisation has tended to become larger scale with the relative decline of the family business and the rise of business corporations owned by public shareholders. There are still very many small businesses, of course, and the trend to larger scale is not by any means universal or inexorable. Indeed, small business has seen something of a revival in the last decade in response to changing business conditions. Nonetheless, for the purposes of the current argument taking the last three hundred years as a yardstick, it is no longer possible to analyse the economy simply in terms of a collection of free-standing individuals operating in the market as producers and consumers.

Ever since the late nineteenth century, the tradition of economic liberalism has attempted to find some way of integrating the firm or corporation into its analytical framework. The simplest and initial way of doing this, as practised by the neo-classical school, was to treat the firm as an individual unit of analysis akin to individual persons. Firms could be expected to respond to the price mechanism in terms of cost–benefit calculations just as an individual was supposed to act. More complex revisions in the analysis of the market were required, however, when firms gained significant measures of market power as dominant producers able to influence or even directly fix prices. Such revisions stemmed from the realisation that large-scale businesses increasingly violated the assumptions on which the model of perfect competition was based.

Under perfect competition it was assumed that no single producer or consumer had sufficient influence or control over the market as to influence the actions of other producers and consumers. Put another way no producer could fix prices higher than they would otherwise be as a result of the free play of supply and demand, because any other producer could undercut him. It was competition not control which fixed prices, implying that consumers always keep a check on producers by looking for the cheapest deal. In the perfect market no one producer dominates the market, nor do producers dominate consumers. Advantage would certainly accrue to those who behaved more rationally or more efficiently than others. However, access to rationality and efficiency was available to all.

This model was of course intended not only as an account of how the economy operated, but also as a normative argument associating the market with rationality, efficiency and individual freedom or liberty. The persistence of the model of perfect competition even in an increasingly large-scale bureaucratic world, is not simply a reflection of the persistence of small business, but also a reflection of continuing normative commitment to the liberal world-view of individual freedom and personal autonomy. Faced with a conflict between the actual trend in economic organisation and such ideals, many economic liberals have placed an even higher priority on defending the normative side of the case than on demonstrating the analytical or descriptive side of the case. In other words they have been more concerned to define what is good and what ought to be, than to analyse what is. This normative focus is, as we shall see, typical of all three great traditions seeking to explain the economy and society.

Nonetheless there has grown up an important current of economic writing concerned with both monopoly over markets and with imperfect competition (e.g. Chamberlin 1948; Latsis 1972). This has attempted to grapple with varying types of producer control over markets. In addition, there has also grown up a literature on the internal structure of the firm, including the analysis of relations between owners and managers, principals and agents (Alchian and Demsetz 1972; Fama and Jensen 1983). This has arisen in response to the increasing internal differentiation of ownership from management within large-scale firms consequent on the decline of the family firm which was generally owner-managed (Chandler 1977).

One problem arising from this literature is how far economic liberalism can remain intact once power differentials within the market are recognised. Can economic liberalism survive as an explanatory tool if perfect competition becomes less and less of a reality? And if it does survive, does it do so as an explanatory theory of the actual structure and operations of economic life? Or does it survive only as an analytical yardstick of what would count as rational and efficient behaviour if markets were perfectly competitive? To the extent that its explanatory power has indeed shrunk we would need to turn elsewhere to other major traditions of analysis to fill the vacuum created by its demise.

Organisation theory, a multi-disciplinary intellectual endeavour, has provided one major terrain in which these kinds of questions have been pursued. The assumptions of organisation theory have been less parsimonious and more pluralistic than those of economic liberalism as such. In particular the strict nexus of rationality, self-interest and maximisation assumptions has been challenged by contributions such as Simon on satisficing.

The most important revisionist contribution to debate on such questions within organisation theory has come from Oliver Williamson (1975). The intention here is not to dispense with economic liberalism but to re-cast it in a manner which distinguishes between markets and organisations, rather than reducing organisations to the original model of perfect competition.

Williamson's work, which draws on the pioneering insights of Coase (1937), enables us to integrate together two important considerations. One is the social fact that most economic life takes place within and between organisations rather than perfectly competitive markets composed of individuals. The second consideration is the epistemological uncertainties of action discussed in the previous section. Williamson assumes neither that actors have perfect knowledge of the situation upon which to make rational judgements, nor that economic exchange takes place instantaneously on the analogy of the self-clearing auction.

Economic liberalism in both its classical and neo-classical form never adequately explained the existence of the firm. Williamson sees the firm as an organisational hierarchy which has the capacity to solve certain types of problems that markets by themselves cannot solve. Markets in particular cannot provide means of dealing with certain kinds of transaction costs associated with economic exchange. Such costs include situations where outcomes are risky or uncertain, or where medium to long-run investments of time, money or energy are required before production outcomes can be obtained. Whereas markets deal well with short-term reallocations of resources that can be deployed in a flexible manner with a high certainty of outcome, organisational hierarchies deal better with longer-term and uncertain economic processes that require protection from the immediate impact of market mechanisms to succeed.

To take one example, firms exist because all the labour requirements of many forms of production cannot be hired day-by-day on a casual labour market. Firms build up through continuous employment of skilled labour a pool of trusted expertise, and a labour-force managed and controlled through a hierarchy of authority. Some skill requirements, e.g. for highly specialised or highly unskilled labour may be met through sub-contracting or casual labour on a one-off basis. Most cannot, nor do such arrangements address issues of authority as well as skill, since outside short-term labour has less stake in employment offered by particular firms.

Underlying this analysis are two major revisions on

Williamson's part. The first involves acceptance of the proposition that markets are not in fact self-regulating and orderly, but rather are prone to opportunism and evasion of responsibility. Firms are required to discipline self-interested behaviour into orderly channels. Second, the rationality of economic actors is imperfect or bounded rather than omniscient. Firms are needed to provide a stable framework able to deal with complex and unforeseen contingencies that occur during the course of economic relations. We are a long way here from the self-clearing, virtually instantaneous market.

Williamson's arguments are of major significance in radically re-casting much of the pre-existing, over-individualised tradition of economic liberalism. Rather than treating perfect competition as the norm against which deviations can be analysed as special limiting cases, organisations and markets are accorded co-primacy as equally plausible poles of economic action, depending on context and conditions. This permits a greater realism of analysis because it recognises the advent of large-scale firms and the mechanisms by which organisations, through their internal arrangements, limit the scope of market relationships. A major attraction of the theory in explaining economic life is its capacity to explain why organisations dominate some sectors, while short-term spot markets dominate others.

There are, however, several weaknesses in the theory. In the first place, critics such as Granovetter (1985) are concerned that it over-estimates the utility of managerial hierarchy in solving economic problems. He challenges Williamson's assumption that hierarchies elicit easy obedience and the employees respond to hierarchy in a manner that maximises the technically efficient resolution of economic problems. A survey by Dalton (1959) of the organisational structure of a major chemical plant shows that organisational hierarchies may place organisational politics above technical efficiency. If the system works it does so through inter-personal networks rather than formal hierarchy, indeed hierarchy may encourage evasion of central authority rather than efficient compliance. Granovetter uses empirical material of this kind to dispute the functionalist claim of Williamson that because large firms exist, they must do so because they perform certain functions more efficiently than do markets. As an alternative Granovetter calls for a more sociological account of the range of economic, political and cultural factors that may enter into economic behaviour.

William Ouchi (1980) has suggested one way of doing this. He recasts Williamson's two-dimensional argument about markets and hierarchies into a three-dimensional argument in terms of markets, bureaucracies and class. Ouchi accepts Williamson's argument that markets may fail to provide effective organisation where economic conditions are uncertain and where individual opportunism in the workforce is high. In such situations, 'bureaucracies' (a concept akin to Williamson's 'hierarchies') provide advantages such as long-term labour contracts, inter-personal trust and professional solidarities. These enable organisations to cope with uncertainty and/or individual opportunism. However, bureaucracies themselves may fail, according to Ouchi, where the evaluation of performance becomes ambiguous and refractory to bureaucratic definition and surveillance. Such conditions typically apply in firms using advanced technology, teamwork, and liable to constant innovation in work practices, all of which create ambiguity in performance evaluation. In such contexts a third type of organisation, neglected by Williamson, namely the 'clan' emerges. This is based on common commitment to goals and procedural norms, operated in an informal way among closely-knit co-workers. This analysis opens up considerable scope for the analysis of organisational culture (see Chapter 8).

A second line of criticism of Williamson, from an entirely different, neo-Marxist direction, sees organisational hierarchies as all too effective control mechanisms by which managerial authority is exerted over the workforce (Marglin 1974). Such criticisms raise the issue of fundamental inequalities of power within economic life between those who own and control the economy, and those who work in it as wage and salary earners. This introduces into the analysis for the first time what we shall refer to henceforth as a political economy perspective. The underlying assumption here for the present line of argument is that there are systematic structures of inequality of power present in the market-place which dictate both the aims of economic life and the distribution of economic rewards. The problem is not therefore organisations or markets since these are both connected with overarching structures of power. From this

95

viewpoint Williamson does not go far enough in bringing issues of organisational authority into the analysis. We now turn, therefore, to the problem of power in the market.

POWER AND THE MARKET: CIVILISING AND LIBERATING OR CONTROLLING AND SELF-DESTRUCTIVE

There is no consensus among analysts on the role and function of the market within society. As we have already seen, the tradition of economic liberalism portrays the market both as a rational, efficient and self-regulating mechanism for supplying human wants and as a key element in individual freedom. This point of view has not stood intact or without challenge over the last two hundred and fifty years. We have already noted certain problems with it, including certain difficulties with the key concepts of self-interest and market self-regulation. An even more fundamental set of problems arises when we look at the treatment of power within the market economy, and ask whether markets do really act as supporters of freedom and liberty.

In its original form, the theory of the market assumed a world of individuals (or at least individual households) more or less equal in power. Markets were seen as a liberating force able to constrain the arbitrary powers of monarchies and tyrants. This premise was the foundation upon which the market was associated with individual freedom. In addition, as Hirschman (1982) points out, market-based commerce was seen by eighteenth-century observers as a civilising agent able to soften the brutish, barbaric and warlike customs of feudal and traditional societies. Interactions between individuals in the market were seen to encourage industriousness over indolence, and rationality over hypocrisy and arrogance.

Such ideals have never been fully instituted, and in some key respects, the late twentieth century may seem further away rather than nearer to their realisation. What has happened in the meantime can be summarised under two main headings. First the scale of firms and corporations has grown enormously, creating vast concentrations of economic power. Second, markets have come to be associated with crisis, conflict and self-destruction rather than civilised manners and peaceable behaviour. This

96

highly critical view has not in any way vanquished the positive evaluation of markets, largely because other types of non-market economic systems, such as command or socialist economies have themselves experienced crisis and collapse. However, the case for markets as agencies of freedom no longer has the monopoly over progressive politics that it did in the eighteenth century.

There are two major issues which should be considered at this point in the discussion. The first of these centres on the implications of concentrations of market power. Do such tendencies completely undermine the claims of the market to underpin individual freedom? The second concerns the necessity or otherwise of a moral framework for economic activity. We shall examine these in turn.

We have noted in the previous section that liberal economists have gradually admitted increasing importance for concentrations of market power. Firms and corporations have been integrated into this tradition through the analysis of imperfect competition and, more radically, in Williamson's analysis of markets and hierarchies. Does this go far enough in recognising the institutionalisation of power? Economic liberals assume that it does because they still regard markets as constraining all economic actions whether large or small, as well as governments concerned with income-raising and public expenditure. While such constraints may be less important for the powerful, they still exist as a factor to be reckoned with. What constraints are we talking of here?

First and foremost is the constraint on producers exercised by consumers through the market. Most of the concentrations of economic power that have been identified focus either on industrial corporations or on financial institutions such as banks. Such concentrations of power may also be linked to government, especially where producers of goods or services rely on government as a principal consumer, e.g. in defence industries. In the USA the term 'military-industrial' complex developed in the 1950s and 1960s to refer to one such concentration. Yet even allowing for producer power of this kind bringing with it access to information and political power, economic liberals insist that consumers are not powerless.

In markets composed of private individuals, economic liberals claim that freedom to purchase at a particular price, to purchase another product or to refrain from purchase remains, and is constrained mainly by available purchasing power and access to information. Even though production is often concentrated while consumption is fragmented among individual consumers, this does not obliterate in the words of Milton Friedman, 'the freedom to choose'.

This argument is hard to evaluate from within the internal resources of economic liberalism because many of the key questions and relevant research findings have not been addressed within this tradition. A number of strong reservations must therefore be noted at this stage, pending more systematic examination later in the study.

First, it is no doubt true that market systems based on differentiation of the economy from government offer the potential for greater individual autonomy in consumer choices within the range of private goods available to individuals. As such they contrast with command or state socialist systems based on the integration of the economy with centralised political decision-making, where choices about what to produce and what price to charge are made centrally. If we are comparing ideals the former system emphasises greater individual autonomy, and if freedom is defined in terms of personal autonomy, then greater individual freedom. Whether market systems deliver greater access to public goods (e.g. an unpolluted environment or social security) is a more complex issue. It appears that market economies may or may not be accompanied by significant public goods provision. High levels are evident in Scandinavia, lower levels in Japan (Esping-Andersen 1990). Part of the reason for this contrast may relate to variations in the importance of democratic participation in decision-making, public goods provision being more likely where democracy is stronger. Market ideals therefore may not be enough to guarantee public goods and collective freedoms. The market needs to be combined with democracy for this to occur. On the other hand, there is no compelling evidence that the ideal of a state socialist or command economy necessarily delivers better access to public goods than market systems – witness the colossal pollution problems generated in Soviet and Eastern European societies in the last three decades. Securing of collective freedoms is therefore a more complex issue requiring further analysis.

Once we move from general evaluation of systems proclaiming specific ideals to actual evidence on the impact of specific concentrations of power in specific situations, then a number of further points can be made. One important set of issues centres on the degree of practical freedom that consumers may exercise in various markets. The question of access to information is a central one here, as is the impact – informative or misleading – of advertising. How far consumers are in a position to make informed choices is not a question that has been adequately researched by economic liberals.

This issue may be linked with a further crucial problem, namely the global distribution of economic power. The concentrations of economic power already noted, are not restricted to particular Western nation-states but have an international and multinational outreach. They include the activities of industrial corporations such as IBM, Exxon, Mitsubishi and ICI, as well as financial institutions and Western development agencies such as the International Monetary Fund and World Bank. We are a very long way here from the eighteenth-century ideal of a world of small producers, unable to constrain each other or other third parties.

If we pick up the question of producer–consumer relations, we may ask how much freedom do Third World consumers have to exercise free choice in purchasing products originating in the West? How typical for example, is the practice of pharmaceutical companies marketing in poor Third World countries medical products already declared unsafe by Western governments? Economic liberals appear to by-pass these awkward questions.

Another set of issues involves not merely consumer access to information, but the very capacity to enter the market as a consumer. If this capacity is impaired by poverty or unemployment, then freedom to choose becomes a rather empty freedom restricted to the purchase of necessities. To push this question further requires analysis of the causes of poverty and unemployment. Economic liberals have devoted rather more attention to this problem. This is partly because it challenges the optimistic assessment they make of the market as a rational and efficient as well as a free system.

Again the answers given do not exhaust the relevant research agendas. Two types of response have emerged over the last two hundred years. One is to treat at least part of poverty or unemployment as the voluntary consequence of irrational or feckless behaviour. This type of explanation was especially prevalent in the nineteenth century and generated a range of policy responses, including denial of public support to those who would not work and promotion of education in work-relevant capacities. From this viewpoint welfare state provision is often regarded as contributing to voluntary unemployment. Another type of response treats poverty or unemployment as the effect of poor political decision-making, focussing on what is regarded as excessive interference in market processes. These are seen as retarding efficiency, economic growth and hence the capacity to generate work and rising incomes for all.

Analysts such as Downs and the public choice theorists have developed this latter line of argument by arguing that politicians, being self-interested, typically seek to buy votes through dispersal of public expenditure to various segments of the electorate, in order to stay in power. This has the effect of arbitrarily increasing public expenditure in response to electoral considerations, and at the expense of market efficiency (Downs 1957).

The problem with this line of argument is the assumption that markets operate at optimum efficiency and make their optimum contribution to human welfare with the minimum government intervention. Even if this were true, according to neo-classical theory, it would only be so for perfect markets. Where markets are imperfect due to concentrations of economic power, there is no guarantee of efficient self-regulation, even if we define this in technical terms relating solely to productivity of the firm. Consequently there is no strict nexus between market freedom, economic efficiency and economic growth. Poverty and unemployment are not therefore to be explained simply in terms of excessive government intervention.

This does not mean that governments can do what they like without reference to market conditions or considerations of efficiency. Public intervention, however, may be supportive of efficiency, especially where it assists private business in meeting costs or provides infrastructural assistance. There is no necessary problem with government involvement as such. Nor is it the case that the trend of public expenditure is necessarily upwards as a simplistic effect of political vote-buying. The research agenda on the relationship between politics and markets is more complex, deserving of more attention than economic liberals have so far given it.

One component of this wider research agenda follows from the Marxist critique of the market – a topic we shall explore in greater depth in following chapters. For the moment, we shall simply note that this critique rejects the liberalistic and civilising approach to the market in favour of a unitary theory of power and domination. This theory claims that the market is necessarily an arena of power, inequality and exploitation. It is not only that producers dominate consumers, that the Western world dominates the global economic system, or that the market generates poverty and unemployment. All these are seen as manifestations of the inner logic of the capitalist mode of production. Instead of the market, the focus of enquiry shifts to capitalism conceived as a system that simultaneously dominates the economy, the political arena and the wider culture. What integrates this system is power over economic resources. This, however, leads to crisis and self-destruction rather than the creation of freedom.

This argument amounts to a separate tradition of enquiry into economy and society. As such, the confrontation between economic liberalism and the Marxist critique will be suspended until the following chapters where a more systematic account of this alternative tradition will be provided. We shall then return to issues raised here concerning power relations as they enter into the relationships between markets and politics, producers and consumers and the global economy.

MARKETS AND THE PROBLEM OF A MORAL FRAMEWORK

A final issue already raised by the foregoing analysis is whether markets are constituted simply by self-interest. This question takes on added significance if we accept that markets generate concentrations of economic power and embrace organisations as well as individuals. Such developments not only provoke the question 'Is the ideal of individual freedom any longer attainable?' but also raise the more fundamental concern, 'Are economies simply arena for the exercise of power in support of

101

self-interest, dispensing with any kind of integrative moral or normative framework altogether'? If so, this would imply either that economic life has nothing whatsoever to do with moral issues, or that what moral framework there may be derives from sources external to the economy.

One influential argument developed in the twentieth century claims that market economies tend to destroy the moral foundations which they initially required to function (Weber 1930; Schumpeter 1961). Compared with the seventeenth- and eighteenth-century values of individual freedom, frugality and probity, it has been argued that contemporary markets have become more amoral. Self-interest and possessive individualism has triumphed over the earlier moral justification for the market.

Hirsch (1976) maintained that this depleted moral legacy was the product of the erosion of integrative values of obligation, restraint and trust, brought about by the decline of religion and tradition. Since the market and economic individualism played its part in this process of erosion, Hirsch claims that market economies are self-destructive. They destroy the moral frames of reference they originally required in which to function. This argument is similar in form to the earlier argument of Schumpeter (1961) who claimed that market economies require the moral support of traditionalism to survive. In this version of the self-destruction argument, the very same critical rationalism fostered by the market is eventually used as a critique of the market and market-based values.

All this does not matter very much to most latter-day schools of economic liberalism who identify in self-interest and amoral opportunism the mainsprings of human behaviour. (The suggestive discussion of economic life and moral order by James Buchanan is very much an exception here.) Nor does it matter very much to critics of economic liberalism who substitute organisational power for individual self-interest as the integrating regulator of economic relations. Accordingly the issue of whether economic systems require moral regulation is not a major theme in the tradition of political economy which we investigate next. Put another way, political economic traditions do not provide an exhaustive response to the problems and inadequacies of the tradition of economic liberalism.

In this chapter we identified some prima facie reasons why we may regard moral or normative regulation as a matter of continuing salience in economic life. This stems from the critique of the pre-social theory of human wants, the neglect of meta-preferences and the inadequacy of self-interest as a means of providing workable guarantees of reliability in economic relations. We noted that the incidence of self-interest varies according to economic, political and cultural variables, rather than appearing as a universal feature of human behaviour in all contexts. We also identified informal networks of trust as an important example of normative regulation. Compared with the impact of power, it may of course be that moral regulation plays a restricted role in economic life. Nonetheless, for the moment we leave the problem of moral regulation as an unresolved issue, pending further classification of the analysis of power, conflict and inequality in the next part of this study.

5

POLITICAL ECONOMY
Bringing power back in

A very simple way of introducing political economy – the second of our three major traditions – is though the phrase 'Bringing power back in'. Whereas economic liberalism has operated with a muted and very limited concern for power and inequality in economic life, for political economy power provides the core insight by which the economy, and the relations between economy and society may be understood.

A PROBLEM OF TERMINOLOGY

As used here, the term political economy refers to a theoretical tradition embracing thinkers like Ricardo, Marx, latter-day Marxists and the world-system theorist Wallerstein and his associates. What all these hold in common is the insight that economic life is constituted through networks of power involving dominant and subordinate social groups. This contrasts with the core emphases of economic liberalism on individual sovereignty and market self-regulation.

Historically, political economy emerged in the eighteenth century as the primary means of enquiry into economic matters. The juxtaposition of the two words 'political' and 'economy' is a reminder that at that stage the economy was not seen as sharply differentiated from political affairs. Political economy, in this sense, still embedded economic issues in a political framework. This practice contrasts with the much more highly differentiated nineteenth- and twentieth-century term 'economics' where political issues generally remain outside the mainstream of economic thought. It is therefore appropriate to use the term 'political economy' to signify the importance of integrating together economic and political analysis, including the analysis of power (for a similar recent usage see Nell 1972).

Having said this, it is equally true that many of the earliest economic liberals, such as Adam Smith regarded themselves as writing political economy, because this was still the conventional term to describe economic enquiry. This historical identification of eighteenth-century economic thinkers with political economy is not followed in this study. Instead, we identify with a more contemporary usage of the term, which refers to a body of thought critical of economic liberalism. Political economy in this sense is regarded as a discrete tradition in its own right, centred on a distinct set of core propositions.

POLITICAL ECONOMY AS AN INTELLECTUAL, MORAL AND POLITICAL REACTION TO ECONOMIC LIBERALISM

Just as economic liberalism emerged from processes of political debate, social conflict and change, so too did the tradition of political economy. In many respects it may be seen as a historical reaction both to economic liberalism and to the establishment of a society in which the market economy was becoming more highly differentiated from the remainder of social life. However, in contrast with the optimistic faith of liberalism in individualism and the self-regulating character of the market, political economy focussed on problems of instability, inequality and crisis that had emerged with the market, and private ownership and control of economic resources. Instead of a harmonious realm of freedom and liberty, what appeared to be emerging by the first half of the nineteenth century was a conflict-ridden society dominated by inequality, exploitation and injustice (Polanyi 1944; Thompson 1963).

One of the main difficulties with the liberal tradition is the problem of social integration. How can a society of individuals hold together, especially now that traditional ties of religion had weakened? Critics of the market economy and the liberal focus on private individual freedoms can be separated into two main kinds. The first or Romantic critics focus on what they regarded as the shrivelled and impoverished view of human personality projected by liberalism. The vision of *homo oeconomicus*, dominated by self-interest, seemed to exclude bonds between individuals, including those of community and ties of passion and emotion. The language of economics stressed rationality and science at the expense of values and feeling. Many Romantics appealed to community as the necessary basis of social integration, but this appeal took many forms. These ranged from a reassertion of the conservative values of tradition, through ideals of nationalism and patriotism to more radical revamped conceptions of community, such as Robert Owen's co-operative commonwealth.

A second response to market society and the world-view of economic liberalism took up the appeal to science and reason rather than values, emotions and community. This second strand maintained that the institutions of private property and the market could not be relied upon to provide a continuing source of improving welfare for human society. Writing in this vein, Marx and subsequent authors in the tradition of radical political economy, argued that private property and the market systematically distorted human capacities. This distortion, which depended on an unequal system of power relations, was identified as a profound source of human alienation (Marx 1964). Within a system dominated by the market and the production of commodities to be exchanged for private profit, individuals lost any creative control over the process of labour through which they endeavoured to satisfy their wants. Market competition not only ruled out any kind of creative self-expression through work, but also isolated individuals from one another as each competed for employment. In this argument competition ruled out genuine co-operation and community because human labour was reduced to a commodity to be bought and sold in an impersonal manner according to requirements of profitability.

As a result of all this, political economists increasingly abandoned the notion of a market economy as a system of natural liberty. They replaced it, over the course of the nineteenth and early twentieth centuries, with the notion of a capitalist economic system necessarily based on inequalities of power. Instead of harmony the prognosis was for conflict. Instead of the focus on free-standing individuals the emphasis was on social groups, more especially classes, possessing different interests and different degrees of power, clashing with each other.

Although a distinction can be made between the Romantic and political economic critiques of the market economy, this should not be pushed too far. While political economy has always appealed to science and reason rather than values and emotions as such, there is quite clearly a strong moral philosophy underpinning it. This projects modern values of individual freedom and equality, but in a rather different way to economic liberalism. Such values are grounded not in pre-social assumptions about individual rationality and sovereignty but in strongly collectivist or communal conceptions of human nature and capacity. Freedom and equality therefore cannot be realised by individuals in isolation, free from external constraint, but only within society, as collective rights embodied in the relations that apply between individuals and groups. The key to these relations is not the freedom of consumers to exercise choice over the purchase of commodities. It is rather the freedom of human beings as producers to both control, and express themselves through the labour process free from arbitrary constraint. It is however conventional for political economy, as for liberal economics to suppress any explicit value-judgements, leaving the impression that these doctrines stand or fall as scientific or positivistic analyses of the facts of economic life.

Just as economic liberalism became a political force as part of general European processes of social and political upheaval, so too did political economy find political expression. Above all, perhaps, it became the intellectual underpinning for an increasingly significant sector of the organised labour and socialist movements as they developed in the nineteenth and early twentieth century. The precise impact of such ideas is a complex matter which has been analysed by a range of labour historians including E.P. Thompson (1963) and E.J. Hobsbawm (1964). Liberalism itself exerted a considerable influence on labour movements throughout the nineteenth century, as did more moralistic religious sources of dissent, especially in Britain. The influence of liberalism was probably of major significance up until the Great Depression when the future of capitalism as a stable economic system appeared to be in real doubt, while socialist or communist alternatives had now become feasible political alternatives. In all of this the intellectual backbone of rational critique available to labour and socialist leaders depended increasingly on the demonstration that the market was not tending in the direction of natural liberty but was, on the contrary concentrating power and influence at a remarkable rate.

THE CORE COMPONENTS OF POLITICAL ECONOMY

The core components of political economy, as analysed here, are an amalgam of ideas taken from a range of sources. These include nineteenth-century thinkers such as Marx and Ricardo, as well as late nineteenth- and twentieth-century neo-Marxist theorists such as Wallerstein, and finally theorists of welfare capitalism such as Esping-Andersen. The key concepts of this tradition include the following:

Power and exploitation
Capitalism
Imperialism, globalism and the world system

Power and exploitation

The tradition of political economy, as defined here, is distinguished from economic liberalism primarily through its treatment of power in economic life. Economic liberalism regards the market, first and foremost, as a system of decentralised power and individual or organisational autonomy. Concentrations of power are one possible consequence of market exchange, but in no way a necessary feature of the market. For the tradition of political economy, by contrast, power is a core structure of economic life which determines economic objectives and the distribution of resources between social groups. Whereas economic liberalism treats concentrations of power as deviations from the norm, political economy sees power relations as a constituent feature of the way social groups produce and distribute goods in pursuit of their interests.

One of the principal ways in which radical political economy developed this argument was by means of a distinction between the surface appearance of social life under liberalism, and the

(a) Surface appearance of
     freedom of individual
     exchange

(b) Underlying reality of
     control by the powerful

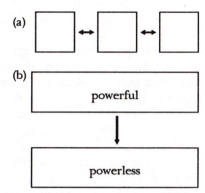

Figure 5.1 Appearance and reality in the market as seen by
political economy.

underlying reality. This argument, developed most powerfully
by Karl Marx in the mid-nineteenth century, states that the
appearance of individual sovereignty and freedom of choice
associated with the institutions of private property and the
market was in fact an illusion (Marx 1976). This argument was
applied not only to the institutions of economic liberalism like
the market, but also to the institutions of political liberalism such
as representative democracy based on citizenship rights. The
form of this argument is represented in Figure 5.1.

In each part of the figure the existence of a relationship
between two parties is indicated by an arrow, the direction of the
arrow pointing away from the source of power towards another.
In part (a) of the figure, the liberalistic view of the market as a
system of reciprocal exchange between individuals involves two-
way arrows. Each and every individual has the power to initiate
and conduct any transaction. In part (b) by contrast, the powerful
and the powerless are organised in separate bounded groups
(represented by the two boxes). In addition, the pattern of
relationships between them is one of superordination and subordination involving arrows pointing one-way and downward.

The substance of this argument about appearance and reality
is that individual sovereignty and freedom of choice are only
surface realities that give a misleading picture of an underlying
reality of constraint, inequality and exploitation. Put another
way, the market freedoms of economic liberalism are regarded

as 'abstract' because they cannot be realised in reality by the mass of the population.

Against the model of the pre-social individual, in which all entered the economy with the capacity to exercise individual freedom, political economy counterposed a world of social individuals divided according to possession of power. The key resource was not simply power as such but economic power defined in terms of private ownership of the means of production, and control over production and exchange.

It is important to note that the discussion of power within the tradition of political economy centres not on the relationship between producers and consumers. It focusses rather on relationships between owners and controllers of resources, on the one hand, and those who work for these owners and controllers on the other. This focus includes both relationships within the labour process itself (i.e. within the enterprise or firm), and relationships within the labour market that influence the terms upon which labour is employed. The argument is that this nexus of relationships establishes a pattern of inequality that influences not merely production and exchange, but wider economic and political processes. Concentrated economic power allows owners and controllers of capital influence not only over production and exchange, and over the organisation of consumption, but reaches further to constrain democratic political systems (where they exist).

One of the most celebrated examples of this argument is contained in the base–superstructure analogy used by Karl Marx (1962) to understand the predominance of economic power in society. This argument is outlined in simplified and schematic form in Figure 5.2. Here, it is the economic base that determines the political and cultural superstructure as represented by the vertical arrow leading from the base to the superstructure. Thus whoever is the dominant power in economic life will also control the state (politics) and the ruling ideas of the epoch (culture).

Much debate has arisen over the interpretation of this approach. In their later life both Marx and Engels emphasised that the analogy was meant to assist exposition rather than comprise an exhaustive theoretical statement. The point about the analogy was that it challenged existing theories which gave exclusive primacy to culture or politics. Marx's own position was

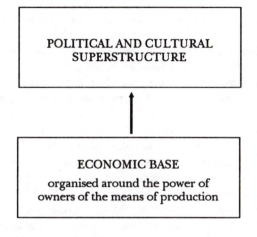

Figure 5.2 Marx's base–superstructure analogy.

actually more subtle than this analogy implies, because he did allow some degree of interaction between base and super-structure. His intention was to argue only that political and cultural arrangements are always conditioned by the economic base. (For more discussion of this interpretive problem see Williams 1973; Hall 1977; Bottomore 1983.)

Such subtleties may allow some autonomy to politics and culture, but they do not displace the fundamental contribution of Marx to the theory of concentrated market power. This con-tribution, building on earlier work by Ricardo, was to establish an alternative line of analysis which reformulated the problem of power in relation to the existence of private economic power and control over the means of production.

The plausibility of this alternative to economic liberalism arose from fundamental changes in the structure of European economies between the seventeenth century (when liberalism first emerged) and the nineteenth century (when political economy in our sense became prominent).

With the seventeenth- and early eighteenth-century world of small producers in mind, early representatives of liberalism were able to conceive of the possibility of a decentralised system of power relations based on free-standing individual sovereignty. One key dimension to this was a belief in the capacity to get access to land as an economic resource. In fact, this picture of small-scale production was even then by no means universal or predominant since large-scale land-ownership and state-sponsored monopolies also existed. Nonetheless, the liberalistic view of a decentralised economic power structure was far more realistic at that time than it was to become after the Industrial Revolution, with the coming of the factory system and urban-industrial society.

A key question affecting the feasibility of a decentralised system of market power is as follows: 'How far can all individuals reasonably gain access to a share of economic resources such that they do not become dependent on the power of others?' By the mid-nineteenth century it had become quite clear that access to land-ownership, in the 'old world' of Europe at least, was getting more difficult. At the same time, access to capital-ownership and an entrepreneurial career was also becoming limited in most key sectors of the new industrial economy, especially in textiles, iron and steel and mining, where the capital costs of entry were getting higher. It is true that many small tradesmen, artisans and small farmers did save, and could accumulate modest sums of capital. However, even small business and self-employment, while widespread, were not growing as rapidly as larger-scale enterprise. Since access to education as an alternative route to advancement remained limited, the only practical options for most of Europe's population were either wage-labour or emigration to areas of white settlement such as the USA and Australia. Here access to land was less difficult and the social structure more fluid, encouraging opportunities for upward mobility. Nonetheless, by the end of the century even these outlets were less buoyant, especially with the closing of the American frontier in the 1890s.

This brief economic history of limited opportunity forms the backdrop to the theoretical analyses by political economy of the evolving pattern of concentrated power. Such analyses presumed that all could not simultaneously be capital-owners or entrepreneurs. Without the transformation of labour into the commodity wage-labour, it would not be possible for the full and unfettered development of a market system, responsive to the supply and demand for commodities to take place. In the absence of wage-labour, market development would be limited by the persistence of peasant-based production, in which integration into the market was only partial. Many peasants seek profits, but an even higher priority is maintenance of the integrity of the peasant household and kinship structure.

The growth in economies of scale also meant that many individuals must become wage-earners selling their labour-power on the market in order for the growth of private businesses and private business-ownership to be possible. Put another way, it was structurally necessary for wage-labour to be present in order for private businesses to grow and capital to accumulate. From this viewpoint concentrations of economic power by the owners of capital over the growing mass of wage-labourers, were necessary features of the market economy. Without the transformation of labour into the commodity wage-labour, market development could not take place.

The effect of these processes was of course to produce a divided social structure based on inequalities of economic power and income, rather than a society of more or less equal, free-standing individuals. Such divisions had, from the early nineteenth-century European experience of industrialisation, been described in terms of divisions between social classes (Briggs 1960; Williams 1963). By 1900, even American observers, brought up on the ideal of the USA as the land of opportunity and egalitarianism, had become concerned about the rise of concentrated economic power in the hands of so-called 'robber barons', such as the entrepreneurial dynasties of Morgan and Rockefeller. Industrial concentration in the USA had fused together the banks and large industrial firms into an interlocking network of concentrated power (see the discussion in Lash and Urry 1987). In the process, the agrarian myth of the free-standing, self-sufficient farmer as the base unit of egalitarian citizenship had been eroded as 'the United States . . . born in the country . . . moved to the city' (Hofstadter 1955, p. 23).

In Europe as in the USA, the scope of this concentrated power was considerable. It was also increasingly moving beyond national frontiers as the larger corporations assembled world-wide interests. While the term 'multinational company' was not coined until 1960 (Sklair 1991), multinational productive enterprise dates from as early as 1867. We shall examine the particular issue of the globalisation of capital in a later section of this study.

The theoretical case made by the more radical political

113

economists such as Marx, took a further step by linking the existence of inequalities of power between social classes with the additional argument that such inequalities amounted to a form of exploitation. The term 'exploitation' is not easy to use in social scientific analysis without some exploration of its moral connotations. By 'exploitation' we usually refer to a social practice in which a group of individuals are systematically deprived of something that is their due, by another group of individuals. This type of argument inevitably raises issues of the *rights* of various groups to certain resources, and whether such rights are grounded purely in morality or in some legal sense as well.

The linking of inequalities of market power with exploitation is typically associated with the deprivation of workers of the value of their contribution to the labour process. This argument generally deploys the labour theory of value which holds that labour is the source of all value. While it originated in medieval Christian theology, this argument as taken up by political economists was utilised to claim that the market was founded on the exploitation of labour rather than free choice and liberty. Political economists pursued this argument in an ostensibly scientific manner through technical attempts to equate the quantity of labour embodied in a commodity with its value on the market. Marx (1976) himself developed a formula whereby the value of a commodity reflected the socially necessary labour time embodied in it.

The presence of exploitation followed from the proposition that while labour was the source of all value, labour did not receive back in wages an equivalent of the value created during the labour process. This is because the capitalist received part of the value created as profit. Radical political economy did not regard this as a legitimate return to the capitalist because it did not believe that the capitalist added anything to the production process. Accumulated capital was regarded instead as the embodiment of previous acts of labour.

It is hard to accept that the labour theory of value, conceived in these terms, is anything other than a moral argument, founded on the moral premise that labour should receive the full value it alone adds to commodities during the process of production. The moral foundations of this argument have become clearer, since political economy failed to produce a convincing demonstration

114

that the value of commodities could be measured in terms of socially necessary labour time. It has also proved extremely difficult to demonstrate how value as so measured approximated to market price. Many contemporary analysts writing in the Marxist tradition reject the labour theory of value altogether (e.g. Steedman 1977; Roemer 1982; Wright 1985).

What remains of the political economic argument, if the labour theory of value is dispensed with, is still a strong argument that economic power controls market arrangements to the benefit of the strong. One consequence of this is a rejection of the liberal economic theory of wage determination, which sees wages set in terms of the marginal productivity of labour. By this is meant the productivity of the least productive worker at the margin between profit and loss. The alternative theory advanced by political economy is that wages, like all other returns of income-bearing assets, are set by the relative bargaining strength of wage-recipients as compared with recipients of other types of income.

This approach owes at least as much to Ricardo, Marx's predecessor as to Marx himself. Ricardo (1973), a liberal adherent of free trade, stands at the juncture of economic liberalism and political economy. While committed like Smith to market institutions, his analysis of the distribution of income in early nineteenth-century England led him to the conclusion that analysis should proceed not so much in terms of individual sovereignty, as in terms of economic conditions affecting the three great social classes of land-owners, capitalists and workers. These classes were defined in terms of their source of income, namely rents, profits and wages. Economic liberals had often used these categories of aggregation, but usually argued that the interests of the individuals comprising each aggregation were mutually compatible with each other and conducive to economic expansion. Ricardo, by contrast, emphasised problems and likely crises arising from the situation now facing each group. In particular, he argued that the interest of land-owners receiving rents was incompatible with the interests of other classes in society (Clarke 1982). This critique was associated in large measure with land-owners' support for the Corn Laws which kept up food prices and agricultural rents, and exerted an upward pressure on wages – all at the cost of profits.

Ricardo's theory of distribution operated as follows. As

population grew with economic expansion, he argued that less fertile land would be brought into production, generating less wealth per unit of land and consequently lowering rents to land-owners. At the same time profits accruing to capitalists would be squeezed by the expansion of wages required to pay to an expanding workforce. However, such a profits squeeze would be a disincentive to further economic expansion, producing a stationary level of development. In contrast to the burgeoning optimism and confidence of economic liberals, Ricardo produced a rather muted picture in which the new market economy would reach an upper limit and then remain in a stationary state.

As events turned out, this pessimistic scenario under-estimated the capacity of the nineteenth-century economy for productivity improvement which helped to obviate the squeeze on profits. Nonetheless, Ricardo's theory of distribution stimulated an interest in the social relationships within which incomes were distributed. Over time this expanded to embrace the bargaining strength or power of the various parties. In modern neo-Ricardian analyses, such power relations form the framework for understanding both the allocation of resources and distribution of incomes within the economy. This is pri-marily because the distribution of incomes to capital or labour at any one stage affects the capacity of capital to allocate resources to productive investment at a later stage.

Ian Steedman (1977), a leading neo-Ricardian, argues that rates of profit and prices of products depend on levels of real wages and processes of wage determination. This line of analysis owes nothing to the labour theory of value. However, it is equally corrosive of the explanations advanced by economic liberals. Put simply, power is more important than efficiency in what really happens in economic life.

Capitalism

Recognition of the centrality of economic power in both economy and society resulted in the development of new concepts with which to understand the relationship between them. While economic liberalism speaks of the market and the development of market or commercial society, political economy developed the alternative concepts of capitalism and social class as a means of integrating power into economic analysis. The foremost contributor to this was Marx who spoke not of capitalism as such but of the capitalist mode of production.

Until the beginning of the twentieth century terms like 'capitalism' or the 'capitalist mode of production' were very much restricted to Marxist discourse (Schumpeter 1961). Thereafter the terminology has become more widely diffused. At the heart of the specifically Marxist usage is the idea of capital as *the* central component of a distinct *system* of economic and social organisation. This usage of the term 'capital' is not intended as a technical economic category referring to movable inanimate resources distinct from land or labour, available for profit-seeking. It is conceived rather as a set of social relationships between people; relationships that are dominated by the power of those private interests who own and control capital over those who sell their labour power for a wage.

Although capital is seen as a relationship not a thing, Marx argued that the operation of the capitalist mode of production turned economic activity into a profoundly impersonal and depersonalising experience. This arose from the primary objective of the system to realise profit through maximisation of the exchange-value of commodities (Marx 1976). Marx contrasted this emphasis on value in exchange – how much will this product realise on the market – with the use-value of the objects of labour – what human wants do products satisfy. He argued that the capitalist mode of production elevated exchange-value over use-value, and in so doing severed any previous connection that may have existed between economic objectives and the satisfaction of human welfare.

The impersonal objectives of the system were related not only to the objective of maximum exchange-value, but also to the transformation of labour into a commodity. Looked at historically, labour within less differentiated economies was directed at the satisfaction of wants. Even though previous economic systems were in most respects poverty-stricken, human labour was at least directed at survival. In hunter–gatherer societies or peasant agriculture people produced what they consumed. With the highly differentiated capitalist mode of production, by contrast, people worked for the profit of others, and need have no connection with what was produced. According to Marx this turned labour into a depersonalising activity in which individuals found little fulfilment. Labour had no control over the objectives of consumption, and was required to be indifferent to the consumption of what was produced. Someone else, in all likelihood, consumed the product of an individual's labour, just as the individual workers consumed products made by unknown individuals. Whereas economic liberals regard the loss of co-operative labour for direct use as justified by the wider range of commodities available for consumption, political economists argue that the social costs of depersonalisation are enormous.

Marx himself referred to the pathological consequence of depersonalisation in terms of the fetishism of commodities (1976). By this he meant that the individual workers encountered a world in which commodities were offered for sale at a particular price, without any visible recognition of the human labour that had gone into making them. Whether this theory of social pathology is accepted as valid depends in large measure on how far production takes precedence over consumption, as a more central aspect of human experience. Put another way, are human desires to control the purpose of work permitting an intimate relationship between production and consumption stronger than desires based on want-satisfaction through the consumption of commodities alone? We shall return to evaluate this question in Chapter 6.

The central feature of power relations within the capitalist mode of production, according to Marx, is the capacity of capital to realise exchange-value through the sale of commodities. Whereas economic liberals regard the market as a means of realising use-values by providing 'utilities' to individuals, political economists regard capitalism as a system that must necessarily seek out profit for capital-owners. Underlying this is an emphasis on the power of producers over consumers and the power of capital over production.

The seeking out of exchange-value – described by political economists as the valorisation of capital – is regarded in this analysis as a structural imperative. This imperative depends on assumptions made about the effect of competition on production for exchange. In order to compete effectively, capital must be deployed to the most profitable extent. Whilst labour was still largely tied to the land in an economically and geographically immobile manner, sufficient flexibility in minimising costs and maximising returns was impossible. In the fifteenth, sixteenth and seventeenth centuries, for example, capital-owners had supplied peasants in their own homes with raw material to make up as saleable commodities, in the putting-out system. These arrangements did not allow capital sufficient scope to satisfy expanding markets, or permit direct control over the pace and intensity of work. Far more advantageous to capital was a situation where attachment to the land was severed, and where workers became solely reliant on a wage to survive. These processes occurred in the eighteenth and nineteenth centuries, partly through over-population on the land encouraging some to seek work in the cities, partly through the attraction of higher wages in cities, and in some cases through labour-displacing enclosures of common land in the countryside (Kriedte et al. 1981).

By whatever mechanism, the commodification of labour power represents the major pre-condition for capitalist control over labour in pursuit of profit. In addition however, continuing control is required to ensure effective power over production. This involves two key aspects of economic life, namely (a) the terms upon which labour is hired in the labour market and (b) the effectiveness of capitalist control over the labour process.

Within the labour market, the power of capital depends on the capacity to hire and fire workers who have no other source of livelihood. Labour market conditions affected the extent of this power. For example, in conditions of depression, increased unemployment increased the capacity of employers to dictate who they would employ and on what terms. On the other hand, differences in the demand for various types of labour could enhance the capacity of some groups, e.g. those possessing skills over the unskilled. While Marx himself treated labour as an increasingly undifferentiated group, not all subsequent political economists agree. Such debates have been reflected in the 'deskilling' debate in which proponents of the increased homogeneity of labour hypothesis (e.g. Braverman 1974) have been challenged by those who see the labour market as segmented by skill and working conditions (Doeringer and Piore 1971; Gordon 1972; Reich et al. 1973), and by those who argue

119

that skills are often retained through trade union struggle or new skills developed to meet production needs (Penn 1982, 1984; Penn and Scattergood 1985).

A related strand of political economic enquiry has focussed on the labour process and the extent to which capital has achieved unilateral control over labour at the point of production. This theme raises for consideration the impact of technological and managerial arrangements on the control of labour. One of the key issues in this area is the extent to which capitalism depends on the highly rationalised measurement and costing of work-tasks, designed to reduce labour to routine cost-sensitive processes of execution. This managerial strategy is known as Taylorism after the founder of scientific management, Frederick Taylor. Such strategies appear to vary in their importance, being more suitable to control of mass production processes than to labour that involves more autonomy and some degree of conceptual input from the worker alongside more routine applications. The view that capital tends towards one overarching strategy of control has been rejected by many political economists (see the essays in Knights and Willmott 1990).

Underlying all such arguments, however, is a common ground within political economy, in which capital and labour are seen as having mutually incompatible interests which conflict. It is such conflicts of interest which require the continuous exercise of control over labour.

Conflict is manifest along two dimensions. The first concerns incomes. While capital seeks the highest profit, labour seeks the highest wages. This conflict, while usually paramount, does not exclude a further second dimension. This involves control issues. Here capital seeks control over the labour process, not only in terms of the allocation of resources (e.g. in terms of how much employment is necessary to meet production objectives), but also in terms of authority (e.g. who should authorise terms and conditions of work). While capital seeks unilateral authority or at the very least ultimate authority in collective bargaining with labour, labour for its part seeks either joint bargaining rights or legislative regulation of economic life.

Such conflicts of interest are seen by political economy in terms of an *asymmetry of power* between capital and labour. Put simply, capital has more advantages on its side than does labour. Such advantages include greater access to economic resources, and greater access to alternative income-generating opportunities. Whereas individual workers have to be able to secure an income to survive, capital-owners are far less vulnerable in terms of survival. In the case of a strike, for example, capital has the resources to hold out longer than labour. There are always a range of options in which capital may invest, whereas alternative employment options may not be so easy to find. Labour will generally be disadvantaged when underlying economic conditions are slack and unemployment high. It is also harder for workers to uproot from one locality to another to seek work, whereas capital-owners need not move when switching assets to other uses. These disadvantages can only be partly overcome if labour organises as a collectivity. However, collective organisation through labour movements may enable labour to challenge capital more effectively than before.

A further dimension to the political economic analysis of capitalism involves linking conflicts of interest to *crisis* and *instability*. In contrast to the economic liberal prognosis of increased harmony among individuals and organisations in pursuit of self-interest, the political economy perspective stresses that conflicts inherent in the capitalist mode of production generate a crisis-ridden performance involving phenomena such as depression, unemployment and industrial conflict. Whereas economic liberals emphasise the capacity of the market for self-regulation, political economy emphasises the incapacity of the market to regulate itself. Accordingly, the theory of capitalism has been extended beyond the earliest formulations of Karl Marx based on the analysis of competitive or *laissez-faire* capitalism. Such extensions have generally taken the form of historical stage theories of capitalist development. This historical emphasis reflects the proposition that capitalism changes a good deal of its structure over the course of time. This concern is in marked contrast with the prevailing liberal economic concern with basic and immutable laws of market exchange, regarded as historically invariant.

The most widely accepted historical approach to capitalist development focussed on a shift from *laissez-faire* to organised or monopoly capitalism. A more controversial third stage has

Table 5.1 Theories of capitalist development

Core concept	Laissez-faire capitalism	Organised or monopoly capitalism	Disorganised capitalism
Chron-ology	High point: mid-19th century	Late 19th to mid-20th centuries	Late 20th century
Character-istics	(1) Largely unregulated market (2) Small to medium-scale enterprise (3) Little state intervention (4) Little welfare state	(1) Increasingly regulated market (2) Large scale enterprises and concentrated production (3) Regulation by cartels and by state (4) Growth of welfare state	(1) Flexible specialisation in production with some shift away from large-scale and concentrated production (2) Growing importance of consumption in relation to production (3) Decreasing significance of the labour market within social stratification

recently been posited around the notion of disorganised capitalism (see especially Offe 1985; Lash and Urry 1987). A brief overview of the process of change involved here is sketched in Table 5.3. Here we outline the main components of the three stage theory against a chronology of Western economic development.

If we limit the discussion for the moment to the shift from *laissez faire* to organised capitalism (i.e. stage 1 to stage 2), we can link the previous discussion of conflict, crisis and instability with the changing structure of capitalist organisation. The key point here is the argument that capitalism generated increasing moves to regulation as a result of crises, and conflicts associated with attempts to operate the market with as little external regulation as possible. This argument advanced by the political economy tradition has made some inroads into economic liberalism in the late twentieth century as we have seen in Chapter 4 in the organisation theory of Oliver Williamson.

It is useful to focus on two types of instability and crisis affecting capitalism that led to greater regulation. The first of these involved problems created by unregulated competition. These included lack of stability for producers always liable to be undercut by others, and also periodic crises of over-production leading to price falls and the squeezing out of the least efficient or least resilient producers. Processes of this kind encouraged a concentration of small producers into larger more robust enterprises able to weather the storm. Such larger producers were increasingly able to influence prices by restricting all-out competition. This was often associated with producer cartels able to enforce stable and regular prices. In addition, large-scale enterprises often encouraged governments to protect markets from overseas competition, thereby protecting prices and limiting competition. Of course, defensive regulation is not the only reason for increasing scale and concentration. Alongside this the effect of market size must also be taken into account, since larger markets tend to produce larger firms.

The theory of monopoly capitalism (Baran and Sweezy 1966) was developed to take account of situations where a few large firms came to dominate whole industries. In this new situation, such firms are protected from competitive pressure given the large scale of their operations and the difficulty of new firms entering. This protection allows a measure of discretion in determining price, output and profit levels. Political economists such as Andrew Friedman (1977) have discussed these processes of discretion, incorporating the satisficing strategies analysed by writers like Simon (1959, 1979). Emphasis on discretion represents a significant revision of Marx's emphasis on structural imperatives driving capital accumulation.

This issue is linked to an important structural change in the corporation linked to expansion in the scale of activity. This is the relative shift from owner-management of small businesses to separation of ownership from management in larger businesses. In the first instance, this separation involved personal owners hiring managers to be able to cope with increased production and complexity of operations. As the scale of capital necessary for viable production increased, however, family or personal owners increasingly took in outside shareholders sometimes to the point where they sold out altogether. The modern structure of the corporation is then typically based on mass share-ownership largely separate from management. This raises the question of whether managers behave as simple agents of capital-owners, or whether they behave with some greater or lesser degree of autonomy.

The majority position within political economy is that managers do have some freedom to manoeuvre especially when protected from competition. This freedom is constrained, however, by an underlying test of performance, namely satisfaction of shareholders in generating profits. While it is true that managers can often defeat shareholder criticism at company meetings, this is less true of major institutional shareholders. In addition, shareholders may sell shares that do not perform, and companies may be taken over if other interests believe they can run the business more profitably. These represent significant checks on managerial autonomy.

A further aspect of the development of a more organised capitalism especially in continental Europe, was the increased involvement of banks and financial institutions in the organisation of industrial manufacturing and raw material extraction. One defining feature for organised capitalism as it was conceived by the Austro-Marxist theorist Hilferding (1981) was the dominance of finance capital over industrial capital. The relations between finance and industry have also been of major interest to political economic analyses of British capitalism, notably in relation to the special role and political influence of the City of London over British economic development (e.g. Foster 1976; Ingham 1982).

The regulation of excessive competition also became one of several responsibilities for the growth of state involvement in economic life in the late nineteenth- and twentieth centuries. This process was even more marked in continental Europe than Britain. Indeed, it is arguable that the first stage of *laissez-faire* capitalism was largely restricted to Britain as the pioneer industrial capitalist nation. For 'late-comers' attempting economic development in the wake of Britain, a greater degree of government-organised capitalism was evident from the outset to help catch up. This included both measures such as protection of national markets, and infrastructural support for industry. Gerschenkron (1962), an economic historian rather than political economist, has developed an interesting general theory which asserts that late-comers will gain economic advantage by starting off with more concentrated and organised forms of economic activity.

If regulation of excessive competition is the first linkage between instability and greater organisation, a second set of linkages involve what came to be called the 'social question' in nineteenth-century discourse. This involved the condition of the working class and the poor under the impact of capitalist industrialisation and limited market regulation. Crisis features of this 'social question' involved new phenomena such as unemployment and poverty created during downswings in the new industrial trade cycle, and harsh conditions of work in the factory system such as long hours. Finally, these employment and labour market conditions were overlaid by poor environmental conditions in the cities involving problems of adequate water supply, housing and sewage disposal. From the viewpoint of nineteenth-century radical political economists, the majority of these problems stemmed from *laissez-faire* capitalism. As a result, they jointed the amalgam of labour activists, middle-class reformers and conservatives seeking in one way or another to alleviate these problems by means of expanded social citizenship rights and social regulation. Such moves built upon the extension of democracy through franchise reform, itself a product of political-economic conflict. By the end of the nineteenth century, much of the cutting edge for social change was emanating from the organised labour movement.

While the complex history of this move to social protection has been well researched elsewhere, what remains of importance to our present purposes is the effect of social pressure on the construction of a welfare state. The underlying assumptions behind this institutional innovation were, first, that the market, left to its own devices, did not guarantee the welfare of all members of the population. Second, the failure of the market to guarantee freedom from unemployment, ill-health and urban over-crowding created social protest requiring state intervention to help redress problems which the market had not solved. Beyond this however, the push for the increasingly organised regulation of capitalism to meet welfare objectives involved two distinct world-views. These may be described as minimum welfare state as against optimum welfare state options.

In the former, the welfare state provides a safety-net of short-term support against economic and social contingencies, rather than comprehensive long-term support. Much welfare-state provision prior to the post Second World War period took this form. It could be supported by liberals on the grounds that short-run minimum assistance did not jeopardise individual self-reliance. If welfare benefits were set at a level sufficient to ward off destitution, but not so high as to act as a disincentive to work and save, then liberals could justify them. Against this the optimal welfare state strategy supported by socialist opponents of capitalism argued for the best possible public welfare services, generally disputing that these would be a disincentive to work. Welfare was seen as a community responsibility in its own right. While some wished to see capitalism abolished, for the moment most argued that an optimal welfare state could be funded through redistribution of the fruits of an efficient economy.

Writers within the tradition of political economy see the Great Depression of the 1930s and the experience of social and economic centralisation during the Second World War as crucial to the rapid post-war expansion of welfare states in most parts of Europe, and especially Scandinavia. The idea is that the two arguments in favour of regulating capitalism, namely economic stabilisation and social support had now come together. Keynesian economic theory during the Depression years of the 1930s had added to the existing arguments against market self-regulation by demonstrating that market equilibrium could under certain conditions be accompanied by mass unemployment and recession (Keynes 1936). This theoretical insight was used to justify macro-economic government planning of public investment to regulate economic activity. Keynesian demand management would not only stabilise capitalism economically but also secure greater social stability by avoiding depression. In this way, Keynesian arguments for increased state regulation of the market, buttressed and coalesced with previous social protection arguments in favour of an expanded welfare state. However, the political will to implement such policies depended not merely on the intellectual force of the arguments involved, nor simply on the manifest market failures of the 1930s, but also on electoral support for labour or reforming governments supportive of these changes. To some degree the coming of the welfare state represents the success of organised labour in off-setting through political means the predominant economic power of private capital.

The high-point of organised capitalism, based on concentrated private economic power, government economic planning and the welfare state, has occurred in the post-war period, culminating in the 1970s and early 1980s. At this point in time, the scale of government spending as a percentage of gross domestic product had reached in excess of 60 per cent in Sweden, nearly 50 per cent in the EEC and well over one-third in the USA and Australia (OECD 1986).

One of the main distinguishing features of recent political economy is the emphasis on the political constitution of economic relationships. In the earlier *laissez-faire* stage of capitalist development, Marxist political economy tended to regard the state as a simple agent of capitalist interests. Not only was the economy differentiated from the political system, but it also dominated it. Within the organised capitalism phase, capitalist interests remained powerful, indeed the concentrations of corporate economic power became in many respects more powerful. However, the increased scope of state intervention became such as to leave the state in a far more autonomous position with respect to private economic interests than had been the case before, during the epoch of *laissez-faire* capitalism.

A typical formulation of this 'autonomy of the state' argument has been provided by Habermas (1976). He argues that, 'Today the state has to fulfil functions that can be neither explained with reference to the prerequisites of the continued existence of the [capitalist] mode of production nor derived from the immanent movement of capital' (p. 52). In this process, states become involved in reconstructing relations previously dominated by market principles. These include labour market reconstruction through quasi-political arbitration and conciliation procedures, and increased political responsibility for capital investment in collective commodities such as economic infrastructures.

Under the impact of this 'political' emphasis, a number of middle-range theories emerged, each seeking to provide an effective characterisation of political economic structures. Foremost among such discussions has been the theory of corporatism and neo-corporatism (e.g. Winkler 1974; Schmitter and

Lehmbruch (eds) 1979; Goldthorpe et al. 1984). This has been designed to shed light on the characteristic tripartite modes of regulation of economic life that developed in the 1960s and 1970s, involving government, labour and capital.

Another way of conceptualising the increased state role has been in terms of the idea of welfare capitalism. As developed by the Swedish sociologist Esping-Andersen (1990), welfare capitalism represents a social formation in which capitalist market and commodity-based relations have become modified by the regulating impact of a welfare state. Whereas the market involves commodification, the welfare state involves what he refers to as de-commodification. What this means is the achievement of social rights to welfare entitlements which are not dependent on the market and which are indeed designed to offset some of the welfare problems created by the market. These problems include lack of adequate income for categories of individuals such as the elderly, sick and unemployed.

However, Esping-Andersen goes further than this to claim that the welfare state is not merely concerned with the delivery of human welfare to address market-based problems. Beyond this role, he sees the welfare state becoming an initiator and moulder of the shape of economic and social relationships. This reflects an accumulation of political power able to challenge the power of private capital. Among the social institutions 'directly shaped and ordered by the welfare state' are 'working life, employment and the labour market', as well as 'personal life' and 'the entire political economy' (1990, p. 141). Within this theory we are talking not of a minimalist but of an optimising welfare state strategy. The evidence for this argument is based on attempts to measure the extent to which de-commodification has entered into key economic and social relationships. Such evidence is stronger for Scandinavian 'social-democratic' societies such as Sweden, than for post-war societies in which *laissez-faire* and deregulation remain powerful influences such as the USA and Britain.

The lack of general applicability of the welfare-state driven theory of social development is one reason for doubting its usefulness as a new stage of capitalist development. Another is the tendency for Esping-Andersen to work outwards from the welfare state rather than from current structures of corporate power. His argument that the economy has now become embedded in the welfare state in a reversal of the trend to social differentiation is certainly in line with Polanyi's prognosis for the reassertion of social protection and integration over excessive differentiation. And Esping-Andersen with other associates has undoubtedly produced a convincing argument for taking the welfare state seriously as a central feature of modern society. The problem nonetheless remains as to its relative *importance* vis-à-vis autonomous centres of capitalist power and with respect to processes of change initiated by private capital. This problem has become of increased significance in the 1980s with attempts by monetarist and New Right governments in the UK, USA and elsewhere to dismantle and privatise a number of welfare state initiatives. Its significance also derives from the continuing globalisation of capital throughout this period.

One alternative line of discussion which came to the fore in the increasingly globalised yet deregulatory context of the 1980s involves the theory of disorganised capitalism developed by Lash and Urry (1987). This identifies a number of recent structural modifications of the organised capitalism model. These include a shift away from highly centralised mass production systems symbolised by Henry Ford's motor vehicles empire to so-called post-Fordist methods of production. These involve smaller production runs organised in less centralised production systems, often by smaller firms or sub-contractors. Such production methods allow what has been called flexible specialisation (see especially Piore and Sabel 1984). This more decentralised approach allows greater attention to non-standardised market segmentation and is more sensitive to changes in consumer incomes and tastes. It also produces less regulation of national markets by large corporations.

Parallel with such economic changes, theorists of disorganised capitalism posit a decline in the political mediation of economic relations through corporatism. A particular example of this is said to be the decline in national quasi-political wage bargaining structures. Drawing on evidence from the EEC, Lash and Urry see an erosion of nationally focussed institutions of economic mediation, as a result of the increasing global mobility and decentralisation of capital, and the destabilising impact of immigration on the national cohesion of labour movements

(Lash and Urry 1987, pp. 309–11). One problem with this approach is that it continues to use a general theory of capitalist development. As such it fails to account for highly significant variations between nation-states. In the case of corporatism, for example, there is no general evidence for decline, but rather a complex mix of national variations over time. This sees a more robust corporatism in Australia and Scandinavia during the 1980s in contrast to deregulated patterns of political economy in Britain and the USA.

A further theme raised in Lash and Urry's theory of disorganised capitalism concerns a *spatial* relocation of capitalist production away from traditional areas of heavy industry associated with the eighteenth- and nineteenth-century Industrial Revolution. Production has been relocated instead, either to new areas within the core Western industrial nations, or to the Third World. Such shifts have undermined the power of traditional labour movements based in the older regions, often allowing a reassertion of managerial authority and unilateral domination of the labour market by employers. Trends of this kind often represent counter-tendencies to the regulatory welfare state developments evident elsewhere. The presence of counter-tendencies – regulation in some contexts, deregulation in others – suggests that disorganised capitalism may not be a coherent theory of a new stage in capitalist development. Its function as a theory may rather be to act as an umbrella concept in which a complex range of new developments may be scrutinised.

The issue of spatial changes in the location of economic activity including global economic restructuring, raises a further fundamental dimension to political economy. This involves the international context of economic relations, and in particular the relationship between power and the spatial distribution of economic life.

Imperialism, globalism and the world system

Economic liberalism has added relatively little to our understanding of the international and global dimensions of economic activity. This is primarily because of the assumption that market institutions, wherever they were located, would act as bearers of efficiency, freedom and liberty. This was thought to apply not only in the West, but also to those non-Western societies able and willing to develop market institutions. Economic liberals see no reason why the market cannot occupy the same strategic position for the non-Western world that they claim for market institutions in the West. Milton and Rose Friedman, in *The Power to Choose* (1980) highlight the *laissez-faire* economy of Hong Kong, with its emphasis on free trade and low taxes, as an example of successful market-led development outside the West.

Underlying arguments of this kind are evolutionary assumptions about the superior economic efficiency of the market. It is claimed that wherever non-Western societies reject or inhibit market processes, their capacity for economic development will be inhibited. All that stands in the way of market-led expansion – whether it be custom and tradition or socialist development strategies – is regarded as economically inefficient. Thus, there is believed to be only one *real* mode of economic development, namely that based on private property rights in economic resources combined with market institutions. Any other development strategy will be inefficient and be outflanked by the superior merits of capitalism. This type of argument has recently received a boost with the collapse of the socialist economies in Russia and Eastern Europe in 1989–90, and the official attempt to institute a transition from socialism to capitalism.

The classical nineteenth-century liberal world-view argued that the economic institutions of private property and the market, once adopted, would permit all nations to trade equitably with one another. The presumption of market effic- iency was buttressed by an argument about comparative advantage, in which it was claimed that market relations enabled all nations to specialise in those types of economic activity best suited to their natural and human resources, i.e. to their comparative advantages vis-a-vis others. The global market was linked, not only to the maximisation of human welfare, but also to the achievement of peace between nations. If economic welfare could be achieved for all, it was assumed there would be no need for war.

This market-led development strategy has also been claimed to be not only efficient but rational and modern. Economic liberal perspectives of this kind are to be found both in economic thought, and in the influential doctrines of modernisation theory developed in the 1950s and early 1960s. A typical example of this school of thought was provided by W.W. Rostow (1960) whose 'take-off' theory of economic development posited the need for a sustained burst of largely privately-controlled capital investment for societies to be able to lift themselves out of economic backwardness through self-sustaining growth. Meanwhile the preference for private rather than publicly-based development has been enshrined in the development strategies of institutions such as the World Bank and International Monetary Fund. These powerful institutions have made limitations on government spending and government regulation a prerequisite for Western capital support for development.

In contrast to this optimistic approach to global development through the institutions of private property and the market, political economy has developed a very powerful alternative. This has addressed many issues that are not adequately dealt with by economic liberalism. The foremost of these is the impact of inequalities of economic power on global development, more especially of the repressive or distorting effect of Western economic power on the chances for economic development of societies and whole regions outside the West. For most radical political economists, Third World societies either cannot develop at all, or cannot develop in a balanced manner within the global mechanisms of capitalism.

The tradition of political economy has developed, over the last hundred and fifty years, a rich and complex set of perspectives on global economic power. Starting with Marx, this body of analysis has expanded its repertoire to take into account international developments which were not apparent to Marx, or which have become more central since his death. The scope of such theories extends through theories of imperialism and dependency theory to the more recent development of world-system theory.

In Table 5.2, we outline in summary form four main contributions of political economy to the analysis of global power relations. Four particular contributions are distinguished in terms of three major dimensions of analysis, namely (a) key social relations, (b) global characteristics and (c) crisis and conflict potential. We shall now discuss each of these four contributions in turn.

Table 5.2 Global power relations and capitalist political economy

Major theory	Capitalism	Imperialism	Dependency	World-system theory
Exemplars	Marx	Hilferding, Lenin	Frank	Wallerstein
Key social relations	1) Social relations of production founded on unequal and exploitative capital–labour relations. 2) Based on competitive markets.	1) Social relations of production founded on unequal and exploitative capital–labour relations. 2) Based on monopoly and industrial and financial concentration to limit competition.	1) Social relations based on exploitative production and exchange relations between capital and both free and unfree labour.	1) Social relations based on exploitative relations of *exchange* between capital and various forms of free and unfree labour. 2) Social relations involve capital, nation-states and household.
Global characteristics	Dynamic and expansive creating a global economy of capitalist nation-states around the globe.	Still dynamic and expansive through capital export, but imperialism intensifies exploitation of non-capitalist world as markets and territories are carved up.	Dynamic and expansive but core capitalist expansion perpetuates under-development of non-Western world. Non-Western world does not follow Western path.	World system creates a global economic system larger than nation-states. Hierarchy of power relations distributed spatially between the core, semi-periphery and periphery.
Crisis and conflict potential	Crisis-prone. Potential for working-class revolt in advanced world.	Crisis-prone in spite of attempts to organise and regulate competition. Conflict between imperial nations. Involvement of non-Western societies in anti-imperialist conflict.	Crisis tendencies and conflict within both Western and non-Western world. Colonial revolt becomes more important.	Crisis tendencies in all sectors, including core, semi-periphery and periphery.

Marx's analysis of the capitalist mode of production emphasised the inherent connection between capitalism and the development of a global market. The assumption was that capitalism was an expansive system which progressively undermined pre-capitalist economic relations, such as those found within the ancient slave empires or within feudal societies. This process of erosion occurred not only as a consequence of the greater economic efficiency of capitalism, but also through the greater economic power of the Western capitalist nations. This power enabled them to dismantle local controls and regulations inhibiting the exchange of commodities, and the transformation of peasants into wage-labourers. In a telling phrase Marx forecast that the advanced world shows to the backward world merely the image of its own future. Marx's discussion of these issues was, however, extremely generalised and lacking in empirical evidence. The end-point of the process of expansion appears to be a world of capitalist nation-states not only in the West but throughout the globe. For Marx, the fate of India, was similar to the fate of Britain. Unlike the economic liberal world-view, history did not stop with the development of capitalism, for beyond capitalism lay socialism and communism. The dynamics of the transition from captalism to socialism involved economic crisis and capital–labour conflict.

It was only towards the end of his life that Marx speculated on the possibility that some kind of direct transition from pre-capitalist to post-capitalist society might be possible. This discussion was prompted by consideration of the social dynamics of late nineteenth-century Russia where capitalism had still to be consolidated, yet anti-capitalist revolutionary movements were of some political significance. In this context Marx offered some speculative support to the idea that the pre-capitalist peasant community might supply some direct support for the development of post-capitalist communism. However, he did not offer any detailed analysis of the possibility that societies might, so to speak, 'jump' a stage of social change, by-passing capitalism altogether. It was left for subsequent Marxists, such as Trotsky (1962), to argue this in more detail.

Marx's highly generalised account of the relationship between capitalism and globalism did not engage in any significant way with the issue of economic imperialism, that is with spatial

134

inequalities of economic power between the West and the world beyond. His vision of a world of capitalist nation-states says very little about the possibility or likely function of such inequalities. By 1914, however, subsequent commentators had begun to offer a more fundamental challenge to economic liberalism. This challenge centred on the argument that the global economy was so stratified by inequality as to subordinate the economies of the less powerful non-Western regions of the globe to the more powerful Western regions.

The theories of imperialism developed in the first half of the twentieth century set out from the proposition that Western capitalism increasingly required control over the non-Western world to ensure its own stability and expansion. The world beyond Europe and America functioned as a market for Western commodities, a source of raw materials, and as an outlet for Western capital, seeking productive openings. Such economic relations with the remainder of the globe depended, however, on a mixture of direct political control, as in colonial annexation, less direct political intervention, as in agreed spheres of influence within independent nations, and economic power. Western nations excused economic power through a variety of means including the contracting of loans on terms favourable to the lender, the tying of loans to commodity trade with the lending nation, and the development of multinational companies able to allocate and reallocate production and marketing on a global basis to maximise profit. Such control mechanisms operated whether or not the non-Western nations in question were colonies of the West (e.g. Africa prior to the 1950s and 1960s) or were nominally independent, as in South America or China.

The development of economic imperialism can also be seen as one element in the growth of organised capitalism, discussed above. Just as internal economic relations within nation-states were becoming more regulated by corporate and government regulation, so the global economy was becoming more regulated through territorial division and agreement of spheres of influence between the Great Powers of the West. The problem with imperialist organisation, however, as with the other types of organisation discussed above, was whether this new stage of capitalist development would be stable and crisis-free, or whether new lines of conflict would emerge.

While some theories believed imperialism would successfully stabilise capitalism, others linked the global economic inequalities involved with new lines of conflict within capitalism. Imperialism, on this line of argument, created conflict between imperial nations over the division of economic spoils and led, in the view of Lenin (1964), to the First World War between economic rivals Germany, on the one side, and Britain and France, on the other. In addition, imperialist political control of non-Western nations created nationalist conflicts between imperialist powers and colonies struggling for political independence. Political economists, while tending to interpret national liberation struggles rather narrowly in purely economic terms, nonetheless helped to incorporate this major twentieth-century theme into the analysis of economy and society.

The underlying presumption within most currents of political economy has been that the powerful Western nation-states have subordinated non-Western societies to overriding Western needs for economic exploitation of resources. Since the liberal ideal of a market of free-standing individuals was totally remote from the experience of non-Western nations faced by multinational companies, Western banks, and powerful Western nation-states, much of the effort to wrest power away from the West has taken political rather than economic forms. Third World nationalism is the characteristic political expression of the drive to gain power and control, uniting peasants, workers, intellectuals, army officers and many sections of Third World business. A further assumption made by Marxist political economists is that effective national economic development in the Third World depends not only on *political independence*, but also on continuing political regulation of the economy, in order to promote national development as against the imperialist priorities of the West. In other words there is no necessity and every reason to avoid *laissez-faire* or liberal capitalism.

The theme of spatial inequalities of economic power, about which economic liberalism is largely silent, has been further developed in post-war dependency theory. This added two further elements to existing discussions of capitalism and globalism within the tradition of political economy.

Within the dependency theory of André Gundar Frank (1969),

136

the conventional definition of capitalism in terms of commodified labour-power is modified to include a range of exploitative relations of production. These embrace both 'free' (i.e. wage-labour) and 'unfree' labour, such as serfdom, slavery, and debt-bondage. The argument here is that capitalism is an exploitative form of exchange, based on the power of private capital. The conceptualisation of capitalism is not restricted simply to the capital–wage-labour relationship within the labour market, since other 'exploitative' modes of labour utilisation have been used by capitalism. What all of these have in common is the extraction of surplus value from labour, by one means or other, and this in turn is linked to the dominant imperatives of capitalist accumulation. Examples of the use of unfree labour include the plantation estates of American capitalism prior to the abolition of slavery in the mid-nineteenth century, and the use of the debt bondage system in Latin America.

The significance of this conceptual revision in dependency theory (and world-system theory) is that it widens the analysis of capitalist economic power to embrace instances of global economic control hitherto disregarded or marginalised.

A second argument, linked with Gundar Frank's dependency theory, concerns the impact of Western capital control on the development outside the West. Within his analysis of post-war Latin America, Frank argued that Western economic control, far from ushering in transformation to fully-fledged capitalist modernisation, resulted instead in the repression of autonomous economic development in the region. The so-called underdevelopment of Latin America, in comparison with Western standards of development, was not caused by some intrinsic or irrational 'failure' on the part of Latin American societies to adopt superior Western models. On the contrary, the underdevelopment of Latin America was actually *caused* by Western control. The mechanisms of control were several. First, Western interests influenced the selection of economic sectors developed and those left undeveloped in Latin America. At its worst this resulted in one-crop over-specialisation in response to Western demands for primary products like sugar, coffee or fruit, rather than diversified development. Second, Western interests sought to undermine Latin American economic autonomy by dictating the terms upon which external capital was available. Such terms included cutting government regulation and government spending. The overall effect of such controls, according to Frank, was the permanent under-development of the region, continuing poverty and social conflict. One immediate problem with this approach is its inability to explain why some Third World countries – the so-called Newly Industrialising Countries (NICs) such as Malaysia, South Korea or Brazil, have managed to secure significant levels of development (Corbridge 1986).

World-system theory, as developed most powerfully by Immanuel Wallerstein (1974, 1980), and his associates (Smith et al. 1984) picks up and expands on many of the themes raised in Frank's dependency theory. In addition, world-system theory has reaffirmed the importance of Karl Polanyi's focus on the patterns of integration that link economy with society. The task, in other words, is not merely to demonstrate that *laissez-faire* economies do not exist, either within the Western world or in the global economy. The challenge is rather to determine, in the context of the global economy with its spatial inequalities of power, how exactly economic life is regulated. As far as world-system theory is concerned, the main patterns of regulation considered are 'political economic' in form.

The major conceptual revision in world-system theory is the shift from a nation-state focus to a global or world focus. This shift is not meant to deny the importance of nation-states. However, it is intended to subordinate nation-states to an even more important set of economic processes. These take place at the global level, and centre on increasingly mobile concentrations of private capital available for potential investment anywhere in the globe. Put another way, it is first and foremost global capital which structures spatial inequalities of power rather than nationally-bounded accumulations of capital. The global economy, in this view, is structured by a world-system of economic power rather than a political system of empires.

Wallerstein's world-system theory builds on this insight by analysing the spatial distribution and spatial inequalities in economic power that arise within the global economy. Within this framework he identifies three regions organised within a hierarchy of economic power. These regions comprise: the *core* regions of the Western economy, dominant players in the world system; the *peripheral* regions of the Third World, lacking power of their economic destiny; and finally, as it were in between these two, the *semi-peripheral* regions possessing some economic autonomy, but still dominated by the Western core.

Wallerstein argues that the political institutions of the nation-state have played an important historical role in the rise of the Western core to dominance within the world-system. By contrast one of the symptoms of peripheral status within the world-system is the incapacity to develop a coherent and autonomous nation-state able to protect and advance the interests and welfare of populations within a particular region or territory. Meanwhile semi-peripheral status has been ascribed either to minor Western regions, such as Australasia, or to Third World societies such as Malaysia which have succeeded in breaking out of complete dependency on the core capitalist societies as the USA, Japan, Germany and Britain.

Political power is therefore important in Wallerstein's theory in acting as a institutional support for the global dominance of private capital. His approach may therefore be regarded as a political economy of globalism, rather than a purely political explanation of spatial inequalities of economic power. As such he rejects the proposition that the world-system is integrated by imperial dominance akin to the geo-political mechanisms of dominance found in the orient Middle East and ancient Rome. The modern world-system is integrated through networks of dominance founded on private capital, but underwritten by the political power of the core Western nation-states. However, as with dependency theory, the approach is liable to the criticism that it undervalues the capacity of some Third World societies to achieve significant levels of development.

We shall evaluate this theory in more depth in Chapter 6. For the moment we will simply note its importance in extending the analytical framework of political economy in new directions. Above all, Wallerstein has done more than any other political economist in demonstrating the significance of world system or global levels of economic activity and political power. In this perspective the world system becomes a distinct system in its own right, linked with but not reducible to a collection of national political economies. This approach offers far more realistic insights into the existence and the causes of inequalities of economic power between regions and states offered by economic liberalism. One important example of research stimulated in large measure by world-system theory is the theory of the new international division of labour (see especially Frobel et al. 1980). This links world-system theory with dependency theory, focussing on the global production strategies of multinational companies.

MULTINATIONAL COMPANIES AND THE NATION-STATE

One of the most important, yet intractable problems raised by political economy has been the relationship between concentrations of private economic power, such as multinational companies and the nation-state. Such issues have typically been neglected by economic liberalism. We have already outlined a range of political economic theories which address this issue in one form or another. Yet there remains a good deal of uncertainty as to the nature of this relationship. Will global capital increasingly undermine national sovereignty, leaving the nation-state as a marginal economic institution? Or can national political integration through the nation-state survive? And if it does is this because global capital organised through multinational corporations, finds it possible to derive benefit from politically-centred institutions of government? Or is it also because nation-states can, under certain circumstances, control or at least influence the operations of multinational corporations.

Martinelli (1982) has analysed a range of theoretical discussion and empirical research on these issues. He advances a number of plausible hypotheses which paint a complex picture of relations between multinational corporations and the state. His argument is essentially that such corporations require nation-states, because the nation-state can meet needs that multinational corporations themselves cannot produce. These include defence of private property rights against political opponents, support for free circulation of factors of production, and integration of subordinate social classes into the social system. However, and simultaneously with this, multinational corporations also tend to undermine the capacity of nation-states to do all this, by insistence on full capital mobility and avoidance of taxation. While nation-states wish to foster inward direct investment and to maximise local value-added production, multinational corporations seek the optimum global profit aggregate rather than profit maximisation in individual countries (Magdoff 1969). Thus while multinational corporations operate in an international world and profit from diversity, governments are more constrained by being national in scope.

Martinelli also makes the point that the destabilising effects of multinational corporation's activities are felt both by developed core nations as well as less-developed peripheral regions. In the developed core, multinational firms can influence the economic welfare of nations through the decisions they take on the location and relocation of investment, which in turn influence levels of national income and the incidence of unemployment. Such effects are especially adverse, as Lash and Urry (1987) point out, where the relocation of production denudes the older industrial regions of large units of private capital investment. Second, wherever multinational corporations locate different stages of production in different countries the prices at which products are transferred within the company can be set so as to minimise tax in high-tax countries. While this is simply an accounting issue for the firm, it has considerable significance for the country involved, not only in terms of reducing tax revenue, but also in terms of adverse effects on the balance of payments.

Meanwhile in less developed societies, multinationals can exert power through control over the terms of trade under which raw materials are sold on the international market. This form of control is especially burdensome where less developed economies are dependent on the export of only one or two commodities. Yet even in such situations, multinationals still rely to a considerable extent on political control. In a number of situations in Latin America (e.g. Chile) and Asia (e.g. South Korea) this has involved destabilisation of radical political initiatives, and support for authoritarian governments (Kaufman 1988). This type of intervention typically results in the repression of labour movements and the channelling of domestic nationalism into forms of accommodation rather than conflict with foreign capital. This strategy of accommodation has proved vulnerable, however, wherever the process of Third World state-building has generated strong anti-imperialist political movements. In certain circumstances, especially where governments can only retain popular legitimacy by radical nationalist control over the economy, the power of multinationals has been limited. This is especially evident in Third World socialist economies such as China (Sklair 1991). Indeed it is preferable to regard nation-state/multinational company relations in the Third World in terms of an endemic power struggle constantly open to negotiation and renegotiation rather than a zero-sum game which one side must win thereby gaining unilateral dominance over the other.

For political economy, markets are populated by corporations, banks and labour organisations, while governments influence and in some cases regulate the terms upon which markets operate. While the symbols of 'individualism' and 'market freedom' continue to resonate in the rhetoric of politicians and economists, political economy argues that this rhetoric is at odds with the reality. This is primarily because markets cannot by themselves solve either the problem of the co-ordination of economic activity, or the problem of the relationship between economy and society. Such problems can only be solved, according to political economy, through the exercise of power.

Political economy sees power as two related forms: first, the concentrated economic power of firms and corporations; second, the power of political institutions to influence economic life, and especially to integrate the economy with the wider society. The second type of power tends to be linked with the first, in the sense that those with economic power will also tend to possess political power. However, political economy does not reduce all political power to that of dominant economic interests, since alternative bases for political power exist. These may include coalitions and political power based on the interests of organised labour, or alternatively political power that places nationalism above the interests of private economic interest.

What is common to all shades of political economy is that economic issues are always to be understood within the context of power relations, whether these are exercised through economic or political mechanisms. In other words political economy rejects the extreme social differentiation basic to economic liberalism, in which the economy is regarded as a self-subsistent domain characterised simply by self-interest, rationality and possessive individualism.

CONCLUDING REMARKS

In this chapter we have outlined the major core concepts and themes brought to bear by political economy on the analysis of economic life. This approach, with its emphasis on power relations, economic inequality and conflict, is as we have seen operative on both a national and on a global level of analysis. Political economy offers, in addition, a fundamental critique of economic liberalism. Market relations are not regarded as vehicles for the pursuit of free, self-interested and rational action by more or less equal parties. They are seen instead as relationships of power in which systematic patterns of control and inequality are evident. Where liberalism focusses mainly on individuals and the market, political economy focusses on organisations, classes and the capitalist system.

The tradition of political economy certainly differs from that of economic liberalism. The question nonetheless remains as to whether it supplies a more satisfactory account of economic life and the relationship between economy and society. The argument of this chapter is that political economy does indeed answer many of the weaknesses identified in economic liberalism. In particular it has succeeded in bringing power back into the theory of economy and society, in a way that generates a greater degree of realism in the analysis of how the economy functions. This theoretical advance has brought into focus the organised as well as the individualistic side of economic life, demonstrating that markets do not spontaneously generate their own order and coherence.

While we are sympathetic to the greater part of this critique, there are grounds for serious doubt as to the complete adequacy of the political economy viewpoint. Such doubts are of several kinds. First there are concerns as to the treatment of power and whether this can be interpreted simply in terms of conflicts between economic collectivities and nation-states. A number of observers have raised problems about the incompleteness of this approach, especially in respect to gender relations between men and women. Why, for example, do men tend to have economic power over women, and why are male economic activities generally more highly regarded than women's? Much previous economic understanding has been gender-blind, and this, it may be argued, has inhibited analysis of important themes such

143

as the division of labour as it affects men and women, and the economic function of the household. The question that arises in all of this is, can gender be integrated into political economy, and if so does this require any significant change to the analysis of power?

A second set of doubts about political economy surrounds the exclusive reliance on power to provide answers to the question of how economies are co-ordinated, and how the economy is integrated with the remainder of society. Many, while sympathetic to the *inclusion* of power into economic analysis, nonetheless doubt whether this provides a *comprehensive* answer to issues of economic and social integration. What appears to be missing is an account of how actors *experience* economic life, including the cultural values and practices that give meaning to economic activity. Political economy, so it is argued, either ignores culture, in a manner very similar to economic liberalism, or reduces cultural questions to those of power. Thus it is the economically powerful groups that are seen as dictating and enforcing meaning, in accordance with Marx's axiom that 'the ruling ideas in any epoch are the ideas of the ruling class'.

A third set of doubts about political economy is whether the critique of economic liberalism has gone too far. Many of those who accept unrealistic and mythical accounts of the spontaneous co-ordination and freedom of the market, nonetheless point to the resilience of market institutions *within* the broader integrative framework of modern societies. Indeed, while markets do not provide a complete basis for human society they have, it seems, outlived every socialist or regulatory attempt to render them outmoded and inoperative. This has been dramatised with the collapse of socialist economies in Russia and Eastern Europe largely as a result of the economic inefficiency and political authoritarianism of socialist allocation and authority mechanisms. The political-economic critique of economic liberalism has not convincingly explained why socialist economies of this type have failed in this way. It has, however, sensitised analysis to the limits of liberal economic development strategies. And, in addition, it has encouraged awareness of a range of alternative development models, such as Third World socialism on the model of China. Yet even here, some accommodation with the market has been evident (see Sklair 1991).

The resilience of market-based economic institutions may owe a great deal to social and political supports such as welfare states and public planning. However, it is difficult to explain all aspects of resilience in this way, without at some point confronting positive claims as to relatively greater economic efficiency of market allocation processes for many types of goods and services. We take up this point again in Chapter 6.

Such considerations encourage us to consider retention of part of the economic liberal framework if not all its core assumptions. Some concern for the significance of the market and private economic institutions seems warranted in order to help make sense of the robustness of capitalism about which political economy has offered only grudging explanations in terms of superior capacity to control and exploit.

These three lines of critical evaluation of political economy will be pursued in Chapter 6, to reach a more precise account of the weaknesses as well as the strengths of this second major intellectual tradition.

6

POLITICAL ECONOMY
A critical assessment

There is no doubt that the tradition of political economy, by bringing power back in, has addressed many problems left un-answered by economic liberalism. Yet for all that, political economy is vulnerable to the criticism that it neglects forms of power other than those linked with economic power and the political expres-sion of economic interest. One way of putting this is to say that political economy has a *reductionist* view of power, in which power relations are reduced to clashes of economic interest, typified in conflicts between capital and labour and in struggles between core and periphery within the world-system. This is to assume a single unitary and overarching approach to power, encapsulated in the focus on the capitalist mode of production and world-system.

One of the major difficulties with this economistic view of power is that it neglects other sources of power that cannot be explained in terms of economic interest. As we have noted in Chapter 2, Michael Mann (1986) has recently argued that human society is composed not of one unitary source of power, but four multiple and overlapping types of power, namely economic, ideological, political and military. He advances a complex historical argument to demonstrate that power cannot be reduced to one single economic source since world history demonstrates many examples of the autonomous operation of ideological, political and military power. Military power is evidenced in the conquering armies of the ancient empires of the Middle East and Ancient Rome, while ideological power, to take another example, is reflected in the impact of the great world religions such as Christianity, Islam and Buddhism.

146

The question nonetheless remains as to whether economic power may have become dominant in modern history under the impact of capitalism, private property and the market. In one sense both political economy and economic liberalism share the assumption that it has, even though these two traditions produce very different analyses of why and how this has come about, and what its effects have been on human freedom and liberty.

THE PROBLEM OF GENDER IN RELATION TO THE ECONOMY AND SOCIETY

One important test-case for this approach to power is posed by the feminist critique of gender-blind and male-centred social science. This critique has focussed on the reasons for the widespread if not universal dominance of men over women. This power relation of male dominance and female subordination is neither to be explained by natural or biological factors, nor in terms of simple economic logic. Biology does not explain why it is, according to a recent United Nations conference, that women 'carry out two-thirds of all work in the world, get one tenth of the income, and own less than one per cent of all wealth' (1985 UN Conference on Women cited Swedberg 1987, p. 66). If women's biology is seen as precluding them from much work they would presumably do less work than men. Instead they do more, yet receive far less monetary reward. All this suggests social rather than biological determinants of women's economic subordination.

Economic liberals have either ignored gender inequalities in economic life or sought to explain them in terms of economic rationality and self-interest. Neo-classical economists, for example, have attempted to explain why it is that men tend to have better, higher-income and higher-status jobs than women in terms of rational economic considerations that exclude power. Sex segregation in the labour force has been explained by some economists, for example, in terms of human capital differences, by which is meant differences in individual skill endowment between men and women, but without any analysis of how power differences between men and women affect access to education and training (for a critical review of this literature see Blau and Jusenius 1976).

While most forms of economic liberalism are liable to the criticism that they treat economic actors as isolated individuals rather than as members of families and households, Gary Becker's 'new home economics' (1981) does at least have the virtue of taking the household seriously as an element of economic life, and as a linkage between economy and society. He has also tried to explain the conventional division of labour, in which men are first and foremost 'bread-winners', and women 'home-makers'. This is explained by Becker very largely in terms of the choices made by men and women, given their different biological and social endowments. The problem with this type of explanation is its simplistic view of social life. For one thing, it neglects the overarching structure of role expectations about gender roles and their institutionalisation in the family and education system, which channel aspirations and exert constraints. Choice of social role can be interpreted in a different way as constrained rather than free. This challenge applies even though resistance to previously dominant gender relations has undoubtedly helped to improve women's educational and labour force access over recent years.

If we do begin to analyse gender relations between men and women in terms of power relations, the next question that arises is whether the tradition of political economy is able to identify the type of power relation involved. Much recent debate among feminists and Marxist political economists has centred on the question of whether women's social subordination is explained by capitalist economic power or whether it is necessary to conceive of another dimension of power centred on patriarchy (Mitchell 1971; Rosaldo 1974; Hartmann 1976; Walby 1986). By 'patriarchy' is meant a power relation between men and women, which acts as an autonomous source of domination and inequality, irreducible to economic considerations.

As in many debates of this kind, it many be necessary to think of these two theories as mutually compatible rather than mutually exclusive. This is because of difficulties in reliance on either theory by itself as an adequate explanation of male dominance and female subordination.

The main problem with theories linking women's subordination with economic power is the historical near-universal nature of this phenomenon. Women's subordination did not begin with

capitalism. Indeed capitalism may have helped to open up opportunities for women in the workforce, opportunities which have
been partly constrained by patriarchal power. On other hand,
women's subordination is not confined to societies in which the
economy is differentiated from the remainder of society.
Women's subordination within the less prestigious areas of social
life is evident in tribal societies as it is modern industrial societies.

It is of course true that in tribal and pre-modern societies
women have always been an economic resource, bringing with
them the capacity to bear children, who are themselves an
economic resource, and often dowries which may include land.
On the other hand, there are major problems with an exclusively
economistic or political economic approach to power in gender
relations, notably neglect of psycho-social and symbolic aspects
of gender relations. Much of women's historic subordination may
be linked with male desires to control female sexuality as an end
in itself, reinforced by physical segregation of women, male
dominance over the household, legal doctrines dispensed by
male judges and elders denying women a role in public
community life, and by sexual violence such as rape.

These psycho-social and symbolic phenomena may of course
be linked with economic power and economic inequality, yet the
link is not a necessary one. Gender relations cannot be reduced
simply to economic or class relations, even though the two may
be closely related. Applying the sociology of power developed by
Max Weber, we may analyse gender relations in terms of both
class and status (Weber 1978). In class terms, women's inequality
is related to unequal participation in paid employment, where
women typically lack property or marketable skills compared
with men. This analysis is especially applicable to women in the
labour market. However, for all women, including women
outside the labour market, considerations of status also structure
gender relations. Here, following Weber, male and female
activity is *evaluated* according to notions of honour and prestige,
and *expressed* in social life through mechanisms of group inclusion
and exclusion. Male activity is typically evaluated more positively
than women's and this is used to justify separate categories of
'men's work' and 'women's work'. This is then reinforced by male
exclusion of women from their conventional preserves.

In the analysis so far we have argued that economic power is not the sole explanation of women's subordination to men either in economy or society. However, if the matter were to be left here, we might think in terms of the development of a feminist political economy as the means by which the broad tradition of political economy could be strengthened. The combination of feminism and Marxism has certainly been a powerful one in seeking to explain phenomena like gender segregation within the labour market, and also the social function of households. Within the Western world women are seen as servicing male wage and salary-workers, while also bearing and socialising the next generation of the labour force. In addition, within world-system theory, the Third World household has been seen as increasingly integrated within analyses of the international division of labour, through the use of household production methods in a number of global markets (Smith et al. 1984).

The political economic research agenda of Marxist feminism has proved to be a very fruitful one. Yet the problem remains that it may be insufficiently broad to confront many of the key questions affecting gender relations in economy and society. What the research agenda does best is to examine the power relations, including both structures of domination and forms of resistance, that arise from conflicting economic interests, and the expression of patriarchy in economic forms. What is does less well is to analyse those features of social and economic life, involving women, which cannot be explained in terms of the core concepts of economic power, and conflicts of interest. These include normative and cultural issues, and issues of sexuality and personality formation. This is one reason why many feminists reject an intellectual alliance with Marxism and political economy.

It is plausible to take the view that the challenge of feminism to political economy is more fundamental than we have suggested so far. The challenge extends not merely to the identification of a new structure of power, but also to the conventional terms within which both the 'economy' and 'labour' are defined. Such definitions, depend, as we have already seen, on the comparatively recent processes of social differentiation which separated production and paid employment generally from the household. Under the impact of such changes, 'work' became defined as paid work, while unpaid labour in the household became almost invisible and regarded as the 'natural' domain of women. Whereas the economy or *oikos* had once largely depended on the household as both a unit of production as well as a unit of human reproduction and child socialisation, the economy and work were now regarded as activities that happened elsewhere.

As a number of observers pointed out, this division between 'work' and 'home', and between the economy and the household is highly arbitrary. It takes a historically-specific way of dividing tasks between the paid and unpaid, or between tasks done inside and outside the household, as a yardstick for distinguishing the economy as such from the world beyond. The arbitrariness of this approach would not matter so much if such arrangements were relatively unchanging, or if the 'economic' part of the society, as so defined, could be regarded as operating autonomously and under its own momentum. However, if the boundaries are subject to change and/or the 'non-economic' component exerts significant determining influence on the 'economic' then arbitrariness becomes far more of a problem.

It has recently been argued that contemporary changes in the boundary between paid and unpaid labour require a reconceptualisation of key categories. Gershuny and Miles (1983) for example have argued that there has been a significant shift of activities previously satisfied through the market back to household 'self-servicing'. Pahl (1984) has investigated aspects of the informal economy, whereby household needs are satisfied by mutual aid and informal collaboration outside the market. From the point of view of the household, therefore, there is an overarching household division of labour in which wants may be satisfied either through incomes from paid work allocated to market-based consumption (e.g. buying food at the supermarket) through direct self-servicing and mutual aid (e.g. growing and eating your own food) or through the use of income to support self-servicing (e.g. buying labour-saving devices enabling needs to be satisfied by do-it yourself rather than buying in services).

Another simple point that emerges from this is that 'housework is a distinct form of work' (Walby 1986, p. 34). According to Gershuny, if we examine allocations of time, the typical married women performs more work (paid and unpaid) than her husband. Such women's work may also involve a high

151

component of emotional and interpersonal activity (James 1989), as well as routine instrumental 'chores', compared to that of men.

All this suggests the need for theories of economy and society to take account of the problem of arbitrary distinctions between paid and unpaid work. First, this reconstruction requires a generic overarching conception of *labour* – whether paid or unpaid, and also a conception of the *household division of labour*. Gershuny (1985) sees the need for a more systematic examination of the household division of labour and work strategies, including 'the processes of inheritance of values . . . and decision-making, which determine both how households get the things they need, and how work responsibilities are allocated among household members' (p. 129). Without these generic concepts and research questions, women's labour remains largely invisible. Second, reconstruction demands that attention be given to the household as a linkage between economy and society, in which women's role is critical. From this viewpoint, we may profitably focus attention on the household mode of integration of economy and society, not as the sole mode of economic integration in the modern world, but as a major and robust component of it.

A third aspect of this reconstruction involves a closer analysis of the interplay of power relations on the one hand, and normative and emotional aspects of the household on the other. It is important not to lose sight of the feminist emphasis on gender inequality *within* the household, as well as *between* the household and the public world of socially recognised paid work. This corrects any simplistic view of the household either as the terrain of free and rational choice between individuals or as a 'haven in a heartless world'. Yet alongside power and inequality it is important to retain a sense of both the differentiation and autonomy of household actors from economic functions of capitalisation and production.

Within the household, a number of economically-relevant activities are located. These include private consumption. Because political economy has tended to be production-centred and thereby male-centred, it has failed to provide an adequate treatment of consumers, except as dupes of producer power and mass advertising. Women's involvement in consumption has been neglected in the general neglect of consumer activity (for further discussion of consumption see Chapter 8).

Additionally the household operates as the source of primary socialisation of children, an activity with which women remain disproportionately associated. Part of this socialisation process, involving personality formation and motivation, is of considerable importance in the reproduction of individuals capable and willing to take on economic roles, including entrepreneurship and wage-labour. The household is not, of course, the only, or necessarily *the* major form of socialisation. There is no functional necessity that children will or must be socialised through the household. Nonetheless there is evidence that household and family practices and commitments do influence economic behaviour. Involvement in small business for example is strongly connected with previous family business activity. Family business, however, typically depends on high levels of unpaid or poorly-paid women's labour (Carr 1988). Women may in such circumstances support the family independence and freedom they believe will ideally come from family businesses, even though their financial dependence on husbands or fathers may become intensified.

The general conclusions that may be drawn from this discussion of gender and the relationship of economy and society may be listed as follows:

1 Gender relations can be usefully analysed within a political economy approach insofar as they involve power, especially economic power.
2 Political economy needs to be augmented by a feminist account of patriarchy before it can analyse the multiple sources of power affecting women's economic position.
3 The challenge of explaining gender relations within economy and society requires a reconstruction of the key concepts of 'economy' and 'work' in terms of generic concepts of 'labour' and the 'household division of labour'.
4 Political economy, even augmented by feminism, is still insufficient to analyse normative, emotional and cultural aspects of gender relations, especially those associated with the household.

THE PROBLEM OF CULTURE AND VALUES

Another fundamental criticism levelled at the tradition of political economy is that it neglects or ignores altogether the question of culture and its effect on economic life. This line of argument claims that the political economic emphasis on power in pursuit of economic interest occurs at the expense of cultural considerations. Culture in this context is generally taken to refer to values which may shape all forms of human action, economic action included.

It is interesting to note that this criticism has been applied with equal force to the tradition of economic liberalism. In this case it is the notions of self-interest and rationality which have come under criticism on exactly the same kind of grounds, namely that they exclude a concern for the operation of values in economic life. It is important to emphasise, therefore, that economic liberalism and political economy share certain common elements, notably heavy reliance on economic interest, as a key component in the explanation of economic life. While they may differ on the form interest takes (e.g. individual *versus* collective) and on the mechanisms by which it operates (e.g. individual sovereignty in the market place versus hierarchies of power), they are united in emphasising the dynamic of economic interest as a core element in both the *structure* of economic relations, and in the *motivation* of economic actors.

One symptom of this common ground is the methodological preference of *many* economic liberals and political economists alike for economic explanations of economic phenomena. If an economic explanation can be found there is no need to look elsewhere, especially not to the area of cultural explanations. This economistic preference usually takes the form of asking whether the actions in question are consistent with the operation of *either* self-interest guided by rationality *or* alternatively of the organised economic interests of powerful collectivities such as capital or labour. If such an explanation can be found, it is assumed that cultural explanations are irrelevant. At best, culture will only appear as a residual to which recourse is made when all else fails.

We have already discussed certain disabling problems connected with the core assumptions of the pre-social self and of individual sovereignty within the tradition of economic liberalism (see Chapter 4). As we saw, these assumptions fall foul

154

of two key sociological axioms. In the first place, they deny the social constitution of wants or needs, which are both formed and satisfied within human society. In the second place, they ignore the meaning of action to the actors involved and therefore fail the test of being adequate on the level of meaning. Not all schools of liberalism do this, but most economists have done. As a result, the mainstream traditions of economic liberalism cannot analyse the full cultural context of economic activity, unless recourse is made to extra-economic assumptions. It is important, in spite of this to note that liberalism, with its focus on individual autonomy is, in this sense, far better placed than political economy to analyse the authenticity of the contemporary culture of individualism, providing, that is, that the social determination of individual action is accepted. We shall return to this point below.

For the remainder of this section we shall therefore switch attention to the tradition of political economy to determine whether any more adequate account of culture is available there.

At this point, there is some value in attempting provisional definition of what is meant by the term 'culture'. This is necessary in view of the loose and ill-defined nature of the term in most social science disciplines outside anthropology and, to a lesser extent, sociology. In particular, some kind of ground clearing exercise is necessary to identify and address certain misconceptions or confusions. For purposes of provisional analysis we therefore define culture as that set of values and processes in which individuals and groups seek meaning.

One area of confusion, often linked with the Marxist base–superstructure model (see Chapter 5) arises where culture is associated with 'ideas' or 'thought' as contrasted with 'material life' or 'action'. In this approach 'culture' is relegated to the insubstantial spheres of contemplation and commitment to 'ideals' as distinct from the more immediate practical realities of everyday life. This argument makes the arbitrary assumption that 'ideas', 'thought' or 'values' are somehow separate from practical realities, including the economic realities of material survival and earning a living. Within the base–superstructure model such realities are regarded as primary elements in social life, which determine the ideas and values individuals hold. This position, which few Marxist political economists now actually hold, may be labelled *vulgar* Marxism.

It is but a short step from here to the view that culture is for those whose lives are not dominated by everyday economic exigencies and pressures. This results in the association of culture with 'high culture', that is with an exclusive preserve of high status activities such as opera and drama. Here again the arbitrary assumption is made that practical people in the material world do not have 'culture'. The confusion or conflation of culture with high culture is not, however, characteristic of political economy. Within this tradition of analysis two principal intellectual strategies are evident. The *first* is simply to ignore culture, defined in the sense of values and the meaning of social action. The *second* is to assimilate culture, as defined in these terms, to the structure of political economic power.

To ignore the question of values and the meaning of action to those involved, as in the first of these options, is to assume that material or economic interest is the dominant and invariable source of human action. The initial plausibility of this view is its emphasis on the material necessity of biological survival and reproduction for the human species, associated with food, clothing and shelter. The majority of the world's population is still preoccupied with precisely these objectives. Beyond this, it is also possible to regard the struggle for survival as being connected, not simply with immediate material needs, but also with the search for satisfying and meaningful labour in the broadest sense. If all of this can be taken for granted then special consideration of culture seems unnecessary.

This viewpoint is often buttressed by a historical argument about the fateful impact of capitalist social differentiation on the possibility of culture. The argument is that capitalism so profoundly differentiated economy from society, and so powerfully elevated the influence of economic life on the remainder of society, that modern society is no longer embedded in a broader social framework, including culture. In many of the bleaker passages of Marx's critique of capitalism we meet this historical argument. It assumes that while the economy of pre-capitalist societies was embedded in cultural forms such as religion, tribalism and mysticism, under capitalism these forms have been swept away to leave economic life and economic realities as the sole reference point for individuals. Marx deployed Carlyle's notion of the 'cash nexus' to symbolise this process. The final element in this historical argument is that under a socialist or communist system, the excessive differentiation of economy from society and the concomitant elevation of economy over society under capitalist relationships would be overcome. The economy would now be reintegrated into society and reconnected with culture.

For Marx (1977) and for more recent Marxists such as Mandel (1976), the analytical framework of political economy is apparently designed specifically to analyse differentiated capitalist societies, rather than all societies. While cultural anthropology may be relevant to Third World or non-capitalist societies, it is political economy that is most relevant to capitalist societies. The economic reductionism of political economy, is thereby seen as a reflection of a society which has reduced cultural issues, including the meaning and value of social life, to narrow economic criteria.

This argument raises the question 'Is culture – defined provisionally as the domain of values and meaning – necessary at all to differentiated capitalist societies, or put another way, to markets?' As far as markets are concerned, we have already accepted much of the political economic argument that they are not self-regulating, and are fundamentally influenced by economic power and economic inequality. However, this is by no means the end of the analysis. For in addition, there is need to ask the question 'How far can power serve to dominate and integrate society?'

Political economy has emphasised that within a capitalist economy capital has greater economic power than labour. This is reflected in the general capacity of capital to be mobile and to dictate the forms of capital investment to society, as compared to labour. As a 'living' entity labour is less easily mobile, and must sell itself somehow to survive, often in conditions of unemployment. Marx emphasised the 'dull compulsion of economic circumstance' (Marx 1976) as the key to capitalist economic power.

The main problem with this whole line of argument is not that it lacks plausibility, but rather that it fails to come to grips in a direct manner with the multi-faceted experience of living in differentiated societies, and with the complex range of meanings individuals give to their actions. Over time even those working within the tradition of political economy, or within the Marxist version of this tradition have felt the need to place greater emphasis on what is often termed the 'subjective' element in social and economic life, or what we would prefer to call the 'cultural' element. This difference in terminology is not a purely semantic one, since reference to the subjective harks back to the narrow identification of culture with ideas and inner thoughts, while the broader term 'culture' embraces actions, practices and institutions that embody ideas as practical realities.

The attempt to reconstruct political economy, and especially Marxist political economy, to embrace culture has often broken the bounds of political economy itself. Indeed as we shall argue in the remainder of this study that the dynamic of Marxist scholarship in pursuit of culture represents one major source in the construction of a third, synthetic tradition of scholarship, namely economic sociology. In the remainder of this section we shall limit discussion to the attempt of political economy to embrace culture, pending an explicit account of the third tradition in the latter chapters of the book.

The assimilation of culture to political economy has proceeded on the assumption that naked power – whether in dictating terms in the labour market or through state support of capital against labour – neither obliterates the experience of the powerless, nor guarantees their everyday consent to the actions of those who control economic power. Power, in short, requires cultural supports to have any credibility, yet the experience of power and control may as readily generate a culture of resistance as a culture of submission. This argument focusses attention both on bodies of ideas or values, and on institutions embodying such values, as key elements in the dominance of powerful economic interests.

Several examples may be cited which related cultural institutions to the dominance of capitalism, and which claim that cultural ideologies are functional to the reproduction of capitalist dominance.

The first example is drawn from world-system theory. While dubious about the value of culture as a coherent concept or social institution, Wallerstein (1990) argues that the ideologies of universalism and of racism–sexism act as cultural supports for the capitalist world-system. The liberal ideology of universalism in which, according to Wallerstein, merit is universally rewarded, is claimed to function as a support for hard work and greater efficiency at the expense of a concern for social inequality in incomes and rewards. The ideologies of racism and sexism function meanwhile to justify the causes of low income and status among blacks and women. For the former, low income levels are explained by lack of effort put in, for the latter by cultural characteristics. The net effect is to ignore what Wallerstein sees as the capitalist roots of inequality. Furthermore, Wallerstein also claims that anti-systematic movements seeking to challenge capitalism cannot incarnate 'any culture other than that of the capitalist world-economy' (1990, p. 51). This argument reflects the typical tendency of much political economy to reduce culture to dominant economic interests. This in turn reflects a belief that no alternative capacity to assert alternative cultural forms exists. Thus in relation to the challenge of feminism, world-system theory even assimilates the household as 'part and parcel of the capitalist world' (Smith *et al.* 1984, p. 7) This is, of course, rampant economic reductionism.

The second example is again drawn from a global approach, and involves the claim that the USA exerts an increasing world-wide cultural dominance through the mass consumption of American goods and an American dominated mass communication media. Leslie Sklair (1991) cites the example of Coca-Cola and Pepsi-Cola as means whereby an American-dominated cultural ideology of consumerism induces utilitarian and symbolic wants among Third World populations. These not only include wants for American products that generate profit, but also wants to participate in an Americanised lifestyle. A serious problem with this argument, however, is the actual experience and meaning that such Third World consumers bring to their lives, and whether they passively internalise externally-generated cultural practices.

The Americanisation argument is in fact just as reductionist, in its own way, as that of Wallerstein. For as Appadurai (1990) has argued, the 'global cultural economy' is far more pluralistic with the forces of indigenisation growing at least as rapidly in fields such as music and housing styles as are the forces of Americanisation and metropolitanisation. If fears of absorption into an external system are present, these are by no means exclusively fears of Americanisation. Thus 'for the people of Irian Jaya, Indonesianisation may be more worrisome than Americanisation, as Japanisation may be for Koreans, Indianisation for Sri Lankans, Vietnamisation for the Cambodians, and Russianisation for the people of Soviet Armenia and the Baltic Republics' (Appadurai 1990, p. 295). Once again the original presumptions of the political economy approach obscure the complexity of culture and, in this case, the autonomy of cultural difference based on ethnicity.

The problems of integrating culture into Marxism or radical political economy without resorting to the crude reductionist tendencies evidenced in these two examples have generated a considerable general literature over the last century. Several systematic attempts to produce such an integration have been made. One of the foremost of these is Frankfurt School critical theory, associated with the work of Horkheimer, Adorno and, more recently, Herbert Marcuse.

Frankfurt School theorists writing in inter-war Europe brought together three major strands of social analysis, namely Marxist political economy, Weberian sociology and Freudian psychoanalysis. From the tradition of political economy they drew a critique of capitalism and the inequalities and repression which Marxists have typically seen as flowing from capitalist economic power. From Max Weber, they took the theory of rationalisation. This argued that social evolution was tending to produce the domination of instrumental reason over social life at the expense of human values. By instrumental reason, Weber referred to the process where social action became preoccupied with the choice of means to reach a given end, rather than debate about the choice of ends. The growth of instrumental rationality involved an expansion of calculation and intellectualisation within social action typified in the cost–benefit calculations evident within market economies driven by self-interest (Weber 1978, Part 1, Chapter 2).

For Weber, following the German sociologist Simmel, the dominance of instrumental reason was symbolised by the elevation of money as a universal measure of value, and a universal equivalent against which commodities can be exchanged. Money represented the medium through which cost–benefit calculations were made, yet it was itself indifferent to the goals or moral values that individuals sought to realise through economic life (Simmel 1978).

Frankfurt School theory took up Weber's analysis of capitalism as a manifestation of rationalisation, thereby rejecting the political economic assumption that the mode of production was *the* fundamental underlying reality of social life. Rationalisation was regarded as the overarching theme in the history of the West reflected in law, religion and literature as well as economic life. The major cultural characteristics of Western society, symbolised by the eighteenth-century Enlightenment in social thought, were associated with the dominance of instrumental reason, which sought mastery and control over resources at the cost of meaning and purpose. Frankfurt School critical theory shared the negative critique of rationalisation that is to be found in Weber, without quite appreciating that Weber saw reason as enabling as well as constraining.

Weber sensitised critical theory to certain major cultural features of Western life. However, in developing their own critique of reason and capitalism as culturally repressive institutions, additional intellectual resources were drawn from Freudian psychoanalytic theory. Freud had emphasised the repressive features of society, and especially civilisation, with respect to inner personality drives, resulting in structures of self-control that tended to dissipate or sublimate the chaotic inner passions, notably sexuality. Critical theory took up this type of theory, but gave it a stronger sociological dimension by emphasising the repressive effect of social and cultural institutions. In particular, it enabled an integration of the critique of capitalism and rationalisation, with analysis of culture and the personality. The argument was that rationalisation, which had reached its most mature form under capitalism, had resulted in a repressive culture and repressed personality types.

In answer to the question 'Why do not exploited workers rise up against capitalism or against economic inequality?' critical theory focussed on this repressive apparatus as it affected personality and personal identity. It was not economic power as such which explained social consent, but the creation and reproduction of personality structures favourable to conformism and to cultural roles prescribed under rationalised capitalistic arrangements. These were embodied in the family which

161

inculcated obedience to authority, in the labour market, and through mass advertising. In his book, *One-Dimensional Man* (1968), Herbert Marcuse argued that the role of passive consumer, purchasing the latest commodities under the manipulative affect of mass advertising, produced a repressed and shrivelled human personality. In so doing, Marcuse demonstrated an expansion in the intellectual scope of social theories of capitalism beyond the economistic production-centred focus of political economy, to embrace culture and personality. While linking culture with economic power, he emphasised the autonomy of culture with respect to economic life, and encouraged analysis of the impact of society on the economy, as much as the impact of economy on society. Marcuse himself argued by means of theoretical speculation rather than empirical research on actual consumer behaviour.

The relative autonomy of culture has become a widespread feature of Marxist-influenced social thought during the twentieth century, not confined to the Frankfurt School. It is evident in the work of rather different theorists such as Gramsci, the literary theorist Raymond Williams and the social historian E.P. Thompson. One of the striking achievements of these intellectual developments has been the demonstration that culture is not a homogeneous or monolithic phenomenon, but has its own internal variations and conflicts. Of particular importance is the proposition that there is not one totally dominant culture, in the sense of one set of values or meanings embodied in action, that suffuses society to the exclusion of all else. The situation is far more complex in a number of ways.

First, subordinate classes or social groups may have their own distinct and alternative cultural practices to those of dominant social classes. This has been brilliantly portrayed for England during the Industrial Revolution by Edward Thompson. He emphasises both continuities and changes in pre-industrial cultural practices as they affect responses to the market and to factory work (Thompson 1963). He shows how such cultural traditions may generate resistance as much as conformism or obedience. Herbert Gutman has developed a similar type of analysis for the USA (Gutman 1977).

A striking contemporary example of this theme is to be found in Michael Burawoy's influential study, *Manufacturing Consent*

(1979). This account of American blue-collar production workers emphasises that, although subject to capitalist control, workers are largely 'self-organising'. In spite of the cultural controls which present the interests of dominant classes as the interests of all, Burawoy identifies tacit skills and unofficial opportunities for autonomy which enable workers to cope with pressures and problems on the shop floor. This may involve 'game-playing' to maximise production bonuses, or the subversion of rules, or the informal modification of work processes to overcome formal management inefficiencies. By these means, however, tensions and conflicts are deflected away from problems associated with the vertical hierarchy of control. Instead, these processes tend to generate harmony and consent.

Second, classes or social groups may be internally divided with respect to cultural commitments. One example of this is the argument by social historians that working-class people in nineteenth-century Britain were divided between 'respectables' seeking acceptance in bourgeois society, and 'roughs' exhibiting anti-bourgeois sentiments.

While recognising the widening of analytical scope that such developments represent, the question nonetheless remains as to whether these efforts do adequate justice to the analysis of culture and the personality? This question leads to another related concern, namely the adequacy or otherwise of the tradition of political economy. Put simply, can we tack on cultural analysis to political economy, or is a more fundamental reconstruction of social thought required.

One of the main problems with the attempt to hold together political economy and cultural theory is the tendency for political economic themes, such as the power of capital, social class and class conflict and repression, to dominate the agenda. This is evident in much of the 'labour-process' literature, even where, as in the case of Burawoy, an attempt has been made to 'bring the human subject back in'. Put another way, culture has begun to be reinserted in the analysis, but the process has not gone far enough, for it is a one-dimensional view of culture that has tended to emerge. This often treats culture as a unitary phenomenon dominated by struggles over control of the workplace and the mode of production. In such case no independent bases for culture, whether in the household or the

163

community, are presumed to exist. Frankfurt School critical theory has ranged more widely than labour-process theory by embracing psychoanalysis, but in so doing has broken the bounds of the political economic tradition.

A major example of the continuing dynamic breaking of bounds process, within the framework of critical theory, is provided by Jurgen Habermas. He has sought to broaden and transform critical theory well beyond the earlier bounds-breaking activities of his Frankfurt School predecessors. This project has been advanced by reconnecting cultural analysis with alternative non-Marxist traditions in sociology, development psychology and linguistics (1976, 1979).

One element of this reconstruction and reconnection process is Habermas' attempt to demonstrate the dual impact upon human history of instrumental reason involving technical learning, with cultural concerns involving moral learning. Thus alongside desires for technical mastery can be found equally strong tendencies towards moral learning in attempts to combine what is true with what is just. The cultural pessimism of Frankfurt School is not therefore justified. On the other hand Habermas retains a critique of the repressive features of markets, private property, possessive individualism and what he calls 'familial privatism'. He also retains a scepticism towards representative democracy, very much in terms of the conventional Marxist critique of liberalism (see Chapter 5). This emphasises that representative democracy excludes *real* social participation. Moral learning, it seems, occurs elsewhere in the inter-personal 'life-world', and in new social movements, such as the peace, environmental and feminist movements. In this way Habermas goes well beyond political economy. In so doing he provides one manifestation of the emergence of a third tradition of analysis, with respect to the theory of economy and society. We shall examine the relative importance of Habermas' contribution in relation to other components of the third tradition, later in this study.

The development of culture-inclusive theories within Marxism and critical theory represent important changes in emphasis. They either augment or point towards the reconstruction of the analytical framework of political economy. Yet there remains doubt as to whether those working outwards from the intellectual reference points of political economy or Marxism have investigated the relations between economy and culture in sufficient depth. Among the questions not adequately tackled is the extent to which patterns of cultural values and practices are significant for the *transformation* of society and of economic systems. Attention has tended to be focussed on the problem of culture in relation to social *integration* and social *order*. And even within this latter sphere, insufficient attention has been given to the question of whether a universalistic normative framework standing above economic activities (including capital–labour relations), is required for social order to be possible. Instead attention has focussed on the cultural claims and legitimations of different groups of economic actors, where values are seen as functional to the pursuit of class and other economic interests.

In the development of the third tradition of economic sociology, which has been underway since the late nineteenth century, it is important to establish what should be retained from the tradition of political economy in any new synthesis. How far the retention of political economic views is justified depends on how far we accept its explanatory power, which is as much an empirical question as one that can be determined by theoretical analysis. We have already established the undoubted significance of political economy for the analysis of economic power relations and economic inequality, and also emphasised the value of the political economic focus on globalism. Against this we have noted that many of those sympathetic to political economy, including many feminists, have nonetheless found it inadequate as a means of understanding issues of culture and personality.

In working towards a synthesis which retains the valid aspects of political economy while drawing on stronger resources in the analysis of culture in relation to economic life, there is also need to review what resources, if any, should be drawn from the tradition of economic liberalism. In particular, if political economy has exaggerated the impact of economic power over individual cultural autonomy within economy and society, then the political economic critique by no means invalidates the whole of economic liberalism. Put another way, there are two reasons for reinstating a qualified version of economic liberalism within the intellectual agenda of economic sociology. The first is that dominant economic power (especially capitalist power) does not hold unilateral sway over economy and society. Markets may not be ideal worlds of universal freedom, but neither are they unitary structures of repression and exploitation. The second is that economic activity, whether in production or consumption, may, even under capitalism, be culturally authentic for those involved, rather than distorted or alienated manifestations of human endeavour. For both these reasons, it is appropriate to conclude this evaluation of political economy by returning to the issue of economic liberalism and liberal views of the market.

THE PROBLEM OF MARKET RESILIENCE IN RELATION TO THE POLITICAL ECONOMIC CRITIQUE OF LIBERALISM

One of the most striking features of economic life in the post-war period is the resilience of capitalism in terms of the dynamic performance of market-based economic systems. This proposition should be promptly qualified by the observation that capitalism and markets have been significantly regulated by political institutions and through private organisational arrangements (see Chapter 5). Nonetheless by comparison with the pre-war experience of economic depression and the twin challenges of communism and Fascism, there is considerable evidence that market-based economic arrangements remain of increasingly robust significance as core components of modern societies. This applies even though many significant changes are evident in the form of capitalist development, including processes such as the growth of welfare capitalism or the shift from organised to disorganised capitalism. Meanwhile, while capitalism has proved resilient, attempts to organise state socialist or communist economies through command rather than market mechanisms are in disarray with the collapse of communist regimes in Eastern Europe and Russia. The hope of Khruschev in the early 1960s that the Soviet socialist economy would have overtaken the American economy by 1990 has proved unjustified. It is capitalist Japan not socialist Russia which has overtaken the USA, in terms of many key economic indicators.

The question as to why market-based capitalist economies

have proved so resilient raises difficult problems. These have not been adequately answered by writers operating in the tradition of political economy. Two types of answers are typical. First, there is the emphasis on the superior economic, political and cultural power of private capital over other elements in society. Second, there is the more subtle focus on the incorporation of conflict and the management of crisis by means of regulatory arrangements.

What neither of these answers considers is the possibility that capitalist economies are more successful than their rivals in meeting many of the needs of individuals and groups. For political economy, the assumption is that many such needs have either been neglected or distorted through the persistence of inequality and exploitation. Where needs have been met, they have typically been wrung out as concessions through organised pressure. The latter argument does indeed find some empirical support in the work of Esping-Andersen (1990) who shows that successfully organised labour movement pressure is a key variable in explaining differences in the level of welfare rights between Western nation-states.

Nonetheless evidence of this kind does not challenge the basic proposition of capitalist success, as measured by growth in real incomes, productivity and improvements in living standards and consumption opportunities. Assuming that need-satisfaction can be measured in such terms, and assuming such changes have been widely distributed, then they do indicate an increasing capacity to satisfy needs. While it is arguable that political regulation and government planning contributes to capitalist success through a more stable and rational development of resources and through supply of public goods, there is some evidence that economic growth rates are retarded as levels of public expenditure increase (Weede 1986). Why growth rates are negatively correlated with levels of public expenditure is not, however, entirely clear. In particular it is not clear whether the scale of public activity is the causal determinant, or whether it is the impact of distributional interest and pressure group coalitions seeking a share of public spending that is responsible (Choi 1983; Olson 1983b). Olson has argued that such political coalitions may be interpreted as 'mature' features of democratic societies, whereby the age of democratic politics in any nation will be positively correlated with lower growth rates. Put another way, the phenomenon of progressively lower growth rates experienced by societies like the UK or USA is not to be seen as a problem of government intervention, but rather as a symptom of successfully organised democratic politics. Over time, democracies experience a relative shift of emphasis from processes of wealth creation to wealth distribution. There is clear evidence in support of this proposition.

The debate about cross-national variations in growth rates in fact lends little support either to the ideology of *laissez-faire* capitalism or to the ideology of state socialism. While there is no clear evidence that market regulation as such increases growth rates and improves the capacity for need-satisfaction, there is a good deal of evidence that the more successful post-war economies have incorporated a mix of market and regulatory institutions in achieving economic and social advance. The form of this mix, however, varies significantly from the social-democratic modes of market regulation found in Scandinavia (Stephens 1979) to the 'plan-rational' national developmental regulatory strategies developed in Japan (Johnson 1982).

One important feature of this debate is the argument that dynamic economies cannot do without the market as one element in their institutional make-up, alongside other regulatory mechanisms. Without this component of market relationships, the command economies of state socialism appear destined to failure. This economic superiority of capitalism over socialism is not to be interpreted naively, however, as a triumph of *laissez-faire* or of capitalism as a *social* system. This is because market-based systems have by themselves proved unable to co-ordinate political action or to provide cultural legitimacy. It is for this reason that it is untenable to describe Western societies as capitalist *societies*, even in spite of the dynamic and robust character of market economies. A good deal of analytical care is therefore required in analysing the scale and limits of capitalist success.

A useful starting point in this analytical endeavour is through the work of Peter Berger. In his recent study *The Capitalist Revolution* (1987), Berger puts forward a series of bold propositions concerning the impact of capitalism on human welfare. The salient propositions may be listed as follows:

1 Industrial capitalism has generated the greatest productive power in human history.
2 To date, no other socio-economic system has been able to generate comparable productive power.
3 An economy oriented towards production for market exchange provides the optimal conditions for long-lasting and ever-expanding productive capacity based on modern technology.
4 Capitalist development is more likely than socialist development to improve the material living standards of people in the contemporary Third World (1987, p. 213).

In addition, Berger notes that capitalism is connected in a complex way with social inequality, arguing in proposition No. 6 that the initial impact of capitalism is to create a sharp increase in income and wealth inequalities, then a sharp decline in these inequalities, and then a relatively stable plateau (1987). The causes of these patterns, as outlined in Berger's proposition No. 7 are, however, 'relatively independent of the forms of socio-economic organisation', e.g. capitalism or socialism. They relate instead to 'the interplay of technological and demographic forces'.

From this viewpoint it is possible to explain the resilience of capitalism, in spite of the admitted inequalities generated, as a product of its success in meeting needs rather than as a product of its superior power to control society. In fact Berger disputes whether capitalism does have such effective power, especially in the cultural domain. Thus in proposition No. 24 he argues that 'capitalism requires institutions (notably the family and religion) that balance the anonymous aspects of individual autonomy with communal solidarities' (Berger 1987, p. 213), and again in proposition No. 50 that 'capitalism has an intrinsic incapacity to generate legitimations'.

There is also need to qualify propositions about the 'capitalist' origins of economic dynamism, however. While Berger emphasises that capitalism is unable to create its own cultural and social supports, he fails to make the additional point that many of the post-war sources of technological innovation on which economic advance takes place have been generated less by the stimulus of profit in the market than through the stimulus of warfare, or through the autonomous dynamic of university or government-based processes of scientific research. In this respect it is not the economic system alone that is necessarily the source of all dynamic elements in technological change. What has been claimed is that market-based systems permit the more rapid diffusion of technological advances, which may have originated in some other sphere of society.

We now pose the question as to the cultural supports for capitalism. While Berger, following the Austrian economist Joseph Schumpeter, refers to the internal weakness of capitalism in generating such supports, it is arguable that capitalist economic success is one possible basis for cultural legitimacy. Such an argument, going well beyond Berger's propositions, can be constructed on the basis of the cultural involvement of many social actors within key economic processes such as production and consumption.

Taking the labour market first, it is arguable that the political economic emphasis on inequalities of power and the alienation of labour is too over-generalised to capture the more complex mixture of inequality and opportunity that is increasingly evident in modern labour markets. To be sure inequalities of control over the labour process remain considerable. On the other hand the labour market is very heterogeneous in character. In contrast to the nineteenth-century Marxist political economic theory of class polarisation between capital-owners and increasingly unskilled workers, the modern labour market is highly differentiated by both skill and scale of capital owned. Some currents of modern political economy, notably Braverman's deskilling thesis have challenged the idea of labour market differentiation, reasserting the older homogenisation thesis (see especially Braverman 1974). Other Marxist theorists, notably Erik Wright (1985) have by contrast conceded heterogeneity as an economic fact. Developments such as the expansion of managerial, professional and technical occupations and the persistence of small business and self-employment have been integrated into new maps of the class structure. Wright also argues that socialist economies can be analysed in terms of heterogeneity of labour market positions in terms of control over organisation assets rather than the capital and educational assets that are relevant to capitalist labour markets.

Such developments have resulted in a partial convergence of

neo-Marxist opponents of Braverman with non-Marxist analysts of social stratification. Both traditions stress heterogeneity in labour market structures, though non-Marxist research generally gives greater emphasis to possibilities of upward social mobility within the class structure of capitalist economies (Goldthorpe 1980). The question nonetheless remains as to how to balance awareness of the continued existence of better-paid more satisfying work, involving the use of skill and/or job autonomy together with opportunities for upward mobility, on the one hand, with inequalities of power and control over the labour process on the other.

Max Weber's (1978) discussion of class, labour market and work ethic is perhaps a useful starting-point here. In the first place much recent neo-Marxist discovery of labour market heterogeneity represents a discovery of earlier Weberian discussions of labour market fragmentation and pluralism under the impact of market forces. Weber as is well known, argued that labour market positions depended not on general group characteristics of capitalists and workers, but on the extent to which individual economic actors possessed capital or some marketable skill such as education. Labour markets were not dichotomous hierarchies based on power and subordination, but rather stratified within complex gradations of market power. Such power could depend on large or small capital-ownership, or for non-capital-owners on skill. In such a manner Weber made space for the growth of the educated skilled middle classes within the social structure. Put crudely, labour market advantages accrued not only to big business as in Marxist political economy, but also to small business and those possessing skills and credentialled knowledge in demand within the economy. Those excluded were the unskilled and unemployed rather than the mass of labour market participants as such.

This striking of a balance between power and inequality on the one hand, and labour market opportunity on the other, may also be linked to the issue of cultural orientations to work. The question here is whether most people work primarily for instrumental reasons, to generate an income for consumption, or whether instrumental motives are combined with commitments such as those involved in the work ethic. Here work becomes an end in itself, not simply a means to an end. The argument then

171

becomes whether and how far cultural supports for capitalism depend on commitment to the work ethic.

There is no clear evidence on this matter. Max Weber certainly argued for the existence of a work ethic among both capitalists and workers in the early stages of modern capitalist development. However, the sources of this ethic came from outside capitalism, notably Protestantism (see Weber 1930) and its influence declined over time with the general rationalisation of economic life, as capitalism became securely established. More recent research by Rose (1985) argues that commitment to the work ethic remains, but not as a general orientation. Its scope varies according to a number of variables. These include the type of occupation involved (stronger among professionals and human service workers) and the characteristics of labour market participants (stronger among women previously excluded from careers through discrimination). There is also evidence that the extent of the work ethic varies within different nation-states (Yankelovitch et al. 1983) being stronger in Japan and the US and weaker in Britain. Insofar as national variations are salient, this clearly directs attention to national cultural factors as major influences on this aspect of economic life. It is tempting to argue that where the work ethic persists, this indicates an unambiguous cultural support for capitalism. Such a connection appears clearest in commitments to the work ethic within small business and self-employment or where workers identify with the company and product (see Dore 1973 on Japanese engineering workers). However, among other groups such as professionals and/or those involved in human service delivery, evidence of the work ethic may be connected more with fulfilment of professional or service delivery goals, which for many is set within the public rather than private sector.

For those excluded from paid employment by unemployment or, as in the case of many women, by patriarchy or unpaid family labour, the work ethic is either inaccessible or if present at all, is expressed in rather different terms within unpaid mutual assistance (Pahl 1984). For those trapped in unskilled labour or in routine assembly work access to the intrinsic rewards of work is also difficult. Exclusion of these kinds produces demoralisation, ill health and a greater probability of involvement in crime, either as perpetrator or victim. These represent the 'dark' or negative sides of the process of capitalist success, indicating limits to the diffusion of increased economic resources. There is, however, sufficient evidence to argue that for a significant minority of those within the labour market capitalist success has generated broadly positive outcomes with respect to opportunities to pursue intrinsically rewarding work. Put another way the theory of alienation of labour under capitalism grossly exaggerates the negative features of labour market experience.

If we now turn from production to consumption another set of arguments comes into play. For whatever the extent or lack of cultural commitment to work, what also matters, in terms of the cultural supports to capitalism, is how the role of consumer is expressed and organised. If capitalist control over the labour-process has been exaggerated, is it the case that capitalist producer control over consumption has been exaggerated too? In short, are private consumers passive dupes of corporate advertising? Or does consumption in both private and collective forms, represent authentic forms of individual and group expression?

These are fundamental questions, the full extent of which we shall explore in the next chapter. For the moment we shall restrict our discussion to prima facie problems with political economic analysis. First and foremost is the problem that consumption is seen as secondary to production. This is because production is seen as being dominated by the pursuit of exchange-value, rather than of the use-value of commodities for consumers. This dominance is seen as possible because of the superior power of producers not only at the point of production but also in the psycho-social manipulation of marketing through advertising.

If, however, we argue that producer power is less than totally dominant, and follow the sociological axiom that actors (in this case consumers) know what they are doing, then the analysis looks rather different. Consumers may be seen as striving to realise use-values by purchasing cars that work, washing-machines that take some of the drudgery out of housework and so forth, even while producers strive to maximise or optimise profits or exchange-value. Kellner (1983) has argued for such a two-dimensional approach in order to restore to consumers a

173

measure of knowledgeability about their actions, something denied by the elitist approach of the Frankfurt School. At the same time consumers do act under constraints and are indeed subject to the considerable power and psychological influence of advertising. Here we find an attempt to retain the core of persuasive truth in the political economy tradition, while broadening the analysis to embrace themes of autonomy as well as control.

Another line of argument claims that while 'work' itself generates few intrinsic satisfactions under capitalism, and while many are excluded from it, consumption offers some kind of compensation for this. Some analysts emphasise the negative consequences of this by seeing consumption and the dreams of freedom associated with institutions such as home-ownership as a privatised escape from the constricting realities of the workplace (Chinoy 1955). However, this assumes that labour is primary and consumption secondary to need-satisfaction in a manner that cannot be justified except by recourse to evaluative philosophical assumptions about the intrinsic nature of human beings. Looking at the sociological literature it is not clear at all that individuals prefer to express their humanity through creative labour above the enjoyment of consumption for its own sake. Indeed, we are close here to a moral argument which sees work as better than leisure, and labour as creative, while consumption is destructive in the sense of using up resources.

Arguments about the cultural authenticity of consumption may not fit with certain ascetic philosophical assumptions about human nature, but they do appear to recognise a social reality. The authenticity and autonomy of consumption is very much tied up with cultural ideals of individual sovereignty projected by liberalism, and with core institutions such as the household. There is a good deal of evidence that the private household represents an irreducible feature of modern culture and that individuals and small groups see it as a vehicle of autonomy in the face of constraints emanating from the labour market, government intervention in social policy and the public world of political conflict (Stretton 1975; Saunders 1990). This is not to deny the importance of the feminist critique of gender inequalities within the conventional nuclear family. The erosion or rejection of nuclear family households, however, is not the

174

same as rejection of the private household as such. Indeed the proliferation of household types testifies to the cultural resilience of the household as a flexible vehicle for the realisation of cultural goals.

Provided we are mindful of the theoretical flaws in asocial and atomistic versions of liberalism, there is every reason to retain a qualified emphasis on individualism and privatism, provided this is grounded within a social setting. Such an argument accepts that ends are set in society, and that consumer behaviour takes place under constraints of unequal power as well as scarcity. It nonetheless retains a focus on liberal concepts like personal and household 'autonomy', 'choice' and 'privatism' alongside constraint and inequality. Not all consumption is of course individual or private. We may refer to collectively delivered forms of consumption such as public transport and public parks, and to collectively experienced forms of consumption such as concerts and sporting fixtures. Not all consumption takes place in private, separate from the involvement of others. This indicates that the household by itself does not provide exclusive or sufficient modes of cultural integration of consumers within modern society. Its significance, to be analysed further in Chapter 7, nonetheless has been more extensive than many proponents of a public culture of collective participation, as evidenced in the Frankfurt School would suggest.

Another version of the argument that sees consumer culture as central to modern social life has been suggested by Daniel Bell in his important study *The Cultural Contradictions of Capitalism* (1976). In this work Bell argues that contemporary culture has not only been differentiated from the economy, but also contains conflicts with it. He draws a specific contrast between the controlled and disciplined requirements of the work ethic in which individuals strive for efficiency, as against the more expressive cultural search for personal fulfilment and self-realisation. This search is associated with 'art', by which Bell means a pre-occupation with aesthetic concerns. These are pursued through hedonistic activities which effectively idolise the self. For Bell this cultural configuration is seen as a pathological form of differentiation because it neither supplies a stable source of meaning nor ordering principles of experience and judgement.

Bell's argument has been criticised on a number of counts,

including the failure to specify just how widespread cultural hedonism and self-idolatry has become, and how far the argument may apply outside New York City. It nonetheless picks up a number of themes more recently developed in theories of post-modernity. These claim that societies are no longer centred around economic or political institutions, and argue that culture has increasingly become the celebration of symbolic difference and style, free from any intrinsic foundations in rationality or fixed objective meanings (Lash and Urry 1987; Turner 1990). The contrast between Bell and post-modern theorists such as Lyotard (1984) or Baudrillard (1983) is that post-modernists do not regard the proliferation of cultural autonomy outside overarching value frameworks as pathological. Rather, difference and heterogeneity are celebrated together with the incommensurability of cultures and values.

Writers from a wide range of points of view have thereby converged on the notion of the autonomy of culture, and on the authenticity of consumer culture. This body of research is significant because it suggests that consumers are not dupes of capitalist advertising. This in turn lends support to a socialised version of economic liberalism by reinstating the importance of personal choice and individual autonomy within economy and society. The significance of post-modernism for moral liberalism has been recognised by Bryan Turner (1990, p. 11) who argues that 'post-modern critique of hierarchy, unitary notions of authority, and the bureaucratic imposition of official values has a certain parallel with the principles of toleration of difference in the liberal tradition'. In this study, post-modernism is also regarded as having affinities with liberal theories of economic life. This in turn represents a further demonstration of the need to retain 'liberal' themes in the development of an adequate theory of economy and society.

CONCLUSION

We now draw together the many threads of the argument in this critical evaluation of the tradition of political economy.

The major strength of this tradition, vis-à-vis economic liberalism is the bringing of power back in to theories of economy and society. The actual discussion of power is nonetheless deficient in two main respects. First, there is a tendency to narrow power down to one unitary structure based on the dominant class within economic life. This fails to recognise the possibility of multiple dimensions to power, including power emanating from patriarchal control over gender relations which influences patterns of economic and non-economic relationships, and the valuation of male and female labour.

Second, there is the tendency to exaggerate the unilateral impact of the dominant economic power over society. This second problem is especially pronounced in political economic theories of capitalism. Here political economy has often seen capitalist power as dominating all else, including politics and culture. Part of this exaggeration can be dealt with within the tradition of political economy by means of theories of the autonomy of government and the state. These can embrace the theme of the politicisation of power conflicts between capital, labour and other social movements reflected in political changes which limit the power of private capital. These include welfare state construction through the decommodification of welfare delivery.

Nonetheless political economy finds it very difficult to deal with culture except as a reflex of economic power. This has led many theorists to embrace other intellectual resources the better to grasp cultural influences on economy and society. This in turn has led to the reconstruction of theories of economy and society so as to embrace culture as well as power as irreducible social phenomena.

The present chapter is not intended as an extensive elaboration of the relationships between culture and economic life, but rather as a critique of the capacity of political economy to deal with culture. This critique has been illustrated by means of a discussion of cultural aspects of economic life in relation to the market and capitalist economic relationships. The argument advanced here is that the differentiation of economy from society associated with capitalism has not led to the suppression of culture in favour of a 'cash nexus', nor to the total subordination of culture to dominant sources of economic power. Rather the differentiation of economy from society has enhanced the dynamic capacity of capitalist economic mechanisms to create labour market and consumption opportunities that help to satisfy needs.

177

The resilience of market-based economic relations, however, is not to be interpreted as a triumph of *laissez-faire*. This is partly because capitalist economies depend on political regulation – as pointed out by political economy – and partly because of the convergence of many features of Western culture with the liberal model of individual autonomy. Neither economic liberalism nor political economy have fully succeeded in analysing these cultural patterns of contemporary life. In order to understand the modes of cultural expression, conflict and cohesion characteristic of societies with capitalist economies, there remains a pressing need to integrate the analysis of culture with the analysis of markets and politics.

We now build on the prima facie case established in this chapter as to the importance of culture, with a more elaborate analysis of theories of culture relevant to economic life. It should be emphasised that the intention is *not* to substitute a cultural theory for an economic or political economic theory. The aim is rather to synthesise a multi-dimensional theory that is culture-inclusive, but which holds on to the insights rather than the weaknesses of liberalism and political economy.

7

ECONOMIC SOCIOLOGY
Bringing culture back in

In this chapter we commence a discussion of economic sociology, conceived here as the third major tradition dealing with theories of economy and society. The intention is to elaborate a theory of culture as it effects economic life, looking at culture in relation to social order, social change and symbolic exchange. As in earlier sections of the book, this expository chapter will be followed by a second interpretive chapter examining strengths and problems associated with the tradition under scrutiny. It should be emphasised that economic sociology is not being portrayed as an exclusively cultural theory, but rather as a culture-inclusive synthesis of many elements, including certain acceptable features of economic liberalism and political economy.

ECONOMIC SOCIOLOGY AS A CRITICAL COMMENTARY ON ECONOMIC LIBERALISM AND POLITICAL ECONOMY

The roots of economic sociology may be traced back as far as the eighteenth-century Enlightenment when a number of social theorists attempted to develop multi-dimensional theories of economy, polity and culture (Swedberg 1987). However, the explicit emergence of this tradition derives from the late nineteenth and early twentieth centuries, and the work of Weber, Durkheim and their contemporaries. This work may be regarded as a critical, but in certain ways sympathetic, commentary on the previously constituted traditions of liberalism and political economy (more especially Marxist political economy).

179

Neither Weber or Durkheim accepted that the economy could be understood in exclusively liberal or political economic terms, yet each recognised the market and economic power as important social institutions within modern Western societies. With respect to liberalism, both theorists disputed the utilitarian claims that economy and society could be understood in terms of individual sovereignty and the self-interested drive to realise pre-social wants. Yet Weber was profoundly sympathetic to the moral and political aspects of liberalism (Holton and Turner 1989) and identified himself with liberal political movements in Germany (Giddens 1972). Durkheim was more critical of liberal individualism and more committed to the importance of supra-individual social institutions able to evoke solidarity and social integration (Lukes 1973). Yet Durkheim also recognised the key roles of the socialised individual and of the heterogeneity of secularised individual activities within modern society. This aligned him politically with radical liberal-democratic movements as distinct from *laissez-faire* liberalism.

Yet it would be simplistic to interpret the economic sociology of Weber and Durkheim solely as a revised, more socialised version of the liberal tradition. This is primarily because of the impact made upon them by other intellectual traditions. Weber, for example, was profoundly influenced by debates within German Romanticism and idealism and had been strongly impressed by Nietzsche's philosophical discussions of the death of God and the proliferation of heterodoxy in the articulation of human values. (The most balanced recent assessment of Nietzsche's influence on Weber is available in Albrow 1990.) Weber had also been influenced by Marx, agreeing that private property rights in capital gave a fundamental power advantage to capitalists vis-a-vis workers, decisively affecting life-chances.

Durkheim had been far more strongly influenced by rationalism and positivism than by idealism. Marxism was certainly one of a number of reference points in his sociology, but not a very prominent one. His sociology is therefore less of a commentary on political economy than is Weber's, even though he accepts that economic inequality is a potential threat to social cohesion. They key question for Durkheim is whether, and under what conditions, social institutions can be developed that stand above and can defuse the battle of self-interested individuals or of warring economic classes.

In earlier chapters of this study, it was possible to identify the traditions of economic liberalism and political economy with discrete social movements and political programmes. This exercise is less easy with economic sociology. What unites its leading exponents like Weber and Durkheim is a refusal to accept an economistic view of society founded exclusively on the assertion of economic interests and the struggle to realise economic wants. This standpoint is difficult to associate with any single current in twentieth-century politics because much of the political terrain has indeed been occupied by questions of economic policy and economic management. The binary divisions of much contemporary politics between supporters of the free market and deregulation, on the one side, and supporters of public planning and socialised welfare, on the other, leave little room for the articulation of further political options within the organised politics of representative democracy.

Having said this, the significance of culture-inclusive modes of sociological analysis is by no means marginal, since it still engages with a more diffuse set of concerns about the meaning and purpose of human behaviour, and about the need for and limits of social integration and social solidarity as means of controlling or mitigating the effects of individual self-interested power conflict. This concern with culture, embracing values and social solidarity, spans party political allegiances. It is to be found rather less in 'high political' discussions of economic policy or crisis-management, however, and more in social movements outside government seeking to align specific values with processes of social change and social integration. Such new social movements include feminism, environmentalism and pacifism. As such economic sociology occupies a more diffuse critical standpoint than either economic liberalism or political economy. In this respect it stands outside any strong association with one particular organised interest group.

We may also speculate, in the light of this, that the recent revival of economic sociology, chronicled by Richard Swedberg (1987) and reviewed below, is connected with certain major changes in the relationship between economy and society. We have already noted in the work of Bell (1976) and Lash and Urry (1987) an emphasis on the detachment and autonomy of culture from economy – whether we conceive this as 'the cultural

181

contradiction of capitalism' or as an aspect of 'disorganised capitalism'. This increasingly positive reception of economic sociology, embodying a more explicit idiom of cultural analysis, may be seen therefore as an intellectual concomitant of such wider social trends.

We shall further pursue the tradition of economic sociology through the following core concepts:

(a) Culture
(b) Culture, social order and social transformation
(c) Cultural symbolism in economy and society

Culture

It is testimony to the dominance of economic liberalism and political economy, that the term 'culture' has had such a confused and under-developed status in social thought, and such a marginal role in most accounts of economic life. In the case of economic liberalism we have seen how this neglect of culture flows from a conception of the sovereign individual detached from all other social ties. Within political economy social ties are recognised, but these are either constituted exclusively through power or, where culture enters in, it is assimilated to power relations and to conflicts of material interest. And yet we have also seen a gradual expansion of interest in culture in order to tackle problems inadequately dealt with in these two major theoretical traditions.

In the earlier discussion 'culture' was defined provisionally as 'that set of values and practices through which individuals seek out meaning'. Drawing on this working definition it is helpful to summarise three major misconceptions about culture which stand in the way of a culture-inclusive theory of economy and society.

In Table 7.1 three major areas of inadequate or misconceived conceptions of culture are outlined, together with alternative more theoretically powerful reformulations.

In the first of these the point is re-emphasised that culture is not simply about the setting of purposes or the articulation of ideal goals, but is also fundamentally tied up with practical activities to achieve them. Put another way, human actions and institutions may to a greater or lesser extent represent particular

Table 7.1 Three misconceptions about culture

Inadequate and misconceived view	*More adequate view*
1 Culture based on 'ideas', e.g. values as distinct from actions or practices.	Culture based on ideas and actions. It is involved with practical activities.
2 Culture as a separate sphere of society, distinct from other spheres, e.g. culture lies outside economic life.	Culture as a component part of all aspects of society, i.e. there is economic culture, political culture, etc.
3 Culture functions to conserve or integrate together forces unleashed by economic and political action.	Culture may function as a source of change or transformation as much as a conservative force.

meanings or be the terrain where meaning is contested, defined and re-defined. This point has been made by a number of writers including Ann Swidler (1986). She calls for analyses of 'culture in action' rather than the restriction of cultural analysis to the impact of 'cultural end values' on subsequent behaviour. To this extent culture is a practical matter involving matters of technique as well as ultimate beliefs and values.

One reason for the neglect of culture as a practical activity is the widespread belief in the dominance of instrumental reason and rationalisation. If we accept the premise that reason deals simply with technical means to reach a given 'end', then the realm of ends remains outside practical instrumental action. The problem with this interpretation is that it fails to attach practical activity to the realm of values. The separation of values from practice that follows from this is, however, arbitrary. This is because practical or instrumental reason is not completely value-free or indifferent to all particular values. Forms of rationality such as technical efficiency, the choice of the best cost–benefit option or the scientifically valid option depend on value-commitment for their ultimate acceptability as courses of action. Thus, as pointed out by Max Weber, we must believe the fruits of science are worth knowing before we find scientific truth acceptable (Weber 1948a).

This point needs to be made completely clear to avoid misunderstanding. The argument is not that instrumental rationality or science do not rest on autonomous procedures of cognition that prescribe what is more or less rational or what is good or bad science. Nor is the argument meant to be that these rational or scientific standards are casually regarded as open to belief at one moment and to rejection the next. If anything, commitment to practical reason, technical efficiency and scientific procedure have for many been 'given' reference points that are rarely if ever explicitly confronted with values, at least up until the recent flowering of new environmental social movements. This 'taken-for-grantedness', however, is the crux of the problem. The argument is, in other words, that the separation of practice from values obscures the value-commitment on which practice ultimately rests. This was perceived by Max Weber in his discussion of rationalisation which was seen as a process in which reason became an end or value in itself, yet was expressed by its practitioners as a means to an end divorced from consideration of values.

This general discussion of the importance of seeing culture-in-action is connected with a second area of misconception about culture. This involves the view of culture as a separate sphere of its own, distinct from other spheres such as the economy. This reference to separate spheres depends, at least in part, on the distinction between ends (the sphere of culture) and means (the sphere of economy and polity). If we reformulate culture in terms of action as well as thought, this distinction between means and ends is so hard to draw as to become arbitrary. Actions simultaneously involve 'means' and 'ends', especially where there is more than one 'end', and where achievement of one 'end' may become the 'means' to achieving other 'ends'.

One major implication of this analysis is that culture enters into all social activities including economic and political life. We may therefore speak of economic culture or political culture, by which is meant those aspects of economic or political life that involve issues of meaning and values, and the practices in which they are embodied. An example of a key feature of economic culture, to be explored more fully below, is the idea of trust between economic actors. Trust in others is not derivable from naked self-interest, but from a sense that actors will negotiate their own actions in a reciprocally advantageous way. Trust will only be built up over time and typically depends on inter-personal networks which allow the constant monitoring of transactions, and also permit negative sanctions (e.g. exclusion for those who break trust). Without commitment to fulfil certain obligations, trust will break down.

If culture is not a separate realm of society distinct from the economy or the polity, then where does this leave the issue of social differentiation? This study is premised on the fundamental character of social differentiation as the context in which theories of economy and society have arisen. If we deny the separation of economy, polity and culture does this not also deny differentiation?

The answer to this complex issue hangs on how we conceive of differentiation. There are two aspects to this, the first an analytical one, the second an empirical one. It is important not to confuse the two.

In the first chapter of this study, attention was given to the distinction drawn by Parsons and Smelser (1956) between analytical and empirical accounts of differentiation. Within their functionalist framework, the analytical approach focussed on distinctions between the various 'functions' that societies (or social systems) need to address to ensure their on-going survival and development. These functions were identified in terms of adaptation (A), goal attainment (G), integration (I) and pattern-maintenance (L). It is possible to translate these somewhat abstract categories into more familiar terms. For example, adaptation, involving the deployment of resources through social interaction with nature, may be likened to what is conventionally referred to as the economy, while pattern-maintenance involving the institutionalisation of values into stable patterns, may be likened to what is conventionally referred to as culture.

Nonetheless, Parsons and Smelser wanted to insist on the distinction between analytical and empirical aspects of social action, a distinction which applies with particular force to social differentiation. By maintaining such a distinction they were able to argue two distinct propositions. The first, analytical proposition, maintained that the A, G, I and L functions represented challenges faced by all social systems during the course of social life. They are, in other words, generic properties of any type of social system. The second, empirical proposition, is that,

185

although such challenges have led over the course of history to a high degree of institutional specialisation (e.g. between markets, governments, legal systems and so forth), this specialisation or differentiation is never absolute and exclusive. For within the real world even those institutions we see as most highly specialised in the performance of a particular function, and sharply differentiated from the remainder of society, are in fact faced with the full range of multi-functional AGIL challenges. Thus markets, to take one example, have their own pattern-maintenance (L) or cultural exigencies, their own political or goal-attainment (G) dimensions and so forth. One example of the cultural dimension of markets is networks of trust built up within the business community. One example of the politics of markets are the collectivities such as employers' organisations, shareholders' meetings and trade unions that set goals for economic actors.

This argument may be visualised in terms of two stages of reasoning developed by Parsons and Smelser (1956) in their analysis of social differentiation. In Figure 7.1, we outline first of all the basic four-function AGIL paradigm in terms of a basic analytical differentiation between four sub-systems. In stage two we further sub-divide each of the sub-systems (represented by the upper case letters A, G, I, L) by the same four sub-divisions (e.g. the adaptation sub-system A is now sub-divided into A^a, A^g, A^i and A^l).

Where does all this get us? Although this model has been criticised for being unnecessarily abstract and formalistic, it does enable us to present a more elaborated account of the social differentiation of economy and society than is available in any other theoretical tradition. This elaboration involves the simultaneous combination of two levels of analysis. The first involves the differentiation of society into specialised institutions, dealing with A, G, I and L functions, such as markets (A function), governments (G function), law (I function) and so forth. The second involves the proposition that the differentiated parts of society each face common A, G, I and L-type exigencies. The economy faces cultural exigencies, the political system economic exigencies and so forth. Within this framework the interpenetration of economy and society, is not simply a question of the impact of culture (L) on the economy (A), but also of economic culture (A^l) on the remainder of the economy (A^a, A^g

Stage one: the social system composed of four sub-systems

A	G
I	L

Stage two: each sub-system of the social system is internally
differentiated into four sub-systems

A^a A^g	G^a G^g
A^i A^l	G^i G^l
I^a I^g	L^a L^g
I^i I^l	L^i L^l

Figure 7.1 Differentiation and the social system.

and A^i). Put another way, culture is simultaneously external and
internal to economic life.

We shall return to the Parsonian contribution below, attempting to assess whether it can be translated into more detailed
empirical terms. For the moment, the argument has been
developed at a general level to help clarify a misconception in the
theory of culture, where culture is regarded as an external sphere
outside the economy. It is this belief which has contributed most
to the practice of analysing the economy without much reference
to cultural issues.

Culture, social order and social transformation

The major advances towards a more substantive historically-informed integration of culture with economic analysis are founded, as already indicated, on the work of Durkheim and Weber.

Durkheim's contribution (see especially 1933) is founded primarily on his discussion of the problem of social order, or put another way, the question 'How do societies hold together?' Within traditional societies, with a limited degree of social differentiation he emphasised the importance of what he called mechanical solidarity. This involved more or less 'natural', taken-for-granted bonds between individuals requiring no conscious discussion and no need for persuasion. Forms of mechanical solidarity within tribal societies depended on a high degree of homogeneity of social identity and cultural practices. They were reflected in strong cultural codes embracing religion and law, which exacted repressive sanctions against those who stepped outside community solidarity. Criminal codes which demand the capital penalty of death for transgression of the law are typical examples of mechanical solidarity.

Within modern societies by contrast, Durkheim emphasised, with many others, the corrosive effects of social differentiation upon mechanical forms of solidarity. In particular, the differentiation of economy from society, and of the individual from the traditional community created major problems for social order. Within the economy Durkheim emphasised the importance of the division of labour and occupational specialisation as crucial aspects of social differentiation. The freeing of the individual from strict community controls as people migrated from country to city, led not only to the increasing possibility of choice of occupation and government, but also to a greater conscious intellectualisation of social life. This was reflected in the increasing sway of reason and science in society.

Within this changed context, Durkheim asked how a society increasingly based on structural differentiation and individual difference could hold together. Mechanical solidarity had operated through the homogenising pressures of sameness between individuals and through taken-for-granted symbolic codes that were matters of faith, regarded as natural and enduring. How could societies increasingly dominated by dynamic and destabilising institutions such as markets, economic individualism and self-interest, hold together? Was it possible that societies which had enshrined individual difference as a major cultural value could find some general overarching framework of values which would integrate the forces of conflict and change within a relatively orderly framework?

Durkheim rejected the economic liberal assumption that the pursuit of self-interest could generate social order spontaneously in the manner of Adam Smith's celebrated 'hidden hand'. He developed his critique of economic liberalism not simply in relation to economic theory as represented by Smith, but also in opposition to the liberal sociologist Herbert Spencer. While Spencer had argued that self-interested individuals could achieve orderly transaction patterns though the institution of contract, Durkheim countered with the view that contracts by themselves had no binding effect on those who were party to them. Self-interested individuals, unconstrained by any other hand, would always seek to evade or break contracts if it was to their advantage to do so. If contracts worked successfully to tie down self-interested individuals, it must be that some additional moral influence is present to create respect for contracts. Such additional moral influences Durkheim referred to as the 'non-contractual basis of contract'.

In developing this line of argument further, Durkheim made one very important concession to economic liberalism. He accepted that the binding force of moral rules is likely to be weaker and more diffuse in modern individualistic societies than under traditional forms of organic solidarity. For Durkheim, once the dynamic forces of the division of labour, individual autonomy and democratisation have been let loose, it is no longer possible to return to the strong, overt and binding forms of repressive moral rules that existed in the past. Rather the characteristics of morality, if it is to have any binding force at all, must be expressed in terms of individual action, and in particular in terms of the obligations upon individuals. Put another way, Durkheim warns us against portraying an over-socialised conception of human society in which strong moral bonds constrain individual action, in the same manner as in traditional societies.

While Durkheim accepts part of the liberal argument against

over-socialised conceptions of economy and society, he refuses to agree with the liberal tendency to abstract the individual from society itself. To do this is to replace an over-socialised concept of humanity with an asocial or minimally-socialised humanity. This is untenable, according to Durkheim, because new forms of social solidarity are emerging within modern society to constrain individual self-interest. They are not the strong repressive moral bonds of mechanical solidarity but weaker, more diffuse, yet still binding structures of what he called organic solidarity.

Under organic solidarity, processes of differentiation, involved in the division of labour and in individuation, are regulated by bonds that recognise difference, but nonetheless subject it to a higher unity. Durkheim's discussion of the non-contractual basis of contract is designed to illustrate this point. Here the parties to contract have different interests in the transaction (e.g. as buyer and seller). However, where these differences co-exist with a commitment to accept the institution of contract as binding, then we may speak of a general unifying framework which regulates difference. This framework must recognise self-interest and the individual, yet be binding on the individual for it to qualify as a moral bond involving some sense of obligation.

Much of the plausibility of Durkheim's argument is drawn from the fact that most economic action takes place through time rather than instantaneously as in neo-classical models of the market (see Chapter 3). Because economic action has this quality of continuity, self-interest forms an unreliable framework of order within which transactions take place. Reliability does not matter so much in single, momentary, unrepeated transactions, but matters a great deal in relationships that are likely to be repeated, or situations in which most actors want to know that other parties will abide by the arrangements made.

Discussions of whether economic life really contains any kind of moral component to secure order and reliability often ignore the argument developed by Durkheim, because they assume morality must be overt and involve strong moral bonds such as are found in explicitly altruistic behaviour. The debate is often couched in terms of demonstrating the presence or absence of self-interest or altruism, as if they were mutually exclusive options. Thus altruism is often posed as a denial of self rather than, as Durkheim would see it, as the tying of self to moral obligation. From Durkheim's perspective there is no need to limit morality to strong, self-denying bonds, nor to see morality as totally antipathetic to the individual or the self. It is rather to be expected that moral codes, if they exist at all under modern conditions, will need to accept the 'self' and the 'individual' as core units of action. Of course this does not rule out the possibility of self-denying altruism. Yet if this exists it is unlikely to have much binding grip, except in aspects of social life which deny the differentiation of individual from society.

The most compelling evidence for the plausibility of Durkheim's discussion of the non-contractual basis of contract centres on the notion of trust. This has attracted increasing attention among sociologists in recent years (Luhman 1979; Barber 1983). The strategic importance of trust in the analysis of economy and society is that it appears as an aspect of economic culture at the heart of economic relations, rather than as a mode of cultural expression, so to speak, outside the economy but impacting upon it. Economic institutions, through the notion of the 'fiduciary relationship', have explicitly enshrined a concern with trust as a legitimate component of relations between 'managers' and 'organisations', between 'professionals' and 'clients', and between 'buyers' and 'sellers'. Trust relations are built into formal legal codes in such areas as banking, insurance and company law, but they also operate more informally in terms of economic networks. They are typically present for example in the informal understandings – 'a man's word', 'the handshake' or 'common honesty' that underpin the myriad of economic transactions where no formal contract is drawn up (Macaulay 1963). The hidden hand assumptions of economic liberalism provide no adequate account of 'order-maintaining' processes in such networks. Social scientists have therefore had to graft an awareness of the importance of economic culture and organisational culture onto analysis of economic transactions, management and organisational behaviour.

One of the most useful attempts to summarise the variety of links between culture and organisation has been made by Smircich (1983). She identifies five types of potential mechanisms of this kind. These involve cross-cultural or comparative issues in management, corporate culture, the role of culture in organisation cognition, organisational symbolism and, last but not least, the impact of unconscious processes within organisations. It is noteworthy that this check-list contains both external and internal sources of the influence of culture on economic life.

Durkheim's discussion did not of course stop at the analysis of the non-contractual basis of contract, important though this is for discussions of economic culture (the A^1 aspect of society in Parsonian terms). This is because he was concerned primarily with the question of order at the macro-level, rather than order within micro-level transactions. (In Parsonian terms this is more akin to the analysis of how A, G, I and L fit together.) Two attempts were made to address this problem.

In the first, developed in his celebrated study *The Division of Labour*, published in 1893, Durkheim provided an answer to the problem of societal order that challenged both economic liberalism and Marxist political economy. We have already noted the core concept of organic solidarity, and the arguments by which Durkheim criticised self-interest as a sufficient basis for solidarity in economic affairs. In extending his analysis beyond the thesis of the non-contractual basis of contract, Durkheim focussed on the division of labour as the basis for organic solidarity.

In so doing he was impressed by contemporary Marxist arguments that economic life had more grip upon the population than political life. Politics within the sphere of government was too remote from everyday life to be the basis for social order. He therefore turned his attention to everyday economic life. At first glance, this appeared an unpromising terrain for the location of a general overarching framework of social order, since capital–labour conflict was endemic to economic life in late nineteenth-century France as elsewhere. Nonetheless Durkheim argued that such divisions were increasingly being offset by the unifying effects of the division of labour. Such effects were associated first of all with the mutual interdependence of producers, each of whom depended on the other to satisfy individual needs. This sense of interdependence was only strong enough to bind society together, according to Durkheim if it was institutionalised rather than left to individual expression. He saw this institutionalisation process in terms of organisations of producers working in particular occupations, committed to the responsible development of their occupation as a contribution to overall social cohesion. Such organisations stood close enough to everyday life concerns to incorporate individuals, but sufficiently far above individuals to constitute a social bond. They were, in other words, intermediary institutions standing between individual and society, rather like medieval guilds. Durkheim added a third component to this initial attempt to analyse social order, in terms of equality of opportunity. Open access to occupations was necessary if individual variations in aptitude and need were to be adequately expressed. Where meritocracy was constrained, for example by privileged access to higher education by birth, or through the inheritance of wealth, such openness would be violated. Individuals would then be making 'forced' rather than 'free' choices, with subsequent damaging effects on social cohesion.

Although this analysis of social order drew much of its economic frame of reference from political economy, it was nonetheless intended to challenge theories of economy and society based exclusively on power relations. The argument was that the division of labour could provide a basis for social order among individuals, and the institutionalisation of occupational identity and commitment, provided that equality of opportunity was present to secure effective choice of occupation. And the whole argument was designed to bring culture back into economic analysis, because social order was seen as dependent on creating conditions suited to the acceptance of social obligations by economic actors.

The first attempt by Durkheim to develop a theory of societal order is perhaps less successful than his account of economic order and the non-contractual basis of contract. While the non-contractual basis of contract has been successfully applied to empirical analysis through notions of trust, informal networks and organisational culture, the discussion of occupational cohesion and interdependence has had a more restricted empirical outreach. It appears restricted to the discussion of professional ethics which generate moral obligations to client-service (see especially the discussion in Parsons 1951), rather than to the full range of occupations. Outside service professions there is less evidence of commitments of this kind, and far more evidence of an instrumental attitude to work as merely a means to an end. This orientation is magnified in importance where workplace relations are experienced in conflictual ways relating to the closing off of opportunities for meaningful participation in work designs and management. This evidence suggests a reduced salience of workplace activities to individuals' lives, and raises the question whether any alternative basis for the construction of generalised social rules exists.

In his second and later attempts to deal with this question, Durkheim reinstated politics and political culture as the primary basis in the construction of social order. This return to politics was necessary because he came to believe that economic life and occupational order was not capable by itself of generating sufficiently binding general moral rules to stand above difference and self-interest. Durkheim did not abandon his emphasis on the importance of intermediary economic institutions, but now subordinated them to the symbolic primacy of political culture. It was above all within democratic political culture that Durkheim saw generalisable moral rules capable of binding all individuals. These were associated with democratic citizenship. This not only included everyone, thereby rejecting previously exclusive forms of political access based on privilege of birth or property, but also elevated the symbol of the citizen to sacred significance. The potentially divisive effects of individualism were now to be countered by turning active individual citizenship into a moral duty. In turn, the grip of this sacralisation process was to be fostered and periodically rehearsed through national political events celebrating democracy as a universal framework of social cohesion in which each could participate.

Durkheim did not elaborate this account in much detail, and the significance of political ritual in securing social cohesion remains under-developed and problematic (Lukes 1975). Durkheim's attempt to integrate democracy into the theory of economy and society, by means of an argument about social order and social cohesion, nonetheless differs quite considerably from parallel concerns for the importance of democratic politics within the tradition of political economy. Whereas political economy treats democratic politics as a possible vehicle for the expression of the collective interests of classes or political alliances of class fractions, Durkheim sees it in more culturally symbolic terms as a genuinely unifying source of social order. Whereas political economy typically sees the relation between politics and economy in terms of the relative power of various economic interests, Durkheim sees it in terms of the moral regulation of self-interest under conditions of social differentiation. Whereas political economy typically sees political regulation (or deregulation) of economic life in terms of the impact of collective economic interests (including class interests) in pursuance of economic advantage, Durkheim sees it in terms of attempts to secure social cohesion that may co-exist with interest-based conflicts, but which nonetheless stands above them.

How we resolve these contrasting perspectives depends ultimately on how far we believe that there are bases for value-construction and moral regulation that cannot be reduced to questions of economic interest. Of course, it is possible to assimilate Durkheim to political economy and to Marx to assist in demonstrating that power often requires cultural support, and that conflicts of economic interest are often expressed culturally in terms of claims to be acting in the general or universal interest. To argue in this way, however, is to evade the force of Durkheim's challenge, which is precisely that moral rules expressed in politics and law may indeed express general and universal interests.

One way of securing Durkheim's position here is to assert that it is possible to articulate moral interests as distinct from material interests. Even if moral arguments are often put at the service of material interests this does not mean that all moral claims can be simplistically regarded as functioning in this manner. For Durkheim moral interests may rather express forms of obligation to ideals such as unity, cohesion, peace and order, that is, to entities such as society, nation or democracy that stand above individual self-interest or collective class interest. Max Weber, who remained rather sceptical of the organic claims of such entities, developed a similar general argument as to the autonomy of ideal from material interests. In his case, such ideals typically involved symbolic issues of honour and prestige perceived in nations or ethnic groups, as well as religious values that prized activism or asceticism, involvement in the world or rejection of worldliness.

There is by now plenty of evidence that such moral

commitments exist, either in the perpetuation of strong bonds (e.g. in nationalism) or in more diffuse bonds (e.g. in democratic or consensus processes of decision-making). No-one ever died for capitalism, but plenty of people have died for their country or in defence of the democratic way of life. Economic interests are not the only salient point of identification, even in less drastic, everyday situations where questions of personal obligation remain significant. Neither economic liberalism nor political economy have ever fully accepted this and their capacity to analyse economy and society has suffered considerably as a result.

To focus on non-economic cultural sources of identification and cohesion is not necessarily to claim that societies are successfully integrated through such bonds. Indeed, cultural ties may serve as much as a source of conflict as cohesion. Nonetheless, the major significance of Durkheim's work for the theory of economy and society is its consolidation of the argument that self-interested economic transactions must rely on some underlying cultural bonds to remain coherent and workable over time. The extent to which such bonds exist remains an issue for empirical analysis.

We now turn from the problem of order to the problem of social transformation. This change of focus involves concern for the mainsprings of social change. To apply cultural analysis to social change is a surprising move from some points of view, because culture is associated more with the forces of integration and conservation than with processes of social transformation. It is typical of many versions of economics and economic history to explain change in economic or technological terms and then, separately, to examine the cultural impact of such economically-determined modes of change. In this approach culture is involved with the way we adapt to or cope with change, rather than a cause of change itself.

Within the tradition of economic sociology, the importance of culture to processes of social change and social transformation was secured by Max Weber. His contribution is associated with the celebrated, and much criticised Protestant ethic thesis, which asserts a connection between certain religious practices and the spirit of modern capitalism (Weber 1930, see also the important commentary by Marshall 1982). This specific argument was set within a wider sociology of religion, which itself was directed to what might be termed a comparative historical sociology of world civilisation.

It is important to clarify the sociology of culture that underlies Weber's comparative historical sociology. This discussion of culture is strongly influenced by liberalism and by a critical engagement with Marxist political economy. It is axiomatic to Weber that all social action is by definition meaningful to the actors involved. This applies even if meaning is implicit and never made the subject of reflexive scrutiny, as in the case of behaviour from habit. This emphasis on meaning gives all action a culturally-relevant character, even where the action itself is thoroughly technical in form, as in economic calculations of the best means to reach a given end. Put another way, culture is not a separate sphere divorced from economic life.

In asserting the meaningfulness of action Weber parts company from the more vulgar forms of economic liberalism which speak merely of self-interest and rational choice. For Weber explanations of action which leave out consideration of the meaning of action to those involved are incomplete. Self-interest cannot be assumed, but where it is present it requires social and historical explanation. In this respect Weber does not accept that we should assume self-interest as a natural form of behaviour that applies, unless some other motivation can be found. Instead he offers a historical sociology of culture that seeks to explain the incidence of self-interest in terms of underlying historical processes. His emphasis on the religious roots of Western individualism is one example of this method of analysis.

Having said this, Weber was undoubtedly far more positively influenced by liberalism than was Durkheim. This influence took two forms. First, Weber's own liberal Protestant background created a concern for the basis of the individual conscience, and what might be termed individual moral sovereignty. Second, he accepted much of the contemporary liberal critique of organicist views of culture, especially as applied to Germany. Here, many discussions of culture focussed exclusively on collectivities such as nation or people (*volk*), conceived as almost mystical communities of emotion and feeling. Such Romantic accounts of culture may perhaps be seen as an understandable reaction to the crass economic reductionism or utilitarian or economic liberalism, which ignored culture altogether. Nonetheless for Weber this reaction went too far. In particular it mystified culture by associating it with organic entities, the cultural power of which had been significantly eroded by social differentiation. The advent of institutions like the market, he believed, had increasingly severed the ties of individuals to the strong bonds of community, as well as separating economic organisation from the traditional household. Western culture, including German culture, retained cultural ideals such as nationalism, but in his view these should not be confused with older, traditionalistic, Romantic views of culture.

Weber's discussion of culture is neither to be associated with vulgar economic liberalism, nor with Romanticism, nor indeed with political economy and Marxism. For while criticising economic liberalism for its asocial assumptions and Romanticism for its mysticism, Weber's conception of sociality did not assimilate culture – the sphere of meaning – exclusively with economic power. Values were often furthered through assertions of power, but these could as much reflect moral or ideal interests as material interests.

There is also an important point of contrast with Durkheim, in that Weber associated culture as much with conflict and a plurality of competing values, as with integration. Culture is vital for Weber, but it will tend to express clashes of value, especially in an epoch of social differentiation of economy and culture from strong religious bonds. With the death of God (in the sense of faith in revealed religious truth), a plurality of competing secular values was to be expected. Culture in this sense would not guarantee social integration, nor, however, would naked use of power in pursuit of particular values secure integration for very long. If integration was to occur it would come in more muted form through the consent of people to the domination of rulers or social institutions. This consent would not necessarily require overarching value consensus, but rather a minimum acceptance of the legitimacy of existing arrangements. Three basic legitimising appeals are possible – the appeal to tradition, to rationally grounded rules that have been properly enacted (e.g. by legislation) and to charisma. By charisma, Weber means belief that particular individuals possess special qualities that demand acceptance of their personal leadership.

Having clarified the narrow ledge that Weber sought to occupy with respect to a theory of culture, we return to the substance of his comparative historical sociology. This was designed to given an account of the nature of what he saw as unique features of Western or Occidental culture. While emphasising the dynamic importance of modern capitalism and institutions such as private property and the market, he linked these with the more overarching characteristic of rationalisation. As noted above, this was seen as a dominant feature of economy, polity and law. In addition, Weber argued that rationalisation also gave a distinctive character to cultural practices, not only in religion, but in areas such as music, architecture and thought. All were characterised by a formalised, intellectualised, impersonal calculative spirit reflected equally in market-based cost–benefit calculations, the formal codifications of law, the subjection of religious practice to ascetic discipline and in the formal patterns of Western musical structure.

It should be noted that although Weber accepts the importance of social differentiation and value pluralism as emergent features of modern Western society, he sees rational-isation as the predominant integrating force. Rationalisation has a somewhat peculiar character in that it is as much a product of the unintended consequences of human action as the product of human design. If the culture of rationalisation is the predomin-ant culturally integrative force in Western society, it has not achieved this status as the result of human intention or an exclusive single-minded pursuit of cultural values aiming at rationalisation. Nonetheless certain explicit cultural practices, such as science and rational law, are major bearers of rationalisation (Weber 1976). In this sense rationalisation does not produce integration simply by spontaneous means without any reference to prevailing structures of meaning.

These Occidental characteristics are seen as distinguishing the West from other major world civilisations, such as Islam or Confucian China. Such non-Western civilisations were not without dynamic features of their own and they certainly display several types of rationalisation. However, taken over the course of world history they did not generate the same type of this-worldly rational differentiation of economy and society that occurred in the West. Either rationalisation was expressed in an other-worldly form, as in forms of Islamic religious law, or the dynamic potential of social differentiation was obstructed by traditionalism sanctioned by other-worldly religious goals, as in the Hindu caste system. Put another way, economies under such conditions remained strongly embedded in forms of cultural integration that limited the full development of private property rights and market-centred individualism. These limiting conditions did not prevent successful trade or technological innovation, but they did limit the social transformation of non-Western cultures in more thoroughly rationalised directions, as far as Weber was concerned.

Weber's historical argument about the impact of the Protestant ethic was framed in this broad historical context. Since his argument has been regularly misconceived it is important to clarify its nature with more precision. Weber was not arguing that Protestantism caused capitalism. If we define capitalism in a very general way as a drive to acquisition through trade, then it is an age-old phenomenon pre-dating Protestantism. For Weber this kind of capitalism was so widely diffused both historically and spatially, that it failed to contribute much to an understanding of the distinctiveness of the West. Weber's argument was directed not at capitalism in general, but rather at what he saw as modern rational capitalism. This was defined in terms of private ownership of the means of production, the commodification of labour as well as physical products, and through a spirit of calculative impersonal profit-seeking. It was this latter rational spirit that Weber linked, though only in part, with the influence of Protestantism.

The linkage was not between Protestant theology and the spirit of rational capitalism, but rather through certain forms of Protestant pastoral practice. Above all else Weber stressed the affinity between the religious notion of the calling, in which one's life and conduct should be disciplined by and made rationally accountable to God, and notions of personal entrepreneurship and the work ethic. Religious practice was seen as imparting qualities of discipline and rational accountability to economic life. The significance of this influence was that it helped to overthrow both existing moral sanctions against profit-seeking behaviour, and the dead hand of traditionalism and habit in economic life. The implications of the argument are two-fold.

First, economic life prior to modern capitalism was embedded in cultural practices inconsistent with rationalisation. Second, changes in cultural practice were one of a number of pre-conditions for the transition from embedded to differentiated rationalised economic systems. The coming of rational capitalism is not therefore to be understood in terms of the triumph of self-interest over culture (in the form of cultural traditionalism), but rather in terms of transformations in cultural as well as economic practices.

The denouement of Weber's argument, however, is suffused with tragedy rather than triumphalism. This is because the rationalisation process, in his view, undermines the cultural practices that helped bring it into existence through the development of rational capitalism. For, once instituted, ration-alised economic behaviour no longer needs religious sanctions. Instead it may operate within the general climate of secularised individualism oriented to the pursuit of instrumental or goal-directed rationality. This raised the spectre of the withering away of an explicit concern for values and conflicts over cultural meaning as the impersonal aspect of rationalisation became entrenched. For Weber this impersonalisation was associated with the increasingly bureaucratic rather than personalised modes of economic and social organisation. Within the market personalised entrepreneurship was giving way to large-scale corporate bureaucracy (a theme picked up in discussions of the growth of organised capitalism), while within politics, the virtuoso leadership of charismatic figures like Bismarck was giving way to the impersonal dominance of bureaucratic official-dom. Personal virtuosity might be possible for academics, but only on the margins of society, and could only be played pianissimo.

There is some ambivalence then in the legacy Weber leaves to economic sociology. On the one side there are certain general argu-ments which help secure a culture-inclusive theory of economy and society. These may be restated in the following propositions:

1 All social action is culturally-relevant insofar as it embodies cultural meaning.
2 The impact of culture within economic life embraces social change and social transformation, and not merely social order and integration. Culture may therefore be order-transforming, and not only order-maintaining.

Beyond this however, the specific discussion of Western rational-isation and culture raises the question, 'Does rationalisation destroy culture?' This question is similar to the Marxist critique of capital-ism in terms of the domination of the 'cash nexus' over society.

Weber's position here is ambivalent. On the one hand he appears to be saying that rationalisation drives out meaning, in the sense of explicit concern for values. The spectre of the 'iron cage' of rationality, in which individuals no longer feel they have choice over their actions, appears to subdue cultural autonomy altogether. On the other hand Weber encourages us to think of rationalisation and instrumental rationality as forms of culture. That is, concern for technique and the best means to reach a given end, can become an end in itself and hence a value. The fact that the value prizes impersonal and calculative operations does not make it any the less of a value. Modern Western society may therefore be regarded as creating a new set of values such as formal efficiency, scientific reasoning and intellectualisation which give status to the roles of manager, technologist, scientist and professional, that is, to occupations that prize formal educational credentials rather than depending on private property ownership rights.

What is missing from Weber is any sustained discussion of democratic values which also appear to be part of Western processes of differentiation and rationalisation. Democracy arises with the differentiation of a national citizenry from personalised kingship, generating values of popular sovereignty. The rationalisation of politics involves the erosion of partic-ularistic privilege in the face of universal rights and obligations. Weber appears sceptical about the influence of democracy as a force for social integration, believing that it will become dominated either by a rationalised bureaucracy or, on occasion, by charismatic leaders. This scepticism is in part connected with the weak rooting of democratic institutions in Wilhelmine Germany, in which context Weber wrote. But it is also connected with Weber's preference for an individualistic rather than interpersonal model of moral discourse under modern con-ditions. Where Durkheim sees moral order in terms of external obligations that bind individuals to society, Weber tends to see moral order in terms of the projection of the individual moral conscience into social institutions, including economic institutions.

Weber's ambivalence in relation to culture, polity and economic life has limited the impact of his sociology of economic culture to the impact of values on economic life. This ambivalence has helped to produce a large and inconclusive debate on the relative importance of Protestant values to Western capitalism (see Holton 1985). It has helped to stimulate consideration of the role of values in other more recent processes of transformation, notably in Japan (Nakane 1970; Dore 1973) and East Asia more generally (Hamilton and Biggart 1988). It is beyond the scope of this study to summarise the substance of these debates in any detail. What they do reflect, however, is first, an acceptance of the theoretical possibility that culture may be order-transforming and that changes in cultural values may assist in generating changes in economic organisation. A second feature of this literature is considerable scepticism that culture by itself is the decisive explanation of cross-national variations in economic development. Most prefer to combine cultural with other types of economic and political explanation.

One of the problems with debates on the role of culture in economic life is the tendency to abstract culture from economy and politics. The procedure is then to examine the impact of cultural factors, such as religious values, as if they came from outside in an unchanging form to exert their impact on an otherwise culture-free economy. Contrary to Weber's methodology, what is either missing or only weakly articulated is any sense of economic culture. If, however, we think in terms of economic culture a new set of explanatory questions are raised. These include the following 'How far does economic culture vary by nation as against economic sector or firm?'; 'What explains the characteristics of economic culture with respect to change?' and 'How far is economic culture reducible to self-interest or to economic power relations?' These are empirical questions rather than matters which can be solved through theory.

We shall explore and evaluate at least part of the empirical research agenda deriving from Durkheimian and Weberian discussions of culture and economy in Chapter 8. In the meantime, further exposition is required of another key element in economic sociology, namely symbolism in economic life.

Cultural symbolism in economy and society

Symbolism is a major element in many of the leading definitions of culture. The anthropologist Clifford Geertz (1973), for example, linked meaning with symbolism in the following definition of culture as 'An historically transmitted pattern of meanings embodied in symbols, a system of inherited conceptions expressed in symbolic forms by means of which men communicate, perpetuate and develop their knowledge about and attitudes towards life' (1973, p. 89).

The key role of symbolic elements in economic life can be fruitfully approached through a discussion of value theory. In response to the questions 'Why do people want goods?' or 'Why do goods have value?' we have so far noted two types of response. Within the tradition of economic liberalism, a subjective set of answers was given linking the origins of wants to pre-social utilities of individuals. People want goods, in other words, because they have uses, or use-value. This applies in any kind of economic system, but it is only within a market economy that liberals believe such utilities can be maximised.

Within the tradition of political economy, the dominance of use-value is seen as historically eroded with the differentiation of economy and society characteristic of market economies and market capitalism. Here the value of a good is set in terms of the profit that can be extracted from it during exchange. This gives a more objective character to value, in that orthodox Marxism sought to link exchange-value with the labour-power embodied in commodities. This linkage was intended to dramatise the primary importance of production rather than consumption in determining the value of goods. In answer to the question 'Why do people want goods?' political economy directed attention away from the wants of individual consumers, because they are seen as relatively powerless in the face of the power of producers. It is this power which structures the value of goods and their availability in the market.

Within the emerging tradition of economic sociology, this type of answer has been seen as inadequate. It either ignores culture altogether or reduces it to issues of economic power. The alternative culture-inclusive forms of economic sociology have set in train a third set of answers to the question of why people want goods. This has shifted back from the sphere of production to the sphere of exchange and consumption, but has reconceptualised consumption in a rather different manner to the utilitarian framework of economic theory. Essentially the relations of exchange and consumption are analysed as socially constituted rather than deriving from pre-social tastes that are peculiar to the individual. This *social* determination of exchange and consumption is founded on the cultural meaning of exchange relationships and of the meaning of the goods available for consumption. In terms of value theory this represents a shift away from use-value and exchange-value, to notions of symbolic, or sign-value. The symbolism of exchange and consumption involves not only those who are a direct party to transactions – i.e. actual consumers – but also all those others for whom the transactions and goods involved have a cultural meaning.

This emphasis on cultural meaning and symbolic-value provides a way of linking economic sociology with all types of economic and social relations rather than differentiated market-oriented capitalist economies alone. Issues of cultural meaning are generic to society as such, even though their form and expression may vary. This generic status of cultural meaning allies economic sociology with anthropology. Indeed many of the leading attempts to bring culture back into the analysis of economy and society under modern conditions, have either been made by anthropologists, such as Mary Douglas (see Douglas and Isherwood 1978), or have been strongly influenced by anthropology (Thompson 1971).

Douglas and Isherwood argue that there are indeed certain common features linking consumption in 'tribal societies' with that of industrial societies or capitalism. In all societies goods are not 'primarily needed for subsistence', but depend for their significance in 'making visible and stable the categories of culture' (1978, p. 59). These categories define who we are and how we think of ourselves, what the relationships are between us, and how we would like to be seen and related to by others. Wherever goods are objects, they form part of 'material culture' and act as markers or signifiers of cultural meaning. Culture is not exclusively composed of these material markers for it also includes verbal components such as language, and ideational elements such as religion. Nonetheless the goods of material culture play a key role in social interaction, acting both as bridges to others or as fences separating people. Even where destined for private or exclusive enjoyment of a limited group of people, such as a household or individual, they perform public cultural functions in embodying messages about those who wish to consume them.

From this point of view there is no major cultural difference between the Nuer tribe of southern Africa, who express cultural meaning through the exchange and ritual consumption of cattle within networks of kinship (Evans-Pritchard 1940), and modern expressions of cultural meaning through the ritual exchange and consumption of food and gifts at Christmas and Thanksgiving, and at marriage, childbirth or death. In both cases 'consumption is a ritual process whose primary function is to make sense of the inchoate flux of events' (Douglas and Isherwood 1978).

Of course there are also many second-order differences between these two examples of the cultural meaning of consumption in tribal and modern societies. These involve the degree to which culture is 'embedded' or 'differentiated' from the wider society, and also the character of the technology of consumption such as the availability of mass communications media. These will influence the extent of innovation as against traditionalism in consumption behaviour, as well as the sources that can be drawn on for new consumer products. The contrast between traditional modes of consumption of a small range of objects, and the globalisation of Western consumer culture with its endless search for novelty is dramatised in the film *The Gods Must Be Crazy*. Here a Kalahari bushman encounters a mysterious can of Coca-Cola dropped from a passing aircraft, and tries to discover the meaning of this globally familiar product of material culture that is alien to his own way of life.

Analysis of the changing symbolic order of economic life, contingent on the emergence of modern Western society, was advanced more by Simmel than either Durkheim or Weber. Simmel's major study *The Philosophy of Money* (1978) took up the symbolic rather than technical significance of money as a social institution. During the course of human history, money had emerged, for Simmel, as an increasingly abstract measure of value and medium of exchange, indifferent to the goods under exchange or even the substance out of which money was physically constituted. What had begun as a measure of value with an intrinsic value for human life in its own right under systems of barter (e.g. cattle) had been transferred first into valuable forms of precious metal divorced from sources of material sustenance (e.g. gold), and finally into paper money of no intrinsic value, but able to express in the most flexible form the value of all other goods.

For Simmel, money had replaced religious symbols, such as God, as a new secular universal equivalent in terms of which the value of all other goods could be expressed. This created technical economic advantages in terms of its universal applicability, flexibility and portability, but at the same time tended to divorce money and exchange from any connection with transcendent cultural values. Money expressed the ultimate reality, which was the indifference of economic exchange to any fixed organic source of value. Money permits an objectification of subjective value, in a universalistic form. However, this development of a secular universal equivalent frees the individual from particularistic allegiances only to fragment society into a set of transitory, fleeting and fortuitous exchanges (Frisby 1990). This is typified for Simmel, not in industrial organisations or at the point of production, but in the everyday culture of urban centres, and more particularly metropolitan cities, like his own Wilhelmine Berlin. These were suffused with a restless secular individualism and a concern for the vagaries of fashion.

This diagnosis of modern times may be interpreted, in part, as addressing major core components of both economic liberalism and political economy. In relation to liberalism, Simmel takes private individualism and the fragmentation of experience seriously as authentic cultural features of modern society. Although he wishes to socialise and historicise this diagnosis, he nonetheless rejects any attempt to over-socialise modern exchange relations, by linking secular individualism back to underlying social bonds of power or culture. In relation to political economy, there are many affinities between Marx's discussion of human alienation and Simmel's discussion of money as a symbol of the new cultural world. Yet Simmel refuses to see this new world as thoroughly pathological in the manner of Marx's critique of alienation as a distortion of human creativity. Some commentators have tried to interpret Simmel in a Marxian manner by claiming that he demonstrated how capitalism would turn the relations between individuals into relations between their 'objects' or possessions (see for example George Lukács discussed in Frisby 1990). This interpretation, which sees Simmel simply as a critic of reification, understates his ambivalence to modern culture. While a strong critical element is undoubtedly present, so also is a sense of modern metropolitan culture as both an autonomous and authentic aspect of culture. From this viewpoint Simmel is not a socialist or Marxist critic of capitalism, searching for a revival of transcendent communitarian values to destroy reification. Rather he is making a contribution to the sociology of culture – and to economic sociology – by emphasising the key role of economic exchange and consumption within the differentiated secular culture of modernity.

Simmel's particular application of cultural symbolisation in the constitution of economy and society does not incorporate all aspects of symbolism in economic life. In particular it fails to address the persistence of production-centred symbolism, involving the cultural meaning of work, technology, science and invention. The continuing promotion and in some cases lionisation of work-centred values and their personal exemplars remains outside Simmel's framework.

One powerful example of this alternative production-centred symbolism is the cultural identification with heroic entrepreneurial figures such as Henry Ford within the folklore of capitalism. The symbolic importance of Ford lies not only in his heroic personal entrepreneurship, but also in the association with technology and science as benign symbols of progress in human welfare. Moorhouse (1983) cites cultural rituals, such as mass visits to the Ford Museum at Dearborn, Michigan, or to the Ford exhibit at the World Fair of 1939, as symbols of popular attachments both to the ideals of the self-made man and the work ethic, but also to social progress through technological change.

Having noted reservations of this kind, it is nonetheless noteworthy how well Simmel's emphasis on the symbolism of exchange and consumption fits with contemporary theories of disorganised capitalism and the cultural contradictions of capitalism. Such theories, as we have seen, emphasise the growing autonomy of culture in relation to the dominant institutions of private capital and government. Each moves away from a production-centred view of the economy, and from economic determinist interpretations of society. This shift is founded in large measure on evidence of cultural autonomisation and pluralisation rather than the unilateral cultural domination of economic interests.

Recent discussions of cultural pluralisation have several noteworthy characteristics. First, there is the attempt to integrate 'the personality' and issues such as sexuality and the emotions into hitherto excessively economistic and rationalised discussions of economy and society. A leading example of this trend is Colin Campbell's (1986) study of the role of desire and fantasy in consumption behaviour. This neither ignores desire and fantasy as irrational phenomena on the model of economic liberalism, nor reduces such issues to the manipulative impact of economic power on culture, as in political economy and critical theory. Instead Campbell argues that there are autonomous cultural roots of consumer desire and fantasy within European Romanticism. In particular Campbell claims a parallel between the contribution of the Protestant work ethic to capitalist production, and the contribution of Romanticism to capitalist consumption. Just as Weber believed that Protestantism helped to undermine cultural constraints on capitalist productive entrepreneurship, so Campbell believes that Romanticism helped to undermine cultural constraints on market-based consumption.

What Romanticism did was to legitimise dreams and desires as valid bases for consumption choices, especially those involving new goods that had not yet been experienced. This created the yearning to have what has not yet been experienced, a form of desire that Campbell claims lies at the heart of modern consumerism. Such yearnings typically take the form of fantasy, including day-dreaming, based more on feeling than on rationality or cost–benefit calculation. This link with Romanticism, raises a second key element in recent discussions of cultural pluralism, namely the importance of an aesthetic element in consumption. This reference to aesthetics, may be linked to valuation of the 'fashionable' or the 'new', where style counts for much more than use-value. This concern for aesthetics, involving presentation of the self, is interpreted by Daniel Bell as an attempt to universalise the hitherto exclusive role of the artist. In the future, in a secular world dominated by a plurality of stylistic routes of personal expression in taste (including dress, personal appearance and other consumption markers) all are straining to make the expressive impact once reserved for the artist. A third aspect to discussions of cultural autonomy and pluralisation is the argument that modernity has given way to a new cultural formation, namely post-modernism. Theories of post-modernism, associated with writers such as Baudrillard (1983) and Lyotard (1984), have been criticised for their over-blown announcement of a new type of socio-cultural order (e.g. Kellner 1988). Nonetheless certain core features of post-modern theory do represent a coherent contribution to theories of economy society.

Amongst these are the idea of society as decentred rather than concentrated around certain core institutions such as the labour market, system of government and so forth. Instead post-modernism posits an increasingly fragmented society lacking any overarching framework of social order and regulation. This notion of decentredness is linked with a perceived pluralisation of cultural meaning and practice. This pluralisation undermines the privileged status of high culture in relation to mass culture. It is also associated with a depoliticisation of culture, as cultural consumption takes over from political mobilisation.

In the work of the French theorist Baudrillard, these processes of decentering and cultural pluralisation are associated in a striking manner with the sphere of consumption. This is, however, constituted not by use-value or exchange-value but through 'symbolic exchange' or sign-value. In consumption there is an active appropriation of signs or messages, not the using-up of an object. Signs refer not to practical uses but to symbolic meanings that form part of a system of meanings.

Baudrillard occupies a critical stance towards such developments in that he regards them as fundamental distortions of inter-personal communication. He goes so far as to claim that the dominance of sign-value represents the death of the 'social'. This dramatic diagnosis is associated with his belief that the 'signs' appropriated during the course of consumption increasingly lose any clear points of reference with the real world of human subjects and objects. This point is made by means of certain key concepts derived from structural linguistics.

Structuralists of this kind distinguish between linguistic terms (signifiers), the meaning of the terms as intended by human actors (the signified) and objects pointed to by linguistic terms (the referents). Baudrillard's claim is that increasingly the signifier is becoming detached from the signified and the referents. We are left with a pluralistic play of signifiers. The sphere of consumption is not seen as a means of aesthetic symbolic expression and communication as in the anthropological interpretation of Mary Douglas. It is seen rather as a solipsistic activity, dividing human actors from each other as they celebrate and enjoy consumption within private worlds. For Baudrillard authenticity is replaced by a simulation of reality in which private consumption of the sign becomes more real than reality (i.e. social relations between individuals). The realm of consumption is thereby conceived of as 'hyper-reality'.

Baudrillard's version of post-modernism shares with Frankfurt School critical theory a highly critical account of mass consumption and privatised social relations. In Baudrillard's case this conclusion is reached by means of a somewhat different intellectual route. He gives greater emphasis to processes of cultural symbolisation and attempts a more fundamental rupture with Marxist political economy. Like the Frankfurt School, however, Baudrillard's theory is subject to a similar line of criticism, namely the failure to demonstrate empirically that mass culture and private consumption are distorted, in authentic, quasi-social practices. This attack on privatism and consumerism, it should be noted, comes from writers disappointed at the failure of the working class to rise up against capitalism and create a new society. The critique of consumption functions to explain why this scenario has not occurred, but it is constructed in such a way to evade scrutiny of the original expectation in the first place. The working class is being penalised for dashing intellectuals' expectations of it. No penalty accrues to intellectuals, whose expectations have proved false. Instead, consumers are effectively blamed for being seduced by consumption.

Much of the difficulty here is associated with a moral dislike of privatised individualism as against collective or communitarian solidarity. What most disturbs Baudrillard is the perception that people no longer participate politically in society. Consumption merely offers an illusory form of symbolic participation. The one exercise Baudrillard has not attempted is to survey actual consumers on how they experience and use consumption. It remains a strength of the liberal tradition that the privatised individual is treated as an authentic actor, and it is unlikely that any adequate sociology of consumption is possible without some such acceptance of the knowledgeability of actors in pursuing consumption preferences.

In summing up this discussion of cultural symbolisation we emphasise first, its importance as an additional dimension to economic sociology. We also note the importance of cultural symbolisation in terms of the integration of personality and of non-rational expressive elements into the analysis of economy and society through the discussion of consumption. Finally, the connection between cultural symbolisation and the key role of culture in modern social formations is brought out. For many social theorists, the differentiation of culture from economy, and the growth of cultural autonomisation now represent major characteristics of contemporary social life, that can no longer be treated as secondary effects of economic or political determination. What we have yet to establish is how far processes of cultural symbolisation are dominated by systems of power rather than individual market-based sovereignty. This will be attempted in Chapter 8.

CONCLUSION

The primary aim of this chapter has been to outline the importance of culture to the constitution of economy and society. The argument is not only that cultural meaning impacts on the economy, but also that the economy is itself a cultural institution. It is therefore misleading to ask whether economic or cultural factors are more important in explaining how the economy works. All economic practices, whether they be linked with contract, efficiency, the firm or the consumer, have a cultural dimension to them in that they all depend on questions of meaning and action based on agreements to or expectations about meaning.

The importance of culture to economic life is also seen in analysis of the themes of order and change as they are manifest in processes of differentiation and integration. These twin processes, at the core of Polanyi's influential contributions to economic anthropology, also form the theoretical agenda for much of the work of Durkheim and Weber. Durkheim sheds further light on possible integrative mechanisms that overarch the fragmenting effect of differentiation, looking first at the division of labour and later at democracy. His contribution here enriches the discussion in Polanyi by drawing more explicit attention to possible modern *cultural* modes of integration, in contrast with Polanyi's political economy of market vs redistributive politics.

Weber, by contrast, emphasises the order-transforming aspects of culture. In addition he throws some doubt on the existence on strong cultural bonds of integration in modern differentiated societies. Instead he offers a more nuanced account of conflicts as well as patterns of order in which material and moral interest are expressed. Integration, for Weber, may occur without strong value consensus, relying rather on consent and acceptance of legitimacy.

Seidman (1985) has expressed these contrasts between neo-Weberian and neo-Durkheimian contributions as follows. First he contrasts Weber's belief in the disintegration of normatively integrated societal communities, with Durkheim's insistence of a shared moral understanding as the basis for identity-formation and societal community in any society. Second, Seidman draws attention to a contrast between Weberian notions of a shift from dominant religious world-views to rational individualistic secularism, and the Durkheimian notion of the persistence of religious cultural symbolism in new forms including the sacralisation of the individual. We shall return to the unresolved debate between these two differing views of culture, economy and society in Chapter 8. In particular, we shall ask the question, posed not only by Weberians but also by recent theorists of post-modernity, as to how far an overarching framework of cultural order is necessary to, or evident within, modern societies.

This question is one of a number of counter-challenges that may be levelled at a culture-inclusive synthetic economic sociology. We may not only ask how far cultural theory is required to explain social order, but also ask how far social change is illuminated by culturally-inclusive reasoning. In so doing, a further question arises namely 'How much do cultural theories emphasising meaning add to accounts of economic life founded on self-interest and/or power relations?' Is it possible to synthesise all these approaches in a coherent fashion, or are they largely mutually exclusive and contradictory?

8

ECONOMIC SOCIOLOGY
An evaluation of a culture-inclusive theory of economy and society

This chapter provides a critical evaluation of culture-inclusive theories of economy and society in relation to two unresolved issues in the foregoing analysis:

1 The problem of order in relation to self-interest and power.
2 The problem of nation-states and globalism in relation to culture.

THE PROBLEM OF ORDER IN RELATION TO SELF-INTEREST AND POWER

Perhaps the key challenge mounted by economic sociology to both economic liberalism and political economy is that neither tradition possesses an adequate theory of social order. In response to the question 'How do societies hold together?' economic sociology rejects the answers put forward by the other two traditions.

Economic liberalism, as we have seen, answers this question in terms of two main options. These are, first, coercion through control over resources creating command economies and, second, the spontaneous order of the 'free' market. This rather stark choice tends to subordinate close analysis of how economies actually work to a normative choice between what liberals see as freedom and coercion. This rules out alternative conceptions of freedom to those posited by liberalism. It also discourages scrutiny of the complex mixtures of freedom and coercion present in most economies. At its worst, the assumption is made that because the *ideal* of the perfect market encapsulates human freedom in economic affairs, so *actual* markets correspond to the

215

ideal. This not only discourages analysis of imperfect markets and market-based coercion as they actually exist, but also excludes the possibility that non-market or regulated market systems may offer alternative collectivist routes to freedom by delivering freedom from hunger, bad health or illiteracy. In addition, no incentive is given to acquiring an understanding of the value-bases and cultural meaning of order-generating institutions, and their cultural stabilisation in norms such as social justice. The possibility of a shared normative order that transcends or regulates self-interest is rejected by liberal assumptions of spontaneous market order.

These criticisms of economic liberalism as presented so far, do not of course demonstrate that social order is actually achieved through means other than market freedom or coercion. They do, however, challenge liberalism to provide less philosophical and more empirically-based accounts of how markets really operate, whether they do operate so spontaneously to generate order, and whether the support of extra-economic political and cultural institutions is really of such secondary importance.

Such accounts are required, not only to correct the excessively philosophical idiom of many liberal discussions of social order, but also because of the weight of evidence suggesting very significant problems with it. Such problems, identified earlier in this study, include the process of market organisation and regulation through the firm, and the process of increased government involvement in economic life through market regulation over the course of the twentieth century. Neither of these tendencies have led to the abandonment of the market as a core economic institution, but both have set sharp limits to the market freedom of individual actors. This general point remains valid even though the boundary between market freedom and regulation is a constantly shifting one, and even though certain Western nations, such as Britain and the USA, have during the 1980s partly deregulated segments of economic life.

We have also noted earlier in this study that certain recent examples of liberal scholarship have taken up and tried to incorporate trends towards regulation and organisation, as in developments such as Oliver Williamson's transaction-cost analysis of markets and hierarchies and James Buchanan's public choice theory. These important developments indicate that liberalism has not stood still. This in turn means that standard critiques of liberalism in terms of the inadequacies of the theory of spontaneous market order must themselves respond to modifications in the underlying liberal position.

The general direction of such modifications in the liberal position has moved neo-liberals rather closer to political economy than to a culture-inclusive economic sociology. By this I mean that the problem of social order has been linked more closely with issues of power and the representation of interest than with the interaction of markets, power and culture. This emphasis on power relations has been incorporated in a weak sense into Williamson's version of organisation theory as applied to corporate hierarchy. However, Williamson still emphasises the rationality of hierarchical control rather than naked power. The emphasis on power is rather stronger in Buchanan's emphasis on political coalitions of interest in the determination of public policy and the distribution of public goods.

Elements of convergence between liberalism and political economy have not been entirely one-way. While liberals have sought to incorporate power into their understanding of market order, certain representatives of the political economy viewpoint have taken up much of the liberal apparatus of interest-based rational choice in the analysis of economic life. This is most evident perhaps in class theory where writers like John Roemer (1982) and Erik Wright (1985) have interpreted the rationality of social class behaviour and class formation in terms of the pursuit of self-interest, and the mobilisation of assets by collectivities to secure individual interest. They have also taken up the 'free-rider problem' identified by liberal rational choice theory, whereby individuals derive benefits from collective action while not sharing the costs involved. A typical example of such 'free riding' would be an individual who refuses to join a trade union, yet benefits from improved wages and conditions secured by trade unions.

The key mainstream assumption of political economy with respect to social order is that it is achieved through the medium of power and as the result of processes of bargaining and conflict between interested parties. Such parties are generally collectivities such as firms, industries, workforces, trade unions, economic lobbies and social movements seeking various forms of economic regulation. For class theorists, these groups are differentiated and aggregated into social classes, such that political economy is interpreted in terms of class conflict and the formation of alliances in the political arena.

Political economy answers the problem of social order primarily through the mechanisms of power, subordination and control, organised in pursuit of interest. This is clearly a very influential approach which appears to offer plausible insights into processes of market organisation, hierarchy within the firm, government involvement in economic life, and the political regulation of the economy. The claim is that economies do not generate their own order, supported only by a small state, but generate conflict and tensions that require extra-economic political resolution.

The main criticism of this assumption from the viewpoint of economic sociology is that it either ignores culture altogether, or reduces it in a simplistic fashion to the operation of economic power. Whereas economic liberalism neglects culture because it neglects the social 'embeddedness' of economic life, political economy neglects culture because of a primary concern with the sociology of power. Those liberals who have moved closer to political economy in search of a theory of social order, have in one sense moved closer to a more fully social account of economic life. Yet they are in danger of taking on board an inadequate version of social theory.

What is at stake in the neglect of culture? The main problems here are two-fold. In the first case, where culture is ignored altogether, no account is provided of the meaning human actors give to their involvement in economic life, or of the way economy and society interrelate. In the second case, where culture is assimilated to economic power, one of two problems arises. Either culture is regarded as controlled by the dominant economic class, reducing human beings to 'dupes', unable to construct their own autonomous meanings and to act upon them. Or variations in cultural practices in the face of economic power are recognised, but culture itself is seen as wholly composed of meanings and practices that may be traced back to conflicts over economic power. No other dimension to culture is recognised, rendering it a unitary rather than a pluralistic structure.

Within the second option, where culture is at least recognised, the power-focus of political economy has been integrated with a culture-inclusive account of how people think, experience economic life and attempt to build meaning into their actions. In such accounts, as we have seen, the achievement of social order is dependent on cultural integration, which usually takes the form of acceptance of the dominant cultural assumptions and meanings projected by those who hold economic power. The most celebrated example of such a theory within the Marxist tradition is the theory of embourgeoisement, in which potential conflicts within capitalist societies between capital and labour are channelled into orderly directions through significant working-class adhesion to 'bourgeois' ideals such as the sanctity of private property, hard work, thrift and respectability. According to theorists who take this view, it is these culturally-meaningful ideals embodied in orderly behaviour that legitimise inequalities of power and undermine the potential for disorder.

An alternative example of this type of theory of cultural integration involves the theory of consumerism. In this theory the seductive influence of private consumer satisfaction undercuts any commitment to social protest and any funda-mental disorder arising from economic inequality. This is especially evident in Herbert Marcuse's (1968) argument that the products (sic!) of private consumption – the automobile, hi-fi set, split-level home, kitchen equipment – act as a form of indoctrin-ation and manipulation militating against public politics and qualitative social change.

The intellectual fate of class-based theories of cultural order has been predominantly negative. In the first place, doubt has been expressed as to both the existence and influence of dominant cultural systems serving the economically powerful. In their influential critique of the 'dominant ideology thesis', Abercrombie, Hill and Turner (1980) dispute (a) that ruling classes have coherent ideologies, and (b) that insofar as they do, these have led to the successful cultural integration of sub-ordinate groups. They point out both that such vaunted 'bourgeois' cultural formations as individualism have complex, long-term historical origins pre-dating capitalism (Abercrombie, Hill and Turner 1986), and that evidence of successful resistance or indifference to supposedly dominant ideologies is rife. If such ideologies have a significant effect it is more likely to be in securing improved cohesion and morale *among* ruling groups than *within* society.

In the second place, considerable empirical evidence has been assembled against the view that working-class involvement in activities such as home and mass consumption ownership represents embourgeoisement, a loss of autonomy and a retreat from public life. Peter Saunders' recent study *A Nation of Home Owners* (1990) demonstrates that in Britain at least home ownership enhances autonomy and choice for the working class. In providing security and elements of psychological well-being it may also serve as a basis for participation in public life rather than an atomistic private retreat.

In the third place, doubt has been placed on the need for cultural integration, especially under modern conditions, to achieve social integration. Whatever may have been the case within traditional societies, it has been argued that modern capitalism and individualism have developed such a high degree of pluralism and variation, that no overarching cultural framework can any longer claim an effective hold on meaning and action. This critique has recently been embellished in theories of post-modernism, which posit a collapse of universal cultural ideals, the celebration of difference, the dominance of simulated over authentic experience and a privatisation of personal concerns and desires away from the political and public arena (see especially Baudrillard 1983; Lyotard 1984; 1988). In contrast with theories of social order which assume that societies have a coherent centre that is vulnerable to disorder and disintegration unless culturally supported, post-modernism posits an increasingly decentred social life organised around small-scale networks rather than politically-bounded nation-states.

While post-modern theories of decentering and the collapse of the 'political' seem highly exaggerated in a world where nation-states and national polities remain intact and able to wage war or control domestic populations, the basic idea that strong cultural integration may no longer be necessary strikes a chord with older liberal theories. These too focussed, albeit in a less sociological manner, on the plurality of individual purposes and on individual autonomy, at the expense of highly socialised views of human community. In some respects then post-modernism ironically rehearses the older liberal critique of the

Table 8.1 Options for the analysis of social order in relation to economic life

1	The liberal account of spontaneous market order without need for cultural order – lent support by post-modernism.
2	The political economic account of social order achieved through power and domination – lent qualified support by organisation and public choice theories.
3	The culture-inclusive political economic account of social order based on a dominant ideology – but criticised by 1 and 2.

over-socialised conception of human society, just at the point when many liberals had begun to lose confidence in their atomised multi-centred picture of market-based exchange.

To summarise, if we approach the problem of social order from the traditions of economic liberalism and political economy we are left with a set of three options concerning social order. These are summarised in Table 8.1. The missing option in this listing, is a culture-inclusive account of social order that is sensitive to, but not reducible to, economic power. We now return to the culture-inclusive theories of economic sociology discussed in Chapter 7 to determine whether such an option remains credible in meeting the criticisms of liberalism and political economy.

In response to both economic liberalism and post-modernism, economic sociology claims that some measure of cultural cohesion is necessary to all societies – contemporary society included. Without some framework of overarching values that have widespread relevance to all members of society, human communication and co-operation would not be viable for any length of time. This applies both to the 'internal' operation of the economy where order-generating values such as trust and goodwill are important, and to the wider relations between economy and society, where more general cultural values are evident. The form which these values take, and their relationship with other aspects of social life, is however so vulnerable to intellectual misunderstanding that a number of further clarifications are necessary.

First, as emphasised by both Durkheim (1933) and Parsons (1953, 1971), the cultural characteristics of contemporary social life differ from those of older societies in that strong overt moral bonds deriving from religious faith and kinship have been

221

eroded. The mistake is in assuming that the absence of this strong form of cultural integration means a lack of cultural cohesion as such. What has nonetheless to be demonstrated by economic sociology is that weaker ties exist and are capable of binding individuals together. Durkheim and Parsons argue that weaker ties do exist, but often in the form of taken-for-granted rights and obligations that are covert and implicit. Parsons, in particular, emphasised the importance of universalistic rather than ascriptive ties within modern differentiated societies. Where economy is differentiated from society, and individuals from one another, society-wide integration can no longer be linked with the ascriptive claims of kin, religious membership or local community. A good deal of the rich cultural substance of integration (e.g. rituals and ceremonials) is thereby lost. At the same time the individual can be integrated into the new societal community if some common universalistic basis of membership can be found. The promise of economic sociology, and its potential advantage over economic liberalism, is that it can provide a socialised rather than atomistic account of contemporary individualism.

The discussion of social cohesion developed by Durkheim and Parsons interprets individualism and citizenship as inclusive universalistic bases of membership of contemporary society. Individualism, for example, is not simply an assertion of self-interest, but also a cultural norm influencing the expectations that we have of each other, namely that we value the expressive integrity of our individuality. Western culture is committed to fostering and protecting the autonomy of the individual through socialisation in the family, and an achievement-based education and economic system. Individualism is also expressed in the quintessentially economic spheres of choice of occupation and consumer behaviour. Although limits are placed on individual freedom, e.g. through law, these are legitimised in terms of protection of the rights of other individuals. For Durkheim, this idealisation of the individual amounted to a new religion – or sacralisation – of the individual.

Citizenship, according to Parsons, and writing under the influence of T.H. Marshall (1977), is the basis whereby individuals are linked in a universalistic manner with the political system. Here the integrity of the individual is linked with the integrity of individual political choices, and with a democratic system of political representation. What makes a government legitimate is that, under the particular franchise in operation, the pattern of individual votes cast underwrite the governing party. This legitimates the right of government to regulate economic life, including the taxation of private property and the placing of legal limits on economic freedom.

A second area of potential misunderstanding with this argument about social order concerns its basis in popular consent. When Durkheim or Parsons speak, respectively, of 'organic solidarity' or 'value consensus', they do not claim that all or even the overwhelming majority of social actors actively support the cultural patterns in question. Both took some care to reject any view of society as constituted by a culturally regimented set of social puppets constrained to follow one single cultural pattern – though many commentators have been unconvinced by this attempt to avoid the problem of over-socialisation (Wrong 1961). It is nonetheless the case that both Durkheim and Parsons saw conflict as an endemic feature of social life. For them, the mere existence of conflict did not automatically mean that common cultural commitments (including taken-for-granted ties) were absent between the parties to conflict.

Their aim then was to identify the common patterns of cultural organisation that not only existed in the midst of pluralism, but that also gave support and coherence to that pluralism. Both individualism and citizenship may be regarded as interdependent parts of that universalistic cultural pattern. Without effective citizenship rights, for example, much individual economic or cultural freedom would be tenuous and vulnerable to political coercion. At the same time each is consistent with the presence of conflict, either between individuals or between citizens. There is no warrant, therefore to portray Durkheim and Parsons as theorists of 'order', separate and distinct from Marx or Weber as theorists of 'conflict'.

The challenge of economic sociology to political economy in relation to the problem of social order has two elements to it. First, economic sociology claims that cultural meaning and practices are an essential component of social order, in contradistinction to those political economists who would ignore culture altogether. Second, economic sociology claims that cultural meaning and practices cannot simply be reduced to the interests of the powerful, or to social relationships and problems arising from conflicts of interest between the powerful and the powerless. Just as the cultural meaning of medieval Catholicism for economic life was not thoroughly determined by the exigencies of medieval serfdom or feudalism, so the cultural meaning of modern individualism, consumerism or citizenship are not thoroughly determined by the exigencies of the market economy or the capitalist mode of production.

The key to the debate on culture between economic sociology and political economy is whether there exist alternative bases to culture than those associated with economic power and class inequality. The tradition of economic sociology as represented by Durkheim, Weber and Parsons claims that there are. In their different ways, each emphasised the irreducibility of culture to material interest, while at the same time stressing that material interest and culture were often closely connected. Put another way, some cultural formations are seen as representing material interest, while others are seen as transcending material divisions depending rather on ideal interests. These may include religion, nationalism and ethnicity, as well as individualism, citizenship and consumption-based lifestyles (Weber 1948b). Weber sought to secure this argument, in relation to religion, by saying that there was no necessary correspondence between adherence to particular religious practices and possession of particular material interest. The same religious practice could serve those with differing material interests.

A fundamental proposition underlying economic sociology is that there are a multiplicity of dimensions to human culture. If culture is concerned with the meaning of social existence as embodied in both thought and action, then the cultural aspects of social life embrace a range of concerns including personal and group identity, the expression of moral and aesthetic values, the search for security and order, and the legitimisation of change and social transformation. It is these concerns that become institutionalised in religion, nationalism, individualism and so forth. Any of these concerns, as institutionalised in social organisations, may be influenced or even dominated by structures of economic power and conflicts of material interest.

Whether they are or are not is an empirical question, rather than a matter that can be settled theoretically. However, theory needs to be sufficiently multi-dimensional to leave space for this plurality of empirical possibilities.

A legitimate objection to the promotion of a culture-inclusive economic sociology discussed so far is that it is too generalised and programmatic. We now turn to a striking case-study of culture and social order to take the argument further.

MORALS AND MARKETS: A LEADING CASE-STUDY ILLUSTRATING THE ECONOMIC SOCIOLOGY APPROACH TO THE PROBLEM OF ORDER

Another way of grasping the empirical complexity of a culture-inclusive economic sociology able to incorporate themes of order and conflict is by means of case-study material. One of the most impressive examples of work demonstrating the interacting of markets, power and culture in relation to social order is provided by Vivian Zelizer in her study of the development of life insurance in nineteenth-century America (see especially Zelizer 1978, 1979).

Zelizer's study takes up the problem of social order within a market economy through the early development of life insurance. As experienced in the nineteenth-century USA, this raised a difficult cultural problem of whether and how far the value of human life could be translated into monetary terms. Many at that time expressed resistance, if not moral outrage, at attempts to establish monetary equivalences for death, life or human organs, on the grounds that they were sacred, whereas money was profane and base. Such conflicts set increasingly powerful insurance companies against religious leaders and moralists.

From the viewpoint of the household, life insurance offered a means of planning for the exigencies of death of the major breadwinner and the threat of family poverty. As such it may appear as a classic example of the intrusion of the cash nexus into areas which were historically dealt with within inter-personal family, household and community welfare networks. Life insurance nonetheless has a clear utilitarian advantage, and many families took up the new market-based means of financial provision against death.

Nonetheless, as Zelizer points out, life and death are also and simultaneously major cultural events, reflected in the continuing ritual symbolism of birth and death. These cultural pre-occupations did generate significant opposition to what was seen as the impersonal and morally insensitive institutions of market-based insurance. Such opposition was, however, partly overcome in Zelizer's view, not through the power of advertising and high-pressure selling, but through a subtle cultural redefinition of the meaning of money and the life insurance contract. Rather than treating potential insurance clients as cultural dupes, the companies marketed the new product as an altruistic self-denying gift to the remaining family rather than a purely economic transaction designed for profit. As Zelizer points out, money can be and was in this context redefined as bearer of sacred values: 'Money that corrupts, can also redeem: dollars can substitute for prayers' (1978, p. 601). On the occasion of death, she argues, money is transformed from a bearer of exchange-value into a bearer of symbolic cultural values.

Life insurance is not only to be seen as a form of altruism towards the living, but also in two further ways. First, it assists in dramatising the secular ritual of death contributing to the memory of the deceased. Second, life insurance offers a 'social' form of immortality, in which individuals perceive they can live on through their children. Life insurance, as described by the life companies of the time, was a pathway to immortality, contributing to the cultural reproduction of the family by tying the older to the younger generations.

Zelizer's argument, it should be noted, is not that life insurance is simply an exclusively cultural institution. She stresses its utilitarian and material contribution to family security during decades of rapid industrialisation and the erosion of inter-personal networks of welfare provision. Nor is her argument devoid of concern with economic power, witness the analysis of marketing strategies adopted by life companies. What is striking about the argument is its *multi-dimensionality*. Life insurance is neither reduced to utilitarian concerns (as in vulgar economic liberalism) nor to capitalist producer dominance (as in vulgar political economy). Both these dimensions are incorporated, but in addition a further cultural element is also introduced, focussing on the meaning of insurance in relation to the achievement of social security and welfare. Utilitarian matters are important since all is not culture or sentiment. Economic power is important, but it does not turn consumers into passive dupes. Cultural meaning is important but not to the exclusion of the other two dimensions.

This case-study not only offers a powerful example of a culture-inclusive economic sociology approach, but also does so in relation to the problem of social order. It suggests that social order was not achieved spontaneously through the market, nor by the dominant power of producers over consumers, but by mechanisms in which cultural meaning and symbolic values transcend market rationality and divisions of material interest.

Thus Zelizer takes up an important issue raised earlier by Durkheim and Parsons concerning the tendency of modern society to sacralise the individual human being. Far from moral bonds being dissolved by the cash nexus, Zelizer, in company with these earlier theorists, sees a shift in the character of moral bonds in which the individual and individualism assume a moral character. Surprisingly, however, Zelizer's study is one of the few attempts to introduce empirical research data into the debate about whether the social order of capitalism or the market does depend on elements of cultural cohesion. Zelizer's study indicates that the institutional development of nineteenth-century life insurance did indeed depend on cultural integration. The implication is that markets are not necessarily inimical to morals.

THE UNDER-DEVELOPMENT OF
CULTURE-INCLUSIVE THEORIES OF ECONOMY
AND SOCIETY

There is certainly no consensus among social scientists in support of Zelizer (or Durkheim and Parsons), partly as a result of theoretical disagreement and partly because the issue has rarely been researched. Much empirical research on capitalism and culture has been conducted through the methodology of enumerative induction, in which cases supporting a particular viewpoint are collected, rather than eliminative induction, in which all competing viewpoints are identified and evaluated and

Table 8.2 Capitalism, culture, order and morality

Positions:
1 *Capitalism has no morality*
   (a) The cash nexus and the fetishism of commodities destroy
       morality – Marx and Engels (1962)
   (b) Rationalisation destroys values in advanced capitalism, but
       in the process rationalisation also transcends capitalism –
       Weber (1930), Schumpeter (1961)

2 *Capitalism uses morality (e.g. religious values) as an ideology to achieve
   social control*
   Marxist culture-inclusive political economy, including
   Marx, Gramsci (1971), Connell (1977)

3 *Capitalism generates class moralities – a dominant middle-class and a
   subordinate working-class morality*
   Culturalist Marxism, e.g. E.P. Thompson (1963)

4 *Capitalism is constrained by certain externally imposed values
   (e.g. social citizenship and social justice)*
   Radical liberal-democratic tradition, e.g. stressing political
   intervention and the welfare state – T.H. Marshall (1977)

5 *Modern society constrains capitalist relations through an effective moral
   order within as well as external to economic activity*
   Durkheim (1933), Parsons (1951), Zelizer (1978, 1979)

---

the weak eliminated. Zelizer's study challenges this approach
through a multi-dimensional recognition of the irreducibility of
'cultural' perspectives to the core principles of utilitarian liberalism and political economy.

The grounds of disagreement over the existence of a cultural
component in the social order of market or capitalist relations is
summarised in Table 8.2. Here, positions 4 and 5 are consistent
with the economic sociology viewpoint whereas positions 1 to 3
are not.

The challenge of economic sociology offered at a theoretical
level by Durkheim and Parsons, and consolidated empirically by
Zelizer is that the alternative positions 1 through 3 are either
culture-blind or culturally reductionist. This challenge now requires
a fundamental rethinking and revision of both the political
economic and economic liberal positions.

In addition to this, empirical research on cultural dimensions to social order within contemporary societies needs to be done. As Pahl (1990) has pointed out, we still know comparatively little about the extent and limitation of social cohesion, how and why levels of cohesion change over time, and how the various macro-level, micro-level and intermediary levels of cohesion interrelate, conflict and, on occasion, fit together. Pahl places particular emphasis on the importance of further research into how far and in what way the national macro-structures (e.g. democracy and market) fit together with the micro-structures of household and local community. He points in particular to a divide between an excessively speculative macro-level idiom of general theorising about social order, and an empirically rich ethnographic literature on local small-scale cultural identities and organisations (e.g. Gans 1988).

In spite of the underdevelopment of research into social order and cohesion with respect to cultural organisations, it is noteworthy that Parsons' general theoretical account of economy and society does leave space for the intersection of macro-and micro-levels of cultural organisation. Parsons recognises the household as a key aspect of socio-cultural organisation, not merely as a unit of consumption but also as the focus of child socialisation and personality formation, and the base unit linking the supply of labour with the labour demands of the economy (Parsons and Smelser 1956). As such, the household is implicated in both labour and product markets, acting both as an agency expressing consumer wants and supplying labour involving individuals whose personality and values have been significantly shaped by the culture of the household. It is largely here that cultural commitments such as the work ethic and the sanctity of the individual are fostered, and also at the inter-household level that much of the symbolic 'status' elements in consumption behaviour are formed.

From this perspective the macro-level structures of the market may be linked with more micro-level processes of value-formation and cultural expression within households. We shall return to this problem of the macro–micro link in the concluding sections of this study.

Meanwhile, there is one remaining dimension of social order that requires further scrutiny, namely the relationship between national and global organisation. The problem of globalism is relevant, as we shall argue, not only to the liberal analysis of markets and to global political economy, but also to culture and social order. This has become evident with the recent emergence of theories of globalisation and global culture. A culture-inclusive economic sociology must take these new developments into account.

THE PROBLEM OF NATION-STATES AND GLOBALISM IN RELATION TO CULTURE

At first sight the idea of a global culture may seem far less plausible than the notions of global markets and a global political economy. The process of international market development has been under way for many hundreds of years involving processes of intercontinental trade and exchange (Curtin 1984; Abu Lughod 1989). The idea of a global market goes somewhat further than the mere existence of intercontinental trade, by claiming that all geographical entities are integrated into a single economic system. This process – well described by political economy as a capitalist world-system – has been reflected in the development of global institutions such as multinational or transnational corporations, international banks and trading houses, and bodies such as the World Bank and International Monetary Fund.

The idea of a global political economy dominated by such institutions has proved more persuasive, until very recently, than the idea of an international political order. This is primarily because of the weakness of the United Nations, during the epoch of the Cold War and super-power conflict, in achieving a genuine transnational political order able to transcend the sectional interests of particular nation-states. This has not prevented the development of regional blocs such as the European Community where some element of the national sovereignty of individual national members has been ceded to a centralised community body. In the main, however, political order has been achieved more readily within than between nation-states. This is especially true with respect to democratically-based political cohesion based on popular consent.

The existence of a global culture has received some analysis and support (Featherstone 1990) symbolised in the idea of the global village. This notion depends in part on arguments about the centrality of world-wide electronic communications media able to reproduce and diffuse cultural practices and symbols from one part of the globe to another, leading to an accessible pluralistic exchange of cultural products and messages. The question nonetheless remains as to what is the content of this culture, and how far it is really based on some quasi-liberal free cultural exchange. A key question has been posed here by political economy, and especially theorists of imperialism and the world-system, in questioning how far the global culture represents a narrowly Western, or even more narrowly American, set of values? Also put into question is how far such values rest upon the global marketing strategies of multinational firms pursued through aggressive advertising and display of the potent symbols of Western wealth and power.

Featherstone (1990) in an important recent collection of essays on 'global culture' attempts a more precise specification of the meaning of global culture. If by global culture we mean 'something akin to the culture of the nation writ large' (1990, p. 1), then he is sceptical that any such homogeneous integrated entity exists whether in Americanised form or any other. Following the key work of Roland Robertson (1987, 1990a, 1990b; Robertson and Lechner 1985), what Featherstone emphasises instead is the *globalisation of culture*, that is the creation of a single interrelated cultural field composed of a wide range of national, regional, local and transnational elements, all in communication and sometimes in conflict with each other. Put another way, the globalisation of culture does not mean the triumph of transnational cosmopolitanism but rather the creation of a single, yet pluralistic cultural system.

One noteworthy feature of this argument is the compatibility rather than incompatibility of the nation-state with the process of globalisation. This compatibility stems from the creation, during the nineteenth and twentieth centuries, of a global system of nation-states more or less in constant communication with each other. However, nationalistic or xenophobic such nations might on occasion be, they nonetheless created a global system of political relations manifest in treaties, conventions and collaborative agencies to regulate global matters. In the nineteenth century this system was dominated by European powers, quickly joined by the USA. However, by the end of the twentieth century Western dominance has been shaken though not destroyed with the rise of a set of powerful non-Western nations.

We therefore face a paradox that although nation-states were created in large part to express and promote national identity, when taken together they formed a key element in the process of globalisation. A vivid example of this paradox is the creation of the modern Olympic Games in 1896. There competitors are organised in national teams, compete against other nationals and salute national flags at the medal-winning ceremonies, yet the event itself can also be interpreted as a manifestation of global co-operation and cultural exchange.

The globalisation process, according to Robertson, is not dependent solely on co-operation between nation-states. It has also been fostered by improvements in communications, and through the development of processes and agencies not closely tied to the core political institutions of nation-states. These range from cross-national social movements such as environmentalism and the diffuse Band Aid concerts against famine, to the socio-cultural agencies of the United Nations. Such activities have begun to exercise some countervailing pressure on nation-states, not so much in the arena of power, as in the arena of culture and cultural legitimacy. As a result of such developments individuals increasingly see themselves as part of a world community, and threatened by world problems such as global environmental deterioration.

Two analytical issues, raised by this globalisation theory are worth mentioning. The first is that the political economic world-system emphasis on global capitalist power embraces only one dimension of globalisation, namely economic inequalities of power and control. This focus is an extremely valuable one in drawing attention to inequalities between North and South, and in tracing the ways in which Western economic power constrains and regulates much of the economic, political and cultural life of the Third World, and of the peripheral regions of Southern and Eastern Europe. And yet this focus remains exaggerated and incomplete. It exaggerates the dominance of the West by neglecting elements of autonomous national economic advance in Third World (e.g. East Asia). It is incomplete because it reduces global culture to Western and above all American cultural dominance. World-system theorists such as Wallerstein (1990) do recognise the existence of oppositional movements, but they see them as trapped within the cultural parameters of Westernism, and unable to articulate an alternative world-view.

This incompleteness is reflected in the assimilation of both the nation-states and national cultures to capitalism. As such, the involvement of nations in autonomous processes of search for and symbolic promotion of cultural identity are neglected. Simultaneously the unilateral impact of Americanisation and capitalist commoditisation – often linked together – is also exaggerated. As Appadurai (1990) points out, as rapidly as the powerful forces of metropolitan culture are diffused to new societies, they become indigenised (Feld 1988; Hannertz 1989; Yoshimoto 1989). Meanwhile reactions against global homogenisation in terms of the assertion of cultural difference are not monopolised by a concern to withstand Americanisation. Fear of cultural absorption by bigger units is far more complex. Thus for the people of Irian Jaya, Indonesianisation may be more worrisome than Americanisation, as Japanisation may be for Koreans, Indianisation for Sri Lankans . . . and so forth (Appadurai 1990, p. 295).

The complex interplay of cultural homogenisation and heterogenisation within what Appadurai refers to as 'the new global cultural economy' renders redundant political economic models of core–periphery emphasising one-way channels of power from the West to the rest. While retaining a concern with inequalities of power, Appadurai explores further the cultural organisation of the global economy with reference to five types of flows – whether of people, products or images. These are outlined in Table 8.3 in terms of ethnoscapes, mediascapes, technoscapes, finanscapes and ideoscapes – the common factor being that they are all elements of the global landscape.

The choice of the landscape metaphor here is deliberate, in that Appadurai wants to emphasise the cultural relativity of the view seen from different standpoints. Perceptions of each landscape may vary according to the historic, linguistic and political location of the observer. Appadurai's analysis of these landscapes stresses the disjuncture or lack of systematic relations between the five components of the global system. He offers yet another example of the emergence of a culture-inclusive economy. This refuses to reduce culture components in the mediascape or ideo-

Table 8.3 Appadurai's concept of the global cultural economy

Type of landscape		*Key characteristics*
(a)	Ethnoscape	The landscape of mobile people within the global system including tourists, immigrants and refugees, and those who want to move. Ethnoscapes involve the tension between motion and stability.
(b)	Mediascape	The image-centred landscapes offering inter-pretations of the narratives of human lives within the global system. Such narratives involve imagination and fantasy as much as hard reporting.
(c)	Technoscape	The landscape of mobile technology, moving at high speed across national boundaries, organised by multinational companies and/or Governments. Such processes are driven by political possibilities as well as availability of capital and labour.
(d)	Finanscape	The landscape of rapidly mobile capital.
(e)	Ideoscapes	Politically-centred world-views, involving key concepts such as freedom, democracy, sovereignty.

scapes to the dominant logic of the technoscape or finanscape. Beyond this, however, it is not made clear how far the global system rests upon, or is capable of generating, social order and cultural cohesion.

None of the recent contributions to the theory of globalisation are particularly sanguine about the existence or even possibility of global social order in the sense of cohesion between the component national parts. Whether impressed by the post-modernistic emphasis on heterogeneity or not, most analysts have drawn attention to continuing cultural divisions and endemic social conflict. At best the analysis of global social cohesion is cautious, concentrating on the emergence of poten-tial order-generating developments rather than the existing achievement of global cohesion. Here is raised the same difficulty as is found in analysing social cohesion *within* nation-states, namely how to strike a balance between evidence of common norms or commitments as against evidence of conflict and the pursuit of self-or collective-interest by a plurality of actors by means of power.

Parsons' guarded comments on the tentative emergence of world order (1967a) centred on several lines of argument. First he emphasised the historical uniqueness of the United Nations as a truly global and inclusive institution as compared with previous transnational empires or religions. Second, he noted the tacit acceptance of global rules of procedure by those nation-states who comprised the global community – a point developed by Giddens (1987) in his analysis of global norms of reflexive monitoring of sovereignty within the inter-state system. Third, Parsons emphasised the pluralistic cross-cutting alliances made possible within the global political community, presaging a more open system, less tightly regulated by the *real-politik* of the super-powers.

None of this, however, gets at those aspects of globalism which lie outside the political inter-state system. As Robertson and Lechner (1985) point out this neglects the increasing role of transnational social movements and other international organisations. At this stage, however, no convincing analysis of their emergent contribution is available. This leaves the problem of global social order in an analytically under-developed state.

One unanswered question particularly relevant to the analysis of economy and society is the significance of marked-based modes of exchange to global culture. Just as the sociology of consumption has been neglected in the analysis of economy and society within nation-states, so the global consumer and global consumption has yet to be integrated fully into the theory of economy and society.

In working towards a more adequate approach to the process of globalisation, the respective strengths of liberalism and political economy should not be forgotten. From liberalism we may retain the emphasis on market institutions as key elements in the development of a global economy and global cultural exchange. It is striking how limited is the contribution of alternative modes of political redistribution to economic and cultural globalisation, through devices such as foreign aid. At the same time, from political economy we may pick up the critique of liberal market relations as producing fundamental economic inequalities of power and within nations. Global consumption has been constrained not only by scarcity but by inequalities of power and control. At a general level these influence what is produced where and for what price, and the global distribution of income available for consumption. Markets have been dominated by Western interests so as to constrain non-Western patterns of consumption, at the same time as global markets have opened up access to and potential opportunity for wider choice. The mistake of liberalism is to argue that markets are exclusively enabling, while the temptation of political economy is to argue that they are exclusively constraining. They are both, and the complexity of patterns of enablement and constraint cannot be settled through generalised theoretical discourse or moral philosophical speculation about ideal markets or ideal governments.

If the strengths of liberalism and political economy are to be integrated into a culture-inclusive theory of globalisation much greater attention must be given to the cultural meaning and articulation of global consumption. To the extent that the massive Eastern European and Third World demand for Western consumer products such as jeans or compact-discs is not generated by the power of advertising and cultural domination, we need to establish more clearly what this demand means and how it is connected with the autonomy of the household and civil society. Does it reflect a convergence with Western patterns of modernity paralleled in politics with movements towards greater democracy and the collapse of communism? And if so will this generate a global order based on the cohesive institutions of liberal democracy? Or is the appearance of convergence exaggerated, failing to take account of significant cultural and political elements of indigenisation? These questions cannot be answered adequately without far more research into global consumer culture, and the macro–micro links between global, national and household levels of action. The reason such research does not exist is not so much a product of the relative novelty of global culture, as of the theoretical obstacles to research of this kind erected by liberalism and political economy.

GENERAL REMARKS ON THE EVALUATION OF ECONOMIC SOCIOLOGY

In the foregoing discussion two particular problems were explored as a means of testing the claims of a culture-inclusive economic sociology – namely the problem of social order and the problem of globalism. The argument developed cannot be said to have adequately answered *all* aspects of these problems. It is, however, claimed that such questions cannot be adequately addressed without a culture-inclusive approach to economy and society. This claim has been advanced by demonstrating weaknesses in the liberal and political economic approach and, even more important, through positive examples of the merits of a culture-inclusive approach.

The weaknesses of these two traditions are nonetheless easier to demonstrate than the positive merits of a culture-inclusive approach. Many of the arguments in favour of economic sociology are theoretically coherent and intellectually plausible, but rest on a comparatively limited basis of empirical research. This research base needs to be widened before the full potential of an economic sociology approach can be grasped. There is, however, full warrant for attempting this extension of the economic sociology research program given the continuing limitations of the two older traditions. This warrant is underwritten by the impressive promise of recent research reviewed in the Chapters 7 and 8 on the interaction of culture, polity and economy.

While it remains the case that much of the case for economic sociology is theoretical, generalised and programmatic, it is possible to specify more precisely and in a more unified manner than has been attempted so far the terms of a new theoretical synthesis and empirical research program. We turn to this task in Chapter 9.

9

ECONOMIC SOCIOLOGY
Towards a new synthesis

In the previous chapter, certain evaluative problems were discussed in relation to the claims of economic sociology to provide a more powerful theory of economy and society than either economic liberalism or political economy. The intention was not to eliminate these two traditions from consideration, but to show how they share a common weakness in excluding culture from systematic consideration. The problem here is not simply a matter of neglect and omission. It is also a reflection of a tendency in social theory to attempt unitary theories of society around a limited set of causal prime movers such as 'self-interest' and 'rationality' or 'collective interest' and 'power'.

The project of economic sociology can be regarded for its part not simply as a culture-inclusive theory of economy and society, but also as a multi-dimensional theoretical idiom (Alexander 1982, 1988). No causal primacy is accorded to any specific dimension of social organisation or any limited set of prime movers. This means that self-interest or interest-based power are not privileged, but neither are they disprivileged as causal agents. Similarly cultural aspects of social life are neither privileged nor disprivileged as explanations of the functioning of economy and society.

The task of developing a new synthesis which draws the best from liberalism and political economy, integrating them into a culture-inclusive understanding of economy and society, is a complex one. As a first step it is important to clarify exactly which elements of liberalism and political economy should be retained in any theoretical account of economy and society.

The development of theories of economy and society has been

directed, as was argued in Chapters 1 and 2, to address the key problems of differentiation and integration. These centred on the historical processes which differentiated the economy from the wider society, while also generating various potential means of integrating the economy with society. The discussion in this study of the three great traditions seeking to explain these processes has been directed primarily at the last two hundred and fifty years of human history, focussing in particular on the development of markets, the emergence of capitalism, the expansion of political regulation of economic life and the creation of a global economic order. This work has not therefore been intended as a complete economic anthropology of economic relations in time and space.

Clarification of the positive legacies of economic liberalism and political economy is then a matter of identifying which aspects of these two traditions assist most in understanding the twin processes of differentiation and integration. Such processes may be further sub-divided for analytical purposes into those relationships largely differentiated from society and hence 'internal' to the economy, such as production, consumption, investment and saving, and those integrative relationships that link economy and society involving such matters as political regulation and cultural values.

In Table 9.1, the respective strengths and weakness of economic liberalism and political economy are summarised. The main question that arises from this summary is how far the strengths of liberalism and political economy can be synthesised into a consistent 'third' body of theory. Can the emphasis on markets and individualism on the one hand, and power, collectivities and regulation on the other, co-exist within a single general theory in a meaningful way?

Any such attempt at synthesis clearly requires major modifications of core elements in the respective traditions. In the case of economic liberalism it requires abandonment of the proposition that markets are self-regulating and the dominant mode of integration of economy and society. In the case of political economy it requires abandonment of the propositions that markets are regulated solely through relations of power and dominance, that consumption is subordinate to production and that individuals and households lack significant elements of

Table 9.1 Strengths and weaknesses of economic liberalism and political economy

		Strengths		Weaknesses
Economic Liberalism	1	Emphasises the market and private individualism as key social institutions in contemporary society.	1	Neglects power differentials within the market.
	2	Rejects the existence of strong moral bonds regulating economy and society.	2	Unclear about the extent to which markets generate a stable integration of economy and society.
			3	Neglects cultural aspects of economy and society.
Political Economy	1	Emphasises power differentials within the market, and how these can generate inequality, conflict and instability.	1	Neglects autonomous cultural elements in the constitution of the economy and in the integration of economy and society.
	2	Emphasises the integration of economy and society through economic and political power.	2	Neglects consumption and the autonomy of private households.
	3	Introduces a global emphasis into theories of economy and society.	3	Exaggerates the role of political collectivities in relation to small-scale privatised units of action.

autonomy. Upon these two types of modifications, it is then possible to regard markets as generally 'imperfect' in the sense that ideal conditions of decentralised and diffused power and self-centred rationality rarely exist. Rather there is a balance to be struck between market autonomy and market regulation, where autonomy involves both producers and consumers, and where regulation involves both organisations such as firms, and governments.

Such generalised accounts of the nature of relationships between markets and society recognise the robustness of markets as enduring social institutions, while simultaneously recognising the endemic tendencies of public and private bodies to seek regulation in promoting their interests. As such they are more consistent with underlying economic and social trends within the modern world than are economic liberalism or political economy taken alone.

The robustness of the market is to be seen in the post-war revival of Western economies, and in the erosion of state socialist regimes in Russia and Eastern Europe. In the latter case, the institutions of socialist economic planning have proven inefficient in terms of low productivity levels, and unable to satisfy demands for consumer goods (Nove 1983; Lane 1985). In addition the compromise policies of 'market socialism' (Lange 1938; Brus 1972) have also failed. These attempted to introduce an element of marketisation into some sections of the economy (e.g. in product markets), while leaving other sectors involved with investment, capitalisation and credit to planning. One reason for this failure was the inability of market socialism to generate a workable set of 'flows' or 'feed-back mechanisms' between consumption, investment and production, since market signals from the commodified product markets need not be, and often were not acted upon by planners. In addition, socialist economies of this type depended on forms of political authoritarianism whereby blocked welfare improvement through consumption shortages could not be made up through political means of redress.

If the viability of state socialist economic planning has been left in disarray by these developments, this does not, however, mean that current economies function exactly according to the canons of economic liberalism. For, on the other side of the coin, markets within the global economy have neither produced economic stability and cohesion, nor generated prosperity for all.

241

To emphasise the robustness of the market is not to make the claim that markets are self-regulating or that markets are able by themselves to achieve the integration of economy and society. The ideal of market self-regulation has been eroded with the growth of large firms, and with the increase of government involvement in economic activity. This involvement has not only been through government consumption of marketed products, but also through government activity as regulator of markets, enforcer of deregulation by political means and as provider of collective goods, many of them outside direct market determination. Some of these activities are private capital-supporting, but others are private capital-replacing and indeed decommodifying (Esping-Andersen 1990). Alternative models of economic planning to those adopted in the state socialist economies of Russia and Eastern Europe, such as Scandinavian social-democratic corporatism, remain relatively robust.

Another limit on the liberal account of economy and society involves the persistence of global inequalities of wealth, income and power. While many of these are historical in origin as much as market-generated, their existence does mean that much of the world's population cannot participate in market exchange on a par with others. Denial of effective access to the market leads in many cases to famine and death, chronic morbidity and the creation of underclasses of the poor and destitute. Liberalism has not succeeded in demonstrating how the market by itself can reach and benefit such groups. Where disprivileged groups have been able to mobilise politically, or act as a support for political elites, as in a number of cases of Third World nationalism (e.g. China) attempts have been made to regulate markets so as to redistribute welfare by political means. Similarly, in the West a range of welfare arrangements have been instituted to attempt re-distribution. The need for such support, however, is indicative of the incapacity of markets to achieve such supports spontaneously.

The foregoing discussion indicates the terms upon which elements of a market and political economy approach can be synthesised together to make sense of major developments in contemporary economy and society. Within this discussion, the robustness of the market has been combined with the necessity for some kind of market regulation to address problems of economic co-ordination and social welfare. It should also be emphasised that these very general considerations are not meant to imply a simple convergence of all activity to one single market-regulated or welfare capitalist pattern. The diversities between different national relations of economy and society are noteworthy. In Chapter 5, in particular we noted the convincing argument of Esping-Andersen (1990) identifying a range of different patterns of welfare capitalism within the Western world, ranging from Scandinavian public sector welfarism through continental European corporatism to American and British deregulated *laissez-faire*. Such variations are not merely secondary variations of a major pattern in economy–society relations, but indicators of the complex historical interaction of economic and political influences on such patterns within particular nation-states. Esping-Andersen places particular emphasis on the power of the labour movement, for example, in the development of Scandinavian welfarism.

The argument can be further extended by bringing in Japanese and East Asian variants of national capitalist development with their own variations in modes of regulation (Hamilton and Biggart 1988). These range from the strong state-sponsored economic development strategies of South Korea, through the state-guided but more decentralised private oligopolistic business patterns of Japan, to the more free trade policies of Taiwan. Such variations are explained very largely in terms of a combination of political conditions and traditions affecting types of organisational development. Korean state-dominated development arose, so it is argued, very largely from the extreme chaos of war and civil war. The Japanese pattern of a guiding centre and strong corporate power derives, on this analysis, from the emperor/society models of Tokugawa and Meiji Japan.

Having demonstrated the possibility of integrating together certain insights from economic liberalism and political economy we now take the further step of clarifying exactly what a culture-inclusive approach adds to the foregoing type of analysis.

As indicated, in Chapters 7 and 8, the importance of culture within economic life has been seriously neglected by both economic liberalism and political economy. In Table 9.2, we provide a general summary of the strengths of a culture-inclusive approach in relation to the common weaknesses of both economic liberalism and political economy.

Table 9.2 The strengths of a culture-inclusive theory of economy and society in relation to economic liberalism and political economy

Weakness of economic liberalism and political economy		Strength of a culture-inclusive approach	
1	Impoverished interest-based view of the meaning of economic action, and the motivation of economic participants.	1	Provides a deep understanding of issues of meaning and motivation (e.g. through connections between values and economic action).
2	Inability to explain the normative basis of economic and social cohesion solely in terms of interest and/or power.	2	Provides an analysis of the normative basis of economic and social order, including tacit rules as well as explicit modes of political regulation.
3	Inability to demonstrate that economic interest is sufficient to generate changes in cultural practices in economic and social life.	3	Emphasises order-transforming elements of culture at both personal, organisational, national and global levels.

Again the key question that arises here is whether, or to what extent, the culture-inclusive economic sociology approach is consistent with the previously identified amalgam of liberal and political economic elements?

The case for the consistency of these two bodies of thought rests on the gaps and omissions in the former approach with respect to issues of meaning and motivation as they affect social change and social cohesion. The argument developed to this effect in Chapters 7 and 8 rests on the additional insights a culture-inclusive approach yields beyond what is available in the traditions of economic liberalism and political economy.

To take one example, self-interest has been recognised as a key component in market exchange within differentiated capitalist societies. Liberalism cannot, however, tell us in a convincing manner how and why self-interest emerged historically as a cultural practice, how and why the incidence of self-interest varies or how self-interested action can be consistent with any kind of social order and cohesion. Instead it is either posited as part of human nature or regarded as the paradoxical basis from which order emerges spontaneously through the action of a hidden hand. Even liberal social contract theorists presume protection of self-interest as the basis for political regulation rather than demonstrating the social and historical validity of the postulate in the operation of actual societies.

Meanwhile political economy, while transforming individual into collective interest formation, still maintains an impoverished view of human motivation and the meaning of economic action, which takes no account of the rich plurality of cultural life and the impact of different value-patterns on economic life. This is compounded by the failure to emphasise private consumption as an autonomous rather than wholly constrained activity, and by a reduction of the culture of individualism and household to the dominant power of producers. In addition, political economy cannot explain how we avoid endemic open conflict and warfare if power is the only cement – except, that is, by subsuming culture to power. This, however, reduces individuals to cultural dupes in a excessively unitary and one-dimensional view of what culture means. Finally, political economy fails to explore the emergence of cultural globalisation with sufficient care.

The social trends underlying the plausibility of a culture-inclusive economic sociology are much the same as those connected with the robustness of the market, and the concomitant development of various modes of market regulation. By emphasising culture however, it is possible to bring into sharper focus the normative significance of institutions such as individualism, privatism, the household and public political and legal regulatory processes. Individualism and the household, for example, are not only vehicles for utilitarian interest-promotion but also cultural institutions, cementing identity within the personality and creating norms which influence markets and power, in terms of their capacity to satisfy material and symbolic wants.

How far a stable integrated pattern of social cohesion actually exists remains a debated question, which we leave open. What is nonetheless clear is that cultural identity-formation and symbolisation are processes that actually happen and the stabilisation and institutionalisation of such processes in lifestyles and consumer behaviour generate social cohesion, even if at a micro- rather than macro-level.

Culture should not be read exclusively as a private or consumption-oriented matter, since it is equally relevant to issues of production (via the work ethic) and to public politics. Picking up the latter point, the problem with political economy is not the analysis of interest-formation and power-conflict as such, but the neglect of the cultural value-basis around which political interests form and coalesce. Thus it is not enough to assert that market regulation and welfare state development often reflect the pressure of working-class interests, to compensate the disprivileged for economic hardship and market failures by distribution of welfare to all. What is missing is an account of the value conflicts at stake here relating both to the meaning of values like social justice and freedom, and to the processes and institutions capable of generating such valued outcomes.

Part of the problem has arisen from the political economic assumption that markets, and indeed capitalism, are morally neutral or amoral. This has sometimes led political economists, especially Marxist political economists, to occupy a moral standpoint in support of what they regard as the interests of the powerless or exploited, without recognising any need to clarify the value-position thus occupied. If markets and capitalism are seen as morality-free exemplars of the 'cash-nexus', then political economy wins the high moral ground so to speak by default. No explicit moral argument need be presented when arguing against economic liberalism, the task is simply presented as offering a critique of the assumptions and propositions involved.

The problem with this is that economic liberalism is not morally neutral or amoral, but asserts the primacy of certain values such as individual freedom and personal choice, and associates them with institutions like the market. As we argued above, capitalism does have a morality, in the sense of a moral justification of markets, private property and personal autonomy. However, at the same time, the failure of state socialist economies, and the association of collective political regulation and state control with bureaucracy and inefficiency in both East and West have undermined the high moral ground that radical political economy occupied. It is not at all evident that 'collective' rather than 'market' solutions offer a more culturally acceptable general route to improved welfare as far as public perceptions are concerned. This applies in spite of the paradox that collective political solutions, at least in the West, have often been demo-cratically sanctioned with the explicit intention of improving welfare, while market solutions have no such formal political sanction and represent no explicit collective wish for improvement.

Had political economy concerned itself with culture, and recognised the moral arguments for the market together with the liberal argument for regulation where the market fails, this situation might not have arisen. Now that it has, the tradition of political economy is caught in its own dilemma. Either culture must be recognised, including the cultural autonomy of private individuals and the household, in which case the core assump-tions about power and interest are fundamentally challenged, *or* culture is not recognised and the predominance of power reasserted, in which case political economy offers no morally-sensitive rebuttal of the liberal case for market exchange and limited regulation. Liberalism can then easily retain the high moral ground simply by portraying radical political economy as founded on support for coercive regulation and the suppression of individual freedom. This is the basic dilemma now facing Left politics in the Western world.

Having reaffirmed these general arguments in favour of a culture-inclusive theory of economy and society we now move in somewhat schematic fashion to demonstrate more concretely what kind of analytical framework an economic sociology approach makes possible. This is demonstrated by means of a critical commentary on the systematic theory of economy–society interaction developed by Parsons and Smelser (1956). This endeavour is regarded not as a finished or even an extremely satisfactory theory, but as the leading and most influential example of the theoretical and empirical research agenda of economic sociology. The Parsonian research agenda is therefore outlined together with major revisions that go beyond Parsons' position. Much of the argument below draws on a previous work published in Holton and Turner (1986).

PARSONS' MULTI-DIMENSIONAL RESEARCH AGENDA AND BEYOND: TOWARDS A NEW SYNTHESIS

Parsons and Smelser attempted a multi-dimensional theory of economy and society built around the four functional challenges posed to any social system. As outlined (see especially Chapter 7) these four functional challenges involved adaptation (A), goal-attainment (G), integration (I) and latent pattern-maintenance (L). The economic aspect of society was identified with adaptation, meaning the adaptation of available resources to meet given goals in the face of natural environmental exigencies. Put another way, the economy sought to provide goods by combining land, labour and capital, bringing together human endeavour with natural resources.

In so doing, the economic or A sub-system of the social system (be it nation or global society) cannot be self-sufficient standing alone in a *laissez-faire* manner. It is rather dependent upon the three other G , I and L sub-systems dealing respectively with the setting of political goals (G), the integration of the parts of the system through law and other regulatory norms (I), and the development of culturally institutionalised value-systems (L). Each interacts with the others through media of exchange including money and power.

This approach is not to be regarded as yet one more

generalised assertion of the need to integrate our understanding of economic matters with politics and culture. This is because Parsons and Smelser attempt to specify the network of relationships that tie the economy to the wider society. This procedure recognises the differentiation of economy from society, while yet identifying the modes of reintegration or embeddedness that typically develop to create interdependence.

The argument they make moves in several steps. Having identified the analytically distinct A, G, I, L, sub-systems of the overall social system, they go on to argue that each of the four sub-systems can be further sub-divided according to the A, G, I, L, scheme. This means, again as discussed in Chapter 7, that the A sub-system of economy is not simply concerned with narrowly economic matters such as production, but has its own internal differentiation, including goal-setting, integrative mechanisms, and value systems (i.e. A^g, A^i and A^l sub-systems). Paraphrasing this argument, in the words of Niklas Luhmann, 'the economy builds its own values, its own goals, norms, criteria of rationality, and directions of abstraction' (Luhmann 1982, p. 200).

In this step in the argument the economy is seen as culture- and politics-inclusive. At the same time, the overall framework in which the economy is placed, means that it still must retain interdependent links with the remainder of society (i.e. the G, I and L sub-systems) rather than standing alone as a generator of societal politics, norms and values. The internal A^g, A^i and A^l sub-systems of the economy are bounded by a specific validity that applies within the economy (A). They are not therefore directly answerable to all of society as such. In this manner, Luhmann reaffirms Parsons' argument that the economy cannot stand alone, solving all functional challenges faced by human society including the establishment of legitimate political power, truth or stable cultural values. In this sense economic relationships do not, in and of themselves, fulfil all political, familial and other cultural functions, even though the economy itself involves certain bounded political, normative and value-based components. Such functions require interdependent relationships of exchange between economy and society.

The analysis of modes of interdependence comprises the next stage in the argument. Here an attempt is made to move beyond highly generalised abstract propositions to a more concrete analysis of economic and social institutions and the relationships between them. This proceeds by means of an analysis of exchange between the differentiated sub-systems of society, organised in terms of a sociological version of input–output theory. The key questions are what 'inputs' do the various sub-systems of the economy receive from the wider society, and what 'outputs' do they send back to the wider society.

The rather complex set of input–output exchanges posited by Parsons and Smelser can be simplified in terms of the relationships between the economy (A) and each of the other three sub-systems (i.e. G, I and L). These relations can be further divided into four main questions:

1 How are the goals of economic life set? This involves interaction between the goal-attainment sub-system of the economy (A^g) and the wider society.
2 How are the physical and financial resources necessary to conduct economic life obtained? This involves interaction between the adaptation sub-system of the economy (A^a) and the wider society.
3 How are the normative rules directed to the functioning of the economy developed? This involves interaction between the integration sub-system of the economy (A^i) and the wider society.
4 How are the institutionalised values of the economy developed? This involves interaction between the pattern maintenance sub-system of the economy (A^l) and the wider society.

These four sets of economy–society interaction will be explored in turn.

How are the goals of economic life set?

Parsons and Smelser identify two types of economy–society interchange which constitute the goal-setting (A^g) context of economic life. They both deal with the setting of general goals or purposes, e.g. what consumer goods should be produced, rather than detailed technical matters, e.g. how to produce a particular good at the cheapest possible price. The two particular interchanges that take place are identified in Table 9.3 in relation to input–output relationships between what might be

Table 9.3 Interaction between economy and culture

	Cultural input		Economic output
1	Consumer goals embodying cultural values.	1	Consumer goods able to satisfy wants.
2	Workers, socialised to perform and value specific occupational roles.	2	Wages and salaries.

broadly referred to as the economy and the wider culture. They involve, first of all, the input of culturally-influenced consumer demands in return for the supply of consumer goods, and second, the supply of workers socialised to value specific occupational roles in return for wages and salaries.

Within the first 'consumption' interchange, the intention is to emphasise that consumption wants are not wholly economically derived. Nor are they constituted exclusively through power-relations. Consumption is neither to be theorised in terms of self-interested, atomised economic man, or in terms of the coercive manipulation of the mass of consumers through corporate power and mass-advertising. It emerges rather from the sphere of value-commitments.

If value-choices expressed in consumption cannot be reduced to individual atomistic preferences, it is equally misleading to regard them as the outcome of some stifling value-consensus. Although Parsons is often seen as a functionalist theorist of value-consensus it is important to emphasise that he set limits to the effective socialisation and also recognised the heterogeneity of modern individualistic culture. Within the sphere of consumption, he did not believe that consumer demands are necessarily mediated through the societal integration system (I) concerned with development of stable normative order at the societal level. This indicates that Parsons and Smelser see consumption goals as a relatively unstable elements in the social order, and hence subject to change. This is not, however, equivalent to the economists' conception of randomness of ends, but closer to modern and post-modern emphases on the importance of status and fashion, and the proliferation of discrete micro-level life-worlds in contemporary society. In

251

addition, consumption typically involves household networks rather than single unattached individuals.

The empirical research agenda made possible within this framework suggests the following questions for analysis.

1 How much autonomy do consumers have with respect to producers, and what determines the limits to such autonomy?
2 How far do consumer choices constrain or transform the range of products produced, e.g. through product switch?
3 Is consumer autonomy more limited by lack of marketable income and lack of information, than by the power of advertising?
4 How important is sign-value and symbolic gratification as distinct from use-value and instrumental gratification in consumer behaviour?

The questions are of major empirical significance in any account of the input–output relations of economic life. While some work has been done on them, notably in the recent appearance of a sociology of consumption (Otnes 1988; *Sociology* 1990), few general answers are clear. Empirical research of this kind has been impeded by both economic liberalism and, in a different way, by political economy. The development of a satisfactory sociology of consumption is therefore coterminous with the development of a culture-inclusive economic sociology. Such a development however does not mean an abandonment of the political economic focus on producer power, nor a rejection of the problem of over-socialised accounts of individual want-formation raised by economic liberalism.

It should be emphasised that the particular application of an economic sociology framework by Parsons is itself liable to theoretical revision. One major logical problem with it is the assumption that in any set of economy–society interchanges only one single extra-economic reference point is involved. In the case of A^g system interchanges, under discussion here, the posited link according to Parsons and Smelser is with the L^g sub-system and no other. This rules out interchange with other direct 'social' influences including, for example, politics and government. As such the research agenda narrows to personal and private rather than collective and public modes of consumption provided directly by government (e.g. social services). These may themselves be influenced by cultural considerations, such as educational and health values, but they also reflect more directly political considerations such as the power of interest groups in securing redistributive welfare provisions, the level of electoral support for state services as against privatisation.

The economic sociology research agenda needs therefore to be augmented to include questions such as the following:

1 How far is consumption delivered through public rather than private means, and how far is public provision decommodified?
2 What determines variations in the organisation of consumption along public and private lines?
3 How far does privatisation of hitherto public-delivered consumption expand or reduce consumer autonomy?

We now turn to the second interchange relationship between economy and culture, identified by Parsons and Smelser. This concerns the input of human services into the workforce, 'balanced' by the output of wages and salaries. For the economy to establish an internal goal-attainment sub-system of its own, the input of consumer goals must be combined with social actors, socialised to identify with and perform discrete occupational roles. This involves value-commitments relating both to the household as the cultural provider of human services, e.g. to be a 'good provider', and to occupational role.

This analytical framework assumes a relative fit between job aspirations and the availability of appropriate employment. As such it is more appropriate to the post-war years of low unemployment than to the more recent era of mass unemployment in most Western societies. In addition it assumes the effectiveness of the nuclear family in socialising its members to fit available occupational roles without the mediation of power and household structures of inequality of access to employment.

It is certainly the case that Parsons and Smelser's framework, linking culture to the economy, permits a more visible discussion of gender relations and processes of personality formation in relation to theories of economy and society than is made possible within the traditions of economic liberalism or political economy. This is because Parsons and Smelser emphasise the extra-economic culture-inclusive origins of socialisation within the division of labour between occupational roles, rather than limiting the analysis to the logic of self-interest or the demands of the 'economy'. This approach, which has been extended in much recent feminist theory, identifies processes of child social-isation, selection and identification with occupational roles (including household labour as well as paid employment outside the home) and the stabilisation of the division of labour, as cultural processes, and not simply the outcome of self-interested deals or the naked power of men over women. With respect to gender differences, for example, one key culturally significant question is why until recently so many women have wanted to be 'women' or 'mothers' in the traditional mould in spite of the economic disadvantages involved (Chodorow 1978).

Parsons' substantive contribution to the sociology of the family is, however, rather disappointing and inadequate in this respect. Although his general theoretical aspirations to include personality development and culture within theories of economy and society have helped to stimulate feminist research, his comments on the nuclear family and gender divisions within it have not stood the test of time. In particular the argument that the nuclear family is a stable basis for the supply of mobile, educated and motivated labour for the workforce no longer commands support (Fox 1967). Analysis of the family unit has been replaced by analysis of the changing household, and of changing gender relations and gender conflicts within it. This has dramatised the inequalities faced by women in access to employ-ment and economic security, and emphasised the dysfunctional aspects of nuclear family living for women's autonomy.

The economic sociology research agenda suggested by the Parsonian discussion of cultural inputs into employment, as modified by the feminist critique of Parsons is as follows:

1 How far does the household generate a stable and autonomous pattern of socialised entrants into the workforce?
2 Do power differentials within the household create significant gender-based inequalities of access for its members and, if so, what determines variations in women's access to paid employment?
3 How do households cope with unemployment in terms of alternative sources of income, whether through benefits or mutual aid?

254

Once again, the function of this check-list of questions is not to ignore important work already done in answer to the questions posed but to indicate how a general multi-dimensional economic sociology may be formulated so as to combine macro-level theorising with empirical research.

How are the physical and financial resources necessary to conduct economic life obtained?

Parsons and Smelser identify two types of economy–society interchange which constitute the adaptive (A^a) context of economic life. They deal essentially with the capitalisation of the economy in terms of the mobilisation of resources required for production. The two particular interchanges that take place are identified in Table 9.4 in relation to input–output relations between what might be broadly referred to as the economy and 'polity'. They involve, first of all, the social input of capital, 'balanced' by economic outputs of profit for investors and taxation for government.

What is striking about this approach is the separation made between the economy as such and the process of capitalisation. This separation involves two elements. First is the differentiation of finance from production, a distinction Parsons shares with many political economic theorists of capitalism (e.g. Hilferding 1981). Second is the centrality of government involvement through public revenue-raising and expenditure patterns within the capitalisation process. In one sense, Parsons and Smelser's framework here amounts to something like a political economy of capitalisation, drawing attention to the common ground shared by financial institutions and government in capitalising

Table 9.4 Interaction between economy and 'polity'

	Social input		Economic output
1	Capital generated by financial institutions or government.	1	(i) Interest and profit for investors. (ii) Taxes for government.
2	Public and private encouragement through tax relief, subsidies and credit standing.	2	Improved productivity, i.e. improved capacity to deliver goods.

production. In addition, power is seen as the essential mediating influence between goal-attainment and adaptation or, put crudely, polity and economy.

Another important aspect of the analysis is the distinction between producers and investors. Although it is the case that the majority of capital investment is self-generated within the firm via profits (Armstrong, Glyn and Harrison 1984), much investment depends on external loans. It is a feature of the post-war economy that enterprises depend a great deal on investment loans or equity capital in a highly 'geared' manner to remain competitive, to achieve optimal earnings and thus to prevent take-over. Investors – both institutional and individual – are, in such circumstances, important external influences on the process of production. They will be influenced in their investment decisions by the comparative performance of share price levels, the rate of interest and the prices of government securities. They also tend to operate increasingly on a global level.

This distinction between production and investment is therefore closely related to the increasing importance of the separation between management of production and ownership of capital within modern Western economies. The full importance of this separation was not evident to nineteenth-century political economists such as Marx. Many early theories of capitalism were based on a very transitional moment in the development of modern society where capital-ownership and managerial control were fused in the undifferentiated person of the nineteenth-century businessman. 'For a brief historical moment, American capitalism appeared to be creating a new Schumpeterian "ruling class" of family dynasties founded by the "captains of industry". But that moment passed . . . and the trend since then is clear – the occupational manager, not the lineage-based owner is the key figure in the American economic structure' (Parsons and Smelser 1956, p. 290). Managers must therefore interact with financiers and investors to achieve successful capitalisation.

There is, however, a major problem with Parsons and Smelser's discussion of the adaptation–goal-attainment inter-change. This the failure to analyse the power differential between owners of capital (whether producers or investors) and other segments of society (including workers and consumers).

This problem can be grasped when we look at Parsons' discussion of property rights. Parkin (1979, pp. 51–4), for example, has argued that Parsons' discussion of property, set in the context of the separation of capital-ownership and control, serves to minimise the importance of private control over capital as a qualitatively different form of property rights to those simply involving possession of objects. Alexander (1984, p. 198) has also claimed that such inadequacies in the treatment of private capital prevent Parsons and Smelser from appreciating the economic constraints that private ownership typically imposed on government.

This latter criticism involves a failure to differentiate sufficiently between the respective roles of private financial institutions and government in the goal-attainment–adaptation interchange. Thus 'because capital formation is not in fact dependent on "public" political decisions, the national government does not receive the kind of adaptive inputs it needs to function effectively. National government ... rarely receive sufficient funds to achieve their public goals' (Alexander 1984, p. 148). Investment strikes, the mobility of capital overseas or the avoidance of taxation, may also combine to generate fiscal crises for the state.

While the Parsonian framework identifies important elements of differentiation between economy and society, it greatly exaggerates the power 'balance' achieved by exchanges between investors and producers on the one hand, and governments on the other. The challenge is that such balances may reflect an asymmetry of power between 'private' and 'public' interests. Parsons' approach may therefore offer far too benign a view of modern society in stressing harmonious balance at the expense of inequality and conflict. These important questions cannot be resolved, however, simply by reference to the political economy view of the capitalisation process.

Parsons and Smelser also go on to discuss the value-basis of capitalisation. They hypothesise that 'common values' link investors of capital and organisers of production. On the production side, such values are embodied in organisational goals: commitment to growth and to productivity. On the investment sides, value-commitments involve the responsibilities of ownership, not merely with respect to a particular firm, but in terms of the 'public responsibilities' of capital and its management (Parsons and Smelser 1956, pp. 128–9).

These relationships are elaborated in the second important boundary interchange between adaptation and goal-attainment sub-systems. This involves such inputs as encouragement to enterprise either in public form (e.g. tax relief and tax subsidies) or in private form through 'credit standing'. These are seen as 'balanced' by the economic output of higher productivity. This has a private pay-off in terms of higher investment returns, and a public pay-off in terms of increased resources for government to satisfy public goals.

As far as government is concerned, a fundamental problem nonetheless remains as to whether such resource inputs from the economy, reflected in taxation income will be sufficient to meet the political objectives of government (see O'Connor 1973; Habermas 1976). To the extent that they are not, the options remaining include cutting public expenditure, attempting to scale down expectations of government, or higher levels of borrowing. Whether any of these work depends in large measure on extra-economic sources of political pressure, including interest group lobbying, and on the legitimacy of government activity. We may therefore pose the 'fiscal crisis' question in broader form to ask 'How far do insufficient inputs of resources to government pose insuperable strains on the popular legitimacy of government, and how far are crises that arise episodic rather than endemic?'

The research agenda that can be built up on the basis of the Parsonian discussion of goal-attainment–adaptation inter-changes, and the critical commentary upon it, may be summarised as follows:

1 How far are financial institutions and investors both distinct from and dominant over the production process? Does this relationship change over time?

2 How far is there a unified capitalist class uniting producers and investors through common interests and values? If so how powerful is it?

3 Is the power of private capital-ownership the most important single source of power, and how far can this power be balanced or offset through government involvement in economic and social life?

4 How far are relations between private capital and government dominated by permanent crisis reflected in 'fiscal crisis'?

5 How much popular legitimacy does private capital have in relation to government and public revenue devices like taxation. Does the pattern of legitimacy with respect to private and public economic responsibilities vary between nation-states and if so why?

Many have tackled these questions and some of these debates have been reviewed above. For the moment, we simply note the distinctiveness of Parsonian economic sociology in shaping and refining this agenda of questions in particular directions. These include:

1 *The pluralistic rather than unitary structure of relations between economy and society.* Theories must embrace relations between investors and producers, and government and producers, as well as relations between producers and consumers, or producers and workers. Investment and credit markets, together with the fiscal affairs of government must therefore be included alongside analysis of labour and product markets. This pluralism renders inoperable conventional theories of capitalism.
2 *A presumption that pluralism means a diffusion of power* to a complex set of differentiated agents, rather than any simple model of class-based dominance.
3 *The mediation of power through value-commitments* including ideals of fiscal responsibility and credit-worthiness.

These emphases go beyond the economic liberal neglect of both power and culture, and the exclusive political economic search for unitary rather than pluralistic structures of power. They are more consistent with theories of contemporary Western society based on the concept of modernity – as a pluralistic combination of economic, political and cultural characteristics – rather than capitalism – as a unitary political economic system.

How are normative rules directed to the functioning of the economy developed?

Parsons and Smelser associate the normative basis of economic life with interchanges between the integration sub-system of the economy (A^i) and the integration sub-system of the overall integration sub-system (I^i). Such interchanges deal both with the

259

operation of normative rules relevant to economic life and with the agents of normative order within the economy. Two particular types of interchange can be reconstructed from Parsons and Smelser's argument. They are summarised in Table 9.5 below in terms of input-output relations between adaptation and integration processes. They involve, first of all, the development of binding normative rules, capable of overcoming tensions and divisions arising in relations between economy and society.

It is noteworthy that Parsons regarded the successful integration of divergent economic interests and social roles within the division of labour as a 'highly sensitive point in the social structure', fundamental to the successful integration of the social system as a whole. Far from under-estimating economic conflicts he saw them as posing profound problems likely to lead to cleavage and disintegration unless effectively regulated. Following Durkheim, Parsons identified contract as the central economic institution without which economic exchange through markets would not be possible. Nonetheless the origins of the rules upon which contract are based are seen as extra-economic, standing above the sectional processes of bargaining. Fraud and coercion are excluded from the operation of contract by means of 'socially prescribed and sanctioned rules' to which different parties are subject (Parsons and Smelser 1956, pp. 104–5). These rest on a combination of non-contractual commitments, together with the legally enforceable provisions of contract. However, like Durkheim, Parsons paid very little attention to the empirical

Table 9.5 Interaction between economy and normative order

	Social input		Economic output
1	A stable normative framework of predictable rules, notably contract, able to generate solidarity and cohesion.	1	Orderly economic relations.
2	Entrepreneurial agents of integration.	2	*Profit*, in the technical sense of returns due to innovation and new product combinations in relation to consumer demand.

development of this point through concrete analysis. This has come later, as we have seen in the analysis of trust and informal networks of reciprocal confidence.

The second aspect of the boundary-interchange is based on the agency of entrepreneurs. Here Parsons and Smelser draw on the realisation of earlier economists such as Alfred Marshall and Joseph Schumpeter that the bringing together of land, labour and capital did not occur spontaneously through the market mechanism. What is required, in addition, is a fourth 'integrating' factor, designated variously as 'organisation', or 'entrepreneurship'. The organiser or entrepreneur is not seen merely as a routine manager, but rather as a creative and imaginative innovator. In such endeavours, however, the entrepreneur draws on extra-economic sources of motivation and commitment, such as the idea of business as a vocation (Marshall) or the desire to found a family dynasty (Schumpeter).

A fuller account of entrepreneurial motivation involves the society's value system as it affects socialisation of the personality. Analysis includes both the supply of individuals motivated to fulfil entrepreneurial roles, and also the historical emergence of the role of entrepreneur itself. Influenced in part by Parsons, these questions have been addressed by a number of economic historians and social psychologists (Flinn 1961; McClelland 1961; Hagen 1962, 1967). Particular attention has been directed to the influence of different religions and cultural practices on child socialisation into achievement-oriented roles.

Less widely explored is the linkage between entrepreneurial activity itself and patterns of consumer demand. Here Parsons and Smelser continue their integration of consumer autonomy into economic sociology through the issue of consumer stimulus to and receptivity of new product combinations and new services. Here the social input of demand for novelty and new improved means of satisfying wants is 'balanced' by the output of new products as a result of entrepreneurial innovation. Such outputs contribute to greater societal cohesion, by permitting an increasing variety of lifestyles within the universalistic framework of the market. This is perhaps best illustrated in the development of fashion entrepreneurship in dress (e.g. Mary Quant in the 1960s) and music (e.g. the succession of popular musical styles e.g. 'acid' 'house', 'rap' and so forth). Cultural entrepreneurs of fashion and taste play a key role in such developments. Parsons identifies the existence of relative flexibility and lack of traditionalism among consumers as important factors in economic innovation and growth (Parsons and Smelser 1956, p. 267).

The empirical agenda arising from discussions of normative order is a rich and underdeveloped one, spanning the analysis of both rules and agents of normative integration. A number of key questions in empirical debate may be listed as follows:

1 To what extent are normative rules of economic life successful in channelling interest-based conflicts into orderly directions?
2 How widespread is the anarcho-capitalist evasion of rules, and what determines the capacity of interests to operate outside normative regulation?
3 What is the relative importance of formal as against informal mechanisms of normative order in economic life?
4 How important is personal as against impersonal entre- preneurship in the contemporary economy?
5 Do innovators contribute more to normative cohesion than normative disintegration? How do we balance the impact of Parsons' entrepreneurial integrators against the activities of asset-strippers, sanctions-busters and tax-avoiders?

How are the institutionalised values of the economy developed?

The final component of the economy, the latent pattern-maintenance system (A^l) refers to the economy's value-system. The relationship posited between this sub-system of the economy and the wider social system, however, is considerably different to the three instances of boundary interchange considered so far. In such cases, the relationship of economy and society is conceived in terms of interactive exchanges involving input–output 'balances' between different elements of the social system. In the case of pattern-maintenance relationships, by contrast, Parsons and Smelser see the input–output model as inappropriate. This is because pattern-maintenance functions are 'cultural' rather than 'interactive' (Parsons and Smelser 1956, p. 69). By cultural they mean holistic, pertaining to the whole of the social system, rather than one differentiated part of it. The individual pattern-maintenance sub-systems (A^l, G^l, I^l and L^l) are not therefore conceived in a differentiated autonomous manner, but regarded as unified manifestations of 'the general value system of the total society'. Whether, or to what extent such a general system exists is of course one of the most controversial areas in Parsonian sociology. However, even if no such consensus exists, this does not in and of itself rule out a culture-inclusive economic sociology. In practice, most analysts are more concerned with the nature of, and limits to value-patterns within the social system, rather than arguing in a general way for the presence or absence of value-consensus.

Parsons and Smelser, following Weber and Durkheim, insist on the importance of values alongside and in interaction with the instrumental aspects of economic life. This applies to pre-capitalist, non-market, and market-based capitalist economic relations. In general terms, economic life – even in the modern epoch – partakes as strongly in value-concerns as any other part of society.

For Parsons and Smelser the economy's value-system is founded on economic rationality, which is simultaneously a society-wide as well as a specifically economic value. It is defined as 'the valuation of the goals of production and appropriate controls over behaviour in the interest of such goals' (Parsons and Smelser 1956, p. 176). Translated into empirical terms, this emphasis on rationality involves both value-commitments on the part of individuals, and the development of institutional sanctions on behaviour designed to adapt action to changing exigencies by instrumental means. Such institutions include market-based penalties against inefficiency, as well as the practices of key institutions of government and financial capitalisation (e.g. banks) in supporting technical efficiency on cost-benefit grounds.

While emphasis is given in this way to economic rationality, Parsons warns against giving a fixed substantive character to the societal value-system. This is because the overriding function of the society-wide value-system is to determine the relative importance of particular values in relation to the activities of differentiated parts of the social system. This means that the relative importance of economic values is itself a matter for valuation in relation to other types of values, such as democratic political values, or the values of order and stability. In this situation it becomes an empirical question as to whether or not economic values predominate. This may vary by nation, being predominant in his view in the USA of the 1950s, but less well developed elsewhere. This emphasis on variation is consistent with subsequent empirical research on cross-national variations in the incidence of the work ethic (see above Chapter 7).

Two main types of objection have been mounted against the existence of this kind of economic value-consensus. The first political objection stresses the fundamental reality of conflicts of interest within the economic sphere between capital and labour. Such phenomena as strikes, absenteeism, sabotage, factory occupation and movements for workers' control have been taken as indicators of a deep conflict of interest that precludes any kind of value-consensus.

It is arguable, however, that many of the more routine types of bargaining conflict are not necessarily incompatible with economic value-consensus. For example, both capital and labour may share a high valuation of industrial production and the manufacture of 'things' rather than financial paper shuffling. They may also share a high valuation of occupational roles within industry in contrast with non-industrial roles. Flanders (1965) has argued that industrial relations systems, while often defined in terms of conflict-ridden bargaining, may nonetheless be dependent on underlying value-commitments such as the freedom of the parties to pursue bargaining in a voluntary and peaceful manner. This type of value-consensus usually functions in a latent rather than manifest and overt manner to prevent complete collapse into sectional power conflicts.

This discussion is a useful reminder that overt conflict is not, in and of itself evidence of absence of value-consensus. At the same time Flanders warns against another false assumption, namely that any instance of conflict is compatible with some underlying value-commitment. In cases where value-commitments change or where basic values conflict (e.g. over workplace authority) conflict may indeed represent a breakdown of value-consensus. Flanders thereby interprets Britain's post-war industrial relations record as one such example of lack of consensus concerning the regulatory principles that should underlie industrial relations. The implication here is that the presence or absence of economic value-consensus is an empirical issue, rather than one that can be settled within grand theory.

Parsons and Smelser, in their general theoretical approach, take the USA rather than Britain as their model. In addition they do not seek to derive economic value-consensus simply from labour–capital relations between collectivities. This is because they regard the American experience as more typical of modernisation than the European one. The European transition from feudalism to capitalism is regarded as an incomplete instance of modernisation, where quasi-feudal status relations carried over into the development of market capitalism. Parsons interprets European labour–capital conflict as being overlaid with status concerns deriving from the past. 'The bourgeoisie may be regarded as frustrated aristocrats and the proletarians frustrated peasants.' Each of these collectivities sees itself as 'alienated' from the historical status-based communities of the past (Parsons 1967b, p. 113). Such nostalgic collectivist identifications are, however, increasingly eroded by the predominant modernising thrust of secular privatised individualism and cultural pluralisation.

Parsons' alternative approach to value-consensus within what might be called the American 'new world' model, is based on societies which never had an aristocracy or peasantry in the European sense. In this context economic value-consensus is associated with the high valuation of individual occupational achievement, and the universalistic doctrine of equality of opportunity, whose inclusive character enables maximum variation in individual choice.

At this point a second general line of criticism arises concerning the substance and extent of economic value-consensus within such modern patterns of cultural values. Part of the critique here emphasises the recent challenge to economic values from what have been called post-materialist (Inglehardt 1977, 1990) or anti-economic values. In this argument, a heterogeneous set of social movements involving environmental conservation, feminism, peace and counter-cultural lifestyles overwhelms conventional economic values of technical rationality and individual achievement. Meanwhile another line of argument associated with the theory of post-modernism (see Chapter 7) emphasises that cultural pluralisation has gone so far that any overarching value-consensus or any consensus over the priority of economic values is no longer possible. This raises the difficult problem of how, if at all, micro-level economic activity at the level of the household and individual connects with macro-level cultural values institutionalised in politics and the law.

If the Parsonian approach to economic value-consensus is to survive as a useful frame of reference it would be necessary to show that the processes of individualism, privatism and cultural pluralisation do rest upon some kind of emergent consensus. At present this has not been demonstrated. Indeed, it may be that Daniel Bell is correct in diagnosing a fundamental contradiction between economic values such as the work ethic and technical rationality, on the one hand, and secularised cultural hedonism on the other (Bell 1976). Alternatively, it may be that instead of a contradiction at the heart of the relationship between economy and culture, it is to cultural rather than economic values that we should look for the most likely bases of social consensus. Such values as individual autonomy and integrity, household privacy, and cultural autonomy and pluralism seem at present within the Western world to be more influential than strictly economic values as such. To this extent society has changed significantly since Parsons and Smelser developed their theoretical framework, requiring major revisions in the substance of any adequate theory of economy and society.

The empirical research agenda arising from this discussion is as follows:

1 How far is there consensus over economic values within nations, and what are the values that are shared?
2 What determines variations in the scale of value-consensus?
3 How important are specific economic values as against other types of non-economic values, and are the former declining in significance relative to the latter?
4 Are cultural values and economic values developing in an increasingly antagonistic relationship?

Considerable emphasis has been given to Parsons and Smelser's theory of economy and society in demonstrating the scope and explanatory power of a multi-dimensional culture-inclusive theory of economy and society. Written over thirty-five years ago, this theory is inadequate in substance for both theoretical and empirical reasons. The most striking deficiencies of the approach include inadequacies in the treatment of power and property rights, and difficulties with the discussion of economic values and social cohesion as they affect civil society. We need to move beyond Parsons if these problems are to be addressed.

In spite of these criticisms, the general theoretical significance of Parsons and Smelser's work is still a highly positive once. First it provides the most systematic statement yet of a multi-dimensional theory of economy and society able to avoid the economic or political economic reductionism found in liberal and political economic theories. This multi-dimensionality may be regarded as a meta-theoretical approach consistent with a range of different applications in the substance of the analysis. While Parsons developed multi-dimensionality to analyse processes of social cohesion and cultural integration in economy and society, the German critical theorist Jurgen Habermas (1976, 1979, 1984) developed a multi-dimensional approach to analyse conflict and crisis in economy and society. Parsons and Habermas share a commitment to develop a non-reductionist culture-inclusive theory of economy and society, even though they differ in the direction in which their analyses lead. In particular, where Parsons and Smelser see balanced input–output relations between economy, polity, normative order and value-system, Habermas emphasises conflicts, shortfalls and crises.

A second positive feature of the Parsonian project is the attempt to combine an account of the internal working and differentiation of economic life with an account of the inter-actions between economy and society. Previously sociology had placed far more emphasis on the latter than the former. Authors in the political economy tradition, like Parsons himself, had clearly sought to analyse the internal operation of the economy, operating so to speak on the conventional terrain of economists. Yet Parsons' approach remains superior to that of political economy, even within the economic terrain, both in terms of scope and in terms of the analysis of agency. The scope of Parsons' work is not dominated by labour–capital relations to the exclusion of consumption, nor is it dominated by power and constraint to the exclusion of the active role of economic agency and economic culture.

A third positive feature of the Parsonian project is precisely the attempt to balance elements of enablement and constraint in the analysis of economy and society. This radical approach rejects both the bland optimism of liberalism as to the efficacy of simple market solutions under the sole constraint of scarcity, and the pessimism of political economic emphasis on power-based constraints and endemic conflicts of interest. These three aspects of the Parsonian legacy are worth building upon, even though much of the substance of his legacy requires re-casting and fundamental modification.

ENABLING AND CONSTRAINING THEMES IN ECONOMIC SOCIOLOGY

This study has been very much a programmatic manifesto for the tradition of scholarship called economic sociology. The merits of economic sociology have been argued in relation to rival traditions of scholarship, namely economic liberalism and political economy. The tradition of economic sociology stemming from the work of Durkheim and Weber, and consolidated by Parsons, has been portrayed as a multi-dimensional and culture-inclusive.

Economics was once called the dismal science because of its emphasis on the niggardliness of nature, setting limits of scarcity to human wants and aspirations. This implied limits to what we can have. In the contemporary epoch, by contrast, it is often sociology, under the sway of political economy, that has appeared as the new dismal science, while economics now occupies the ground of optimism. The economist James Duesenberry pointed to this new contrast when he compared the sociological preference for telling us what we can't do or have due to social constraint, with economists' preferences for telling us the terms upon which we can have it. At its extreme the dismal sociological emphasis on constraint is manifest in the practice of deconstruction, designed to expose the silences and omissions in any positive set of propositions.

Analysis of constraint is of course fundamental to social thought. Social theorising, as we have seen, rests both on moral foundations and on the hope that social action may be usefully guided by the fruits of theory. Analysis of the social constraints that obstruct the realisation of human purposes and values is clearly a major component of social thought. There are, however, two traps into which such endeavours may fall: one is to exaggerate constraint leading to a fatalistic devaluation of action in pursuit of objectives; the other is to exaggerate the autonomy of action, leading to an undervaluation of constraint and (often) an apology for the concentrations of power that underlie constraint.

In this study, economic sociology is portrayed as capable of avoiding these two traps. It avoids the trap of exaggerating constraint and devaluing agency into which political economy falls. This argument is sustained through an emphasis on the enabling as well as constraining features of the market and market-regulating agencies (including political agencies), on the sociology of consumption and on economic culture wherein power is mediated through values and norms. However, it also avoids the economic liberal trap of undervaluing constraints and apologising for fundamental inequalities of power, by focussing on structures of power and domination, and on conflicts of interest.

The result is a view of contemporary social processes in markets, organisations, governments and cultural practices that is neither strongly optimistic or strongly pessimistic about processes of differentiation and integration in economy and society. There is no necessity that economic sociology be tied to the optimistic theories of modernisation developed by Parsons and others, in which the modern amalgam of markets, democracy and the rule of law are seen as offering a universalistic multi-dimensional means to maximise economic welfare, political participation and cultural cohesion. Nor, on the other hand, is there any necessity that economic sociology be dominated by the pessimistic intellectual agenda of political economy, focussing on the resilience of capitalist economic power and global domination in the face of mounting and increasingly utopian resistance. The spirit of economic sociology is nonetheless closer to the Parsonian liberal-democratic project than to the political economic critique of capitalism, insofar as markets have proved enduring economic institutions that have proved more resilient than alternative state socialist or communist modes of economic planning. In both West and East, markets, in a variety of regulated or unregulated forms, represent a major component of the institutional amalgam of global and national economics. Yet markets cannot, as Polanyi rightly said, generate political order and moral cohesion, hence the importance of political and cultural analysis to the theory of economy and society. Such order and cohesion owes a great deal to the operation of power, but this is based on multiple sources including private capital-ownership, patriarchal gender domination and the organised pressure of democratically represented interests and social movements, rather than on some unitary capitalist structure. Meanwhile markets and power structures are strongly influenced and often regulated by cultural values and the symbolic representation of cultural meaning. It is this cultural dimension which is the most under-explored element of the theory of economy and society, where much more empirical work needs to be done.

Optimistic liberal-democratic theories of economy and society assume that processes of differentiation and economic specialisation will somehow be balanced by modes of integration. In this study, the critical comments made on Parsons' treatment of social integration place this assumption of supposed balance into the realms of the uncertain. Many social agents now act on the basis that the differentiation of economy and society, that created divisions between paid work and leisure, workplace and household, or economy and community, has gone too far. The question is not now one of differentiation and integration, but integration through de-differentiation. This project is manifest in the claims of the environmentalist social movements with their concern for ecological survival, and the accountability of economic investment decisions to ecologically-sensitive concerns of the community. Another example of de-differentiation is to be found in feminist social movements, in terms of bids to change the balance of public and private roles in a way that recognises the social value of unpaid labour, and which challenge male-centred definitions of career achievement based upon the domination of women. Meanwhile the traditional concept of career as a lifetime activity is challenged by changing cultural values as to the relative importance of work and leisure, and by the adaptive ingenuity of the unemployed or the retired seeking alternative means of cultural enrichment and human dignity.

Cultural autonomy and household privatism are in addition very complex multi-faceted social activities, which are not simply creations of markets or economic values. They are not simply to be equated with differentiated social roles such as consumerism or acquisitiveness, but embrace a range of other components including the search for security, processes of child socialisation and intergenerational communication, and bases for identity formation and cultural expression (Stretton 1975; Saunders 1990). At this stage, however, it is difficult to determine how far the cultural encroachment on and, in some cases, domination over economic values amounts to a significant reversal of the differentiation process.

In answer to Polanyi's question of how integration is achieved under differentiated conditions, emphasis must be placed on both household and political modes of integration. Political modes of integration depend on welfare mechanisms that mediate between individuals and the labour market, and seek to secure a minimum standard of life outside labour market participation. However, political integration mechanisms may also underwrite the autonomy of individuals and households through recognition of citizenship rights that protect privacy and through positive fiscal privileges (e.g. tax concessions on house purchase arrangements). Households cannot be regarded as existing spontaneously without any relationship with the state, even though the cult of household privacy often pretends otherwise. At the same time households are not simply creatures of government, but may actually resist political programmes through such developments as revolt against taxation and high-spending governments.

In the future development of economic sociology it is important to emphasise that governments, as well as firms, households and individuals, operate in an environment combining elements of enablement with constraint. Even if large firms and government may often have more formal power, under certain circumstances they are constrained by the autonomous impact of household or consumer resistance and through the capacities of new social movements to influence prevailing cultural values. More detailed analysis of how such patterns of enablement and constraint operate, and how far they remain asymmetrical or unequal is a task that cannot be attempted in this study. The traditions of economic liberalism and political economy cannot meet this challenge. The emergent tradition of economic sociology is able to do so, and has already made a striking contribution towards a new set of answers.

271

BIBLIOGRAPHY

Abercrombie, N., Hill, S. and Turner, B. (1980) *The Dominant Ideology Thesis*, Allen & Unwin, London.

Abercrombie, N., Hill, S. and Turner, B. (1986) *Sovereign Individuals of Capitalism*, Allen & Unwin, London.

Abu-Lughod, J. (1989) *Before European Hegemony: The World System AD 1250–1350*, Oxford University Press, New York.

Albrow, M. (1990) *Max Weber's Construction of Social Theory*, Macmillan, London.

Alchian, A. and Demsetz, H. (1972) 'Production, information cost, and economic organisation', *American Economic Review, Vol. 62*, 777–95.

Alexander, J. (1982) *Theoretical Logic in Sociology Vol. 1: Positivism, Presuppositions, and Current Controversies*, Routledge & Kegan Paul, London.

Alexander, J. (1984) *Theoretical Logic in Sociology Vol 4: Talcott Parsons*, Routledge & Kegan Paul, London.

Alexander, J. (1985) 'Social differentiation and collective behaviour', *Sociological Theory*, 3, 11–23.

Alexander, J. (1988) *Action and its Environments: Toward a New Synthesis*, Columbia University Press, New York.

Alexander, J. and Colomy, P. (1990) 'The structure and dynamics of traditions: toward a postpositivist model of knowledge cumulation and decline in the social sciences', paper delivered to 1990 Meeting of the American Sociological Association, Washington DC, USA.

Appadurai, A. (1990) 'Disjuncture and difference in the global cultural economy', in M. Featherstone (ed.) *Global Culture: Nationalism, Globalisation and Modernity*, Sage, London, 295–310.

Armstrong, P., Glyn, A. and Harrison, J. (1984) *Capitalism since World War II*, Fontana, London.

Arnold, R. (1957) 'A port of trade: Whydah on the Guinea Coast', in K. Polanyi, C. Arensberg and H. Pearson (eds) *Trade and Market in the Early Empires*, Free Press, Glencoe, 154–176.

Baran, P. and Sweezy, P. (1966) *Monopoly Capitalism*, Monthly Review Press, New York.

Barber, B. (1983) *The Logic and Limits of Trust*, Rutgers University Press, New Brunswick.

Barrington Moore, W. (1966) *Social Origins of Dictatorship and Democracy*, Beacon Press, Boston.

Baudrillard, J. (1983) *Simulations*, Semiotext(e), New York.

Baudrillard, J. (1988) *America*, Verso, London.

Becker, G. (1976) *The Economic Approach to Human Behavior*, Chicago University Press, Chicago.

Becker, G. (1981) *A Treatise on the Family*, Harvard University Press, Cambridge.

Bell, D. (1976) *The Cultural Contradictions of Capitalism*, Basic Books, New York.

Berger, P. (1987) *The Capitalist Revolution: Fifty Propositions about Prosperity, Liberty and Equality*, Basic Books, New York.

Blau, F. and Jusenius, C. (1976) 'Economists' approaches to sex segregation in the labor market', in M. Blaxall and B. Reagan (eds) *Women and the Workplace: the Implications of Occupational Segregation*, University of Chicago Press, Chicago.

Bottomore, T. (ed.) (1983) *A Dictionary of Marxist Thought*, Blackwell, Oxford.

Braverman, H. (1974) *Labor and Monopoly Capitalism*, Monthly Review Press, New York.

Briggs, A. (1960) 'The language of class', in A. Briggs and J. Saville (eds) *Essays in Labour History, Vol 1.*, Macmillan, London.

Brubaker, R. (1984) *The Limits of Rationality*, Allen & Unwin, London.

Brus, W. (1972) *The Market in a Socialist Economy*, Routledge & Kegan Paul, London.

Buchanan, J. (1975) *The Limits of Liberty: Between Anarchy and Leviathan*, University of Chicago Press, Chicago.

Buchanan, J. (1986) *Liberty, Market and State: Political Economy in the 1980s*, Wheatsheaf Books, Brighton.

Buchanan, J. and Tullock, G. (1962) *The Calculus of Consent*, University of Michigan Press, Ann Arbor.

Burawoy, M. (1979) *Manufacturing Consent*, University of Chicago Press, Chicago.

Campbell, C. (1986) *The Romantic Ethic and the Spirit of Modern Consumerism*, Blackwell, Oxford.

Carr, J. (1988) 'Family business in Australia and New Zealand: gender, ethnicity and class', unpublished PhD thesis, Flinders University of South Australia.

Chamberlin, E.N. (1948) *The Theory of Monopolistic Competition*, Harvard University Press, Cambridge, MA.

Chandler, A. (1977) *The Visible Hand: The Managerial Revolution in American Business*, Belknap Press, Cambridge, MA.

Chapman, A.C. (1957) 'Port of trade enclaves in Aztec and Maya civilisations', in K. Polanyi, C. Arensberg and H. Pearson (eds), *Trade and Market in the Early Empires*, Free Press, Glencoe, 114–153.

Chinoy, E. (1955) *Automobile Workers and the American Dream*, Beacon Press, Boston.

Chodorow, N. (1978) *The Reproduction of Mothering*, University of California Press, Berkeley.

Choi, K. (1983) 'A statistical test of Olson's model', in D.C. Mueller (ed.), *The Political Economy of Growth Rates*, Yale University Press, New Haven, CT, 57–78.

Clarke, S. (1982) *Marx, Marginalism and Modern Sociology: from Adam Smith to Max Weber*, Macmillan, London.

Coase, R.H. (1937) 'The nature of the firm', *Economica* 4, 386–405.

Connell, R. (1977) *Ruling Class, Ruling Culture*, Cambridge University Press, Cambridge.

Corbridge, S. (1986) *Capitalist World Development: A Critique of Radical Development Geography*, Macmillan, London.

Crompton, R. (1990) 'Class, theory and gender', *British Journal of Sociology* 40(4), 565–87.

Curtin, P. (1984) *Cross-cultural Trade in World History*, Cambridge University Press, Cambridge.

Dalton, M. (1959) *Men Who Manage*, Wiley, New York.

Doeringer, P. and Piore, M. (1971) *Internal Labor Markets and Manpower Analysis*, Heath, Lexington, MA.

Dore, R. (1973) *British Factory, Japanese Factory*, Allen & Unwin, London.

Douglas, M. and Isherwood, B. (1978) *The World of Goods*, Allen Lane, London.

Downs, A. (1957) *An Economic Theory of Democracy*, Harper, New York.

Durkheim, E. (1933) *The Division of Labour in Society*, Free Press, Glencoe.

Durkheim, E. (1938) *The Rules of Sociological Method*, Chicago University Press, Chicago.

Eisenstadt, S. (1964) 'Social change, differentiation and evolution', *American Sociological Review*, 29, 375–86.

Esping-Andersen, G. (1990) *The Three Worlds of Welfare Capitalism*, Polity, Oxford.

Etzioni, A. (1988) *The Moral Dimension: Towards a New Economics*, Free Press, New York.

Evans-Pritchard, E.E. (1940) *The Nuer: A Description of the Modes of Livelihood and Political Institutions of the Nilotic People*, Oxford University Press, Oxford.

Fama, E. and Jensen, M. (1983) 'Separation of ownership and control', *Journal of Law and Economics* 26, 301–25.

Featherstone, M. (ed.) (1990) *Global Culture: Nationalism, Globalisation and Modernity*, Sage, London.

Feld, S. (1988) 'Notes on world beat', *Public Culture* 1(2), 31–7.

Fenoaltea, M. (1975) 'Authority, efficiency and agricultural organisation in medieval England and beyond', *Journal of Economic History* 35, 693–718.

Flanders, G. (1965) *Industrial Relations: What is Wrong with the System*, Faber and Faber, London.

Flinn, M.W. (1961) 'Social theory and the industrial revolution', in T. Burns and S. Saul (eds) *Social Theory and Economic Change*, Tavistock, London.

Foster, J. (1974) *Class Struggle and the Industrial Revolution*, Weidenfeld & Nicolson, London.

Foster, J. (1976) 'British imperialism and the labour aristocracy', in J. Skelley (ed.) *The General Strike*, Lawrence & Wishart, London, 3–57.

Fox, R. (1967) *Kinship and Marriage*, Penguin, Harmondsworth.

Frank, A.G. (1969) *Capitalism and Under-development in Latin America*, Monthly Review Press, New York.

Friedman, Andrew L. (1977) *Industry and Labour: Class Struggle at Work and Monopoly Capitalism*, Macmillan, London.

Friedman, M. (1977) *Oligopology and the Theory of Games*, North Holland, Amsterdam.

Friedman, M. and Friedman, R. (1980) *Free to Choose*, Harcourt Brace Jovanovitch, New York.

Frisby, D. (1990) 'Preface to the second edition', in G. Simmel *The Philosophy of Money*, Routledge, London.

Frobel, F., Heinrichs, J. and Kreye, O. (1980) *The New International Division of Labour*, Cambridge University Press, Cambridge.

Fukayama, F. (1989) 'The end of history', *The National Interest*, summer.

Gans, H. (1988) *Middle American Individualism*, Free Press, New York.

Geertz, C. (1973) *The Interpretation of Cultures*, Basic Books, New York.

Gerschenkron, A. (1962) 'Economic backwardness in historical perspective', *Economic Backwardness in Historical Perspective and Other Essays*, Harvard University Press, Cambridge, MA.

Gershuny, J. and Miles, I. (1983) *The New Service Economy, the Transformation of Employment in Industrial Societies*, Frances Pinter, London.

Gershuny, J. (1985) 'Economic development and change in the mode of provision of services', in N. Redclift and E. Mingione (eds) *Beyond Employment: Household, Gender and Subsistence*, Blackwell, Oxford, 128–64.

Giddens, A. (1972) *Politics and Sociology in the Thought of Max Weber*, Macmillan, London.

Giddens, A. (1987) *The Nation-State and Violence*, University of California Press, Berkeley.

Goldthorpe, J. (1980) *Social Mobility and Class Structure in Modern Britain*, Clarendon Press, Oxford.

Goldthorpe, J. (ed.) (1984) *Order and Conflict in Contemporary Capitalism*, Clarendon Press, Oxford.

Gordon, D. (1972) *Theories of Poverty and Unemployment*, Heath, Lexington, MA.

Gramsci, A. (1971) *Selections from the Prison Notebooks*, Lawrence & Wishart, London.

Granovetter, M. (1985) 'Economic action and social structure: the problem of embeddedness', *American Journal of Sociology* 91(3), 481–510.

Gutman, H. (1977) *Work, Culture, and Society in Industrialising America*, Blackwell, Oxford.

Habermas, J. (1976) *Legitimation Crisis*, Heinemann, London.

Habermas, J. (1979) *Communication and the Evolution of Society*, Heinemann, London.

Habermas, J. (1984) *The Theory of Communicative Action, vol. 1*, Heinemann, London.

Hagen, E. (1962) *On the Theory of Social Change*, Dorsey Press, Homewood, IL.

Hagen, E. (1967) 'British personality and the industrial revolution: the historical evidence', in T. Burns and S. Saul (eds) *Social Theory and Economic Change*, Tavistock, London.

Hall, S. (1977) 'Rethinking the "base and superstructure" metaphor', in J. Bloomfield (ed.) *Class, Hegemony and Party*, Lawrence & Wishart, London.

Hamilton, G. and Biggart, N. (1988) 'Market, culture and authority: a comparative analysis of management and organisation in the Far East', *American Journal of Sociology*, 94 Supplement, 552–94.

Hannertz, U. (1989) 'Notes on the global ecumene', *Public Culture* 1(2), 66–75.

Hardin, G. (1968) 'The tragedy of the commons', *Science* 62, 1243–48.

Harrison, R. (ed.) (1979) *Rational Action*, Cambridge University Press, Cambridge.

Hartmann, H. (1976) 'Capitalism, patriarchy and job segregation by sex', in M. Blaxall and B. Reagan (eds) *Women and the Workplace*, University of Chigaco Press, Chicago, 137–69.

Hayek, F.A. (1937) 'Economics as knowledge', *Economica* 4, 33–54.

Hayek, F.A. (1949) *Individualism and Economic Order*, Routledge & Kegan Paul, London.

Hayek, F.A. (1973) *Law, Legislation and Liberty Vol. 1: Rules and Order*, Routledge & Kegan Paul, London.

Hilderbrand, W. and Kirman, A.P. (1976) *Introduction to Equilibrium Analysis*, North Holland, Amsterdam.

Hilferding, R. (1981) *Finance Capital*, Routledge & Kegan Paul, London.

Hindess, B. (1988) *Choice, Rationality and Social Theory*, Unwin Hyman, London.

Hirsch, F. (1976) *Social Limits to Growth*, Harvard University Press, Cambridge, MA.

Hirschman, A. (1982) 'Rival interpretations of market society: civilising, destructure or feeble?', *Journal of Economic Literature* 20(4), 1463–84.

Hirschman, A. (1984) 'Against parsimony: three easy ways of complicating some categories of economic discourse', *American Economic Review: Papers and Proceedings* 74(2), May, 89–96.

Hobsbawm, E.J. (1964) *Labouring Men*, Weidenfeld & Nicolson, London.

Hofstadter, R. (1955) *The Age of Reform*, Vintage Books, New York.

Hollis, M. (1979) 'Introduction', in F. Hahn and M. Hollis (eds) *Philosophy and Economic Theory*, Oxford University Press, Oxford.

Holton, R. (1985) *The Transition from Feudalism to Capitalism*, Macmillan, London.

Holton, R. and Turner, B. (1986) *Talcott Parsons on Economy and Society*, Routledge & Kegan Paul, London.

Holton, R. and Turner, B. (1989) *Max Weber on Economy and Society*, Routledge & Kegan Paul, London.

Ingham, G. (1982) 'Divisions within the dominant class and British exceptionalism', in A. Giddens and G. McKenzie (eds) *Social Class and the Division of Labour*, Cambridge University Press, Cambridge.

Inglehart, R. (1977) *The Silent Revolution*, Princeton University Press, Princeton.

Inglehart, R. (1990) *Culture Shift in Advanced Industrial Society*, Princeton University Press, Princeton.

James, N. (1989) 'Emotional labour: skill and work in the social regulation of feelings', *Sociological Review* 37 (1), 15–42.

Johnson, C. (1982) *MITI and the Japanese Miracle: The Growth of Industrial Policy, 1925–75*, Stanford University Press, Stanford.

Kaufman, E. (1988) *Crisis in Allende's Chile*, Praeger, New York.

Kellner, D. (1983) 'Critical theory, commodities and the consumer society', *Theory, Culture and Society* 1(3), 66–84.

Kellner, D. (1988) 'Postmodernism as social theory', *Theory, Culture and Society* 5, 239–68.

Keynes, J.M. (1936) *The General Theory of Employment, Interest and Money*, Macmillan, London.

Knights, D. and Willmott, H. (eds) (1990) *Labour Process Theory*, Macmillan, London.

Korpi, W. (1983) *The Democratic Class Struggle*, Routledge & Kegan Paul, London.

Kriedte, P., Medick, H. and Schlumbohm, J. (1981) *Industrialisation before Industrialisation*, Cambridge University Press, Cambridge.

Lane, D. (1985) *Soviet Economy and Society*, Blackwell, Oxford.

Lange, O. (1938) 'On the economic theory of socialism', in O. Lange and F. Taylor (eds) *On the Economic Theory of Socialism*, University of Minnesota Press, Minneapolis.

Lash, S. and Urry, J. (1987) *The End of Organised Capitalism*, Polity Press, Oxford.

Latsis, S.J. (1972) 'Situational determinism in economics', *British Journal for the Philosophy of Science*, 23, 207–45.

Lenin, V.I. (1964) *Imperialism: The Highest Stage of Capitalism*, Progress Publishers, Moscow.

Leontief W. (1985) 'Interview: why economics needs input–output analysis', *Challenge* March/April, 27–35.

Lipset, S.M. (1963) *The First New Nation*, Basic Books, New York.

Luhmann, N. (1979) *Trust and Power*, Wiley, New York.

Luhmann, N. (1982) *The Differentiaton of Society*, Columbia University Press, New York.

Lukes, S. (1973) *Emile Durkheim*, Allen Lane, London.

Lukes, S. (1975) 'Political ritual and social integration', *Sociology*, 9, 289–308.

Lyotard, F. (1984) *The Postmodern Condition: A Report on Knowledge*, Manchester University Press, Manchester.

Macaulay, S. (1963) 'On contractual relations in business: a preliminary study', *American Sociological Review* 28 (1) 55–67.

MacFarlane, A. (1978) *The Origins of English Individualism*, Blackwell, Oxford.

McClelland, D.C. (1961) *The Achieving Society*, Van Nostrand, Princeton.

Magdoff, H. (1969) *The Age of Imperialism*, Monthly Review Press, New York.

Mandel, E. (1976) *Late Capitalism*, New Left Books, London.

Mann, M. (1986) *The Sources of Social Power Vol. 1: A History of Power from the Beginning to AD 1760*, Cambridge University Press, Cambridge.

Marcuse, H. (1968) *One-Dimensional Man*, Routledge & Kegan Paul, London.

Marglin, S. (1974) 'What do bosses do?' *Review of Radical Political Economy*, 6, summer, 60–112.

Marshall, G. (1982) *In Search of the Spirit of Capitalism*, Hutchinson, London.

Marshall, T.H. (1977) *Class, Citizenship and Social Development*, Chicago University Press, Chicago.

Martinelli, A. (1982) 'The political and social impact of transnational corporations', in H. Makler, A. Martinelli and N. Smelser (eds) *The New International Economy*, Sage, Beverly Hills, 79–116.

Marwell, G. (1982) 'Altruism and the problem of collective action', in V.J. Derlega and J. Grzelak (eds) *Co-operation and Helping Behaviour: Theories and Research*, Academic Press, New York, 207–26.

Marwell, G. and Ames, R. (1981) 'Economists free ride, does anyone else?', *Journal of Public Economists*, 15, 295–310.

Marx, K. (1962) 'Preface to a contribution to a critique of political economy', in K. Marx and F. Engels (eds) *Selected Works*, Foreign Languages Publishing House, Moscow, 361–5.

Marx, K. (1964) *Economic and Philosophic Manuscripts*, International Publishers, New York.

Marx, K. (1976) *Capital*, Penguin, London.

Marx, K. (1977) *Pre-capitalist Economic Formations*, International Publishers, New York.

Marx, K. and Engels, F. (1962) 'Manifesto of the Communist Party', in *Selected Works Vol 1*, Foreign Languages Publishing House, Moscow, 34–65.

Mitchell, J. (1971) *Women's Estate*, Penguin, Harmondsworth.

Moorhouse, H. (1983) 'American automobiles and workers dreams', *Sociological Review*, 31, 403–26.

Nakane, C. (1970) *Japanese Society*, University of California Press, Berkeley.

Nell, E. (1972) 'Economics: the revival of political economy', in R. Blackburn (ed.) *Ideology in Social Science*, Fontana, London, 76–95.

North, D. (1977) 'Markets and other allocation systems in history: the challenge of Karl Polanyi', *Journal of European Economic History*, March.

North, D. (1981) *Structure and Change in Economic History*, Norton, New York.

North, D. and Thomas, R. (1973) *The Rise of the Western World*, Cambridge University Press, Cambridge.

Nove, A. (1983) *The Economics of Feasible Socialism*, Allen & Unwin, London.

O'Connor, J. (1973) *The Fiscal Crisis of the State*, St Martins Press, New York.

OECD (Organisation for Economic Co-operation and Development) (1986) *Economic Outlook* 39, May.

Offe, C. (1985) *Disorganised Capitalism*, Polity Press, Oxford.

Olson, M. (1983a) *The Rise and Decline of Nations*, Yale University Press, New Haven, CT.

Olson, M. (1983b) 'The political economy of comparative growth rates', in D.C. Mueller (ed.) *The Political Economy of Growth Rates*, Yale University Press, New Haven, CT, 7–52.

Oppenheim, A.L. (1957) 'A bird's eye view of Mesopotamian history', in K. Polanyi, C. Arensberg and H. Pearson (eds) *Trade and Market in the Early Empires*, Free Press, Glencoe, 27–37.

Otnes, P. (ed.) (1988) *The Sociology of Consumption*, Solum Forlag A/S, Oslo.

Ouchi, W. (1980) 'Markets, bureaucracies and clans', *Administrative Science Quarterly* 25, March, 129–45.

Pahl, R (1984) *Divisions of Labour*, Blackwell, Oxford.

Pahl, R. (1990) 'The search for social cohesion: from Durkheim to the European Commission', unpublished paper presented to the ESRC/CNRS Workshop on Citizenship, Social Order and Civilising Processes, Windsor, September 1990.

Parkin, F. (1979) *Marxism and Class Theory: A Bourgeois Critique*, Tavistock, London.

Parsons, T. (1937) *The Structure of Social Action*, McGraw-Hill, New York.

Parsons, T. (1951) *The Social System*, Free Press, Chicago.

Parsons, T. (1953) *Working Papers in the Theory of Action* (in collaboration with R.F. Bales and E. Shills), Free Press, Chicago.

Parsons, T. (1964) 'Evolutionary universals in society', *American Sociological Review*, 29(3) 339–57.

Parsons, T. (1966) *Societies: Evolutionary and Comparative Perspectives*, Prentice-Hall, Englewood Cliffs.

Parsons, T. (1967a) 'Polarisation of the world and international order', in *Sociological Theory and Modern Society*, Free Press, New York.

Parsons, T. (1967b) 'Some comments on the sociology of Karl Marx', in *Sociological Theory and Modern Society*, Free Press, New York, 102–36.

Parsons, T. (1971) *The System of Modern Societies*, Prentice-Hall, Englewood Cliffs.

Parsons, T. and Smelser, N. (1956) *Economy and Society*, Routledge & Kegan Paul, London.

Penn, R. (1982) 'Skilled manual workers in the labour process, 1856–1964', in S. Wood (ed.) *The Degradation of Work*, Hutchinson, London.

Penn, R. (1984) *Skilled Workers in the British Class Structure*, Cambridge University Press, Cambridge.

Penn, R. and Scattergood, H. (1985) 'Deskilling or enskilling?', *British Journal of Sociology* 37 (4) 611–30.

Perrow, C. (1986) 'Economic theories of organisation', *Theory and Society* 15, 11–45.

Piore, M. and Sabel, C. (1984) *The Second Industrial Divide*, Basic Books, New York.
Pirenne, H. (1925) *Medieval Cities*, Princeton University Press, Princeton.
Polanyi, K. (1944) *The Great Transformation*, Rinehart, New York.
Polanyi, K. (1957) 'Marketless trading in Hammurabai's time', in K. Polanyi, C. Arensberg and H. Pearson (eds) *Trade and Market in the Early Empires*, Free Press, Glencoe, 12–26.
Polanyi, K. (1977) *The Livelihood of Man*, Academic Press, New York.
Polanyi, K., Arensberg, C.M. and Pearson, H.W. (eds) 1957, *Trade and Market in the Early Empires*, Free Press, Chicago.
Popkin, S. (1979) *The Rational Peasant: The Political Economy of Rural Vietnam*, University of California Press, Berkeley.
Rapoport, A. (1985) 'Provision of public goods and the MCS experimental paradigm', *American Political Science Review* 79(1), 148–55.
Reich, M., Gordon, D. and Edwards, R.C. (1973) 'A theory of labour market segmentation', *American Economic Review* (Papers and Proceedings) 63, 359–65.
Ricardo, D. (1973) *Principles of Political Economy and Taxation*, Dent, London.
Robertson, R. (1987) 'Globalisation theory and civilisation analysis', *Comparative Civilisations Review* 17, Fall, 20–30.
Robertson, R. (1990a) 'After nostalgia? Wilful nostalgia and the phases of globalisation', in B.S. Turner (ed.) *Theories of Modernity and Postmodernity*, Sage, London.
Robertson, R. (1990b) 'Globality: global culture and images of world order', in H. Haferkamp and N. Smelser (eds) *Social Change and Modernity*, University of California Press, Berkeley.
Robertson, R. and Lechner, F. (1985) 'Modernisation, globalization and the problem of culture in world-systems theory', *Theory, Culture and Society* 2(3), 103–118.
Roemer, J. (1982) 'New directions in the Marxian theory of exploitation and class', *Politics and Society* 11, 3.
Rosaldo, M. (1974) 'Woman, culture and society: a theoretical overview', in M. Rosaldo and L. Lamphere (eds) *Women, Culture and Society*, Stanford University Press, Stanford, 17–42.
Rose, M. (1985) *Re-working the Work Ethic*, Batsford, London.
Rostow, W.W. (1960) *The Stages of Economic Growth*, Cambridge University Press, Cambridge.
Sahlins, M. (1972) *Stone Age Economics*, Aldine-Atherton, Chicago.
Samuelson, P. (1976) *Economics*, McGraw-Hill, New York.
Saunders, P. (1990) *A Nation of Home-owners*, Unwin Hyman, London.
Schmitter, P. and Lehmbruch, G. (eds) (1979) *Trends Towards Corporatist Intermediation*, Sage, Beverly Hills.
Schumpeter, J. (1954) *A History of Economic Analysis*, Oxford University Press, New York.
Schumpeter, J. (1961) *Capitalism, Socialism and Democracy*, Allen & Unwin, London.
Scott, J. (1976) *The Moral Economy of the Peasant*, Yale University Press, New Haven, CT.

Seidman, S. (1985) 'Modernity and the problem of meaning: the Durkheimian tradition', *Sociological Analysis* 46(2), 109–30.

Sen, A. (1977) 'Rational fools: a critique of the behavioural foundations of economic theory', *Philosophy and Public Affairs* 6, 317–44.

Silver, M. (1983) 'Karl Polanyi and markets in the ancient Near East: the challenge of the evidence', *Journal of Economic History* 43(4), 795–829.

Simmel, G. (1978) *The Philosophy of Money*, Routledge & Kegan Paul, London.

Simon, H. (1959) 'Theories of decision making in economics and behavioural science', *American Economic Review*, 49, 3, June, 253–283.

Simon, H. (1979) 'Rational decision making in business organisations', *American Economic Review* 69 (4) September, 493–513.

Simon, H. (1982) *Models of Bounded Rationality*, MIT Press, Cambridge, MA.

Sklair, L. (1991) *Sociology of the Global System*, Harvester, Hemel Hempstead.

Smircich, L. (1983) 'Concepts of culture and organisational analysis', *Administrative Science Quarterly* 28, 339–58.

Smith, A. (1976) *An Enquiry into the Nature and Causes of the Wealth of Nations*, Oxford University Press, Oxford.

Smith, J., Wallerstein, I. and Evers, H.-D. (1984) *Households and the World Economy*, Sage, London.

Sociology (1990, vol. 24, no. 3) 'Special edition: the sociology of consumption', 1–152.

Steedman, I. (1977) *Marx after Sraffa*, New Left Books, London.

Stephens, J.D. (1979) *The Transition from Capitalism to Socialism*, Macmillan, London.

Stretton, H. (1975) *Ideas for Australian Cities*, Georgian House, Melbourne.

Swedberg, R. (1987) 'Economic sociology', *Current Sociology* 35, spring, 1–221.

Swidler, A. (1986) 'Culture in action: symbols and strategies', *American Sociological Review*, 51, 273–86.

Thompson, E.P. (1963, *The Making of the English Working Class*, Gollancz, London.

Thompson, E.P. (1971) 'The moral economy of the English crowd in the eighteenth century', *Past and Present* 50, 76–136.

Toennies, F. (1967) *Community and Society*, Michigan State University Press, Michigan.

Trotsky, L. (1962) *The Permanent Revolution*, Pioneer, New York.

Turner, B. (ed.) (1990) *Theories of Modernity and Postmodernity*, Sage, London.

Walby, S. (1986) *Patriarchy at Work*, Polity Press, Cambridge.

Wallerstein, I. (1974) *The Modern World System*, Academic Press, New York.

Wallerstein, I. (1980) *The Modern World System II*, Academic Press, New York.

Wallerstein, I. (1990) 'Culture as the ideological battleground of the modern world-system', in M. Featherstone (ed.) *Global Culture: Nationalism, Globalisation and Modernity*, Sage, London, 31–55.

Weber, M. (1924) *Gesammelte Aufsatze zur Sozial- und Wirtschaftgeschichte*, Mohr, Tubingen.

Weber, M. (1927) *General Economic History*, Allen & Unwin, London.

Weber, M. (1930) *The Protestant Ethic and the Spirit of Capitalism*, Allen & Unwin, London.

Weber, M. (1948a) 'Science as a vocation', in H. Gerth and C.W. Mills (eds) *From Max Weber: Essays in Sociology*, Routledge & Kegan Paul, London, 129–56.

Weber, M. (1948b) 'The social psychology of the world religions', in H. Gerth and C.W. Mills (eds) *From Max Weber: Essays in Sociology*, Routledge & Kegan Paul, London, 267–301.

Weber, M. (1949) 'Objectivity in social sciences and social policy', in *The Methodology of the Social Sciences*, Free Press, New York.

Weber, M. (1976) 'Author's introduction' (1920), in *The Protestant Ethic and the Spirit of Capitalism*, Allen & Unwin, London.

Weber, M. (1978) *Economy and Society*, 2 vols, University of California Press, Berkeley.

Weede, E. (1986) 'Catch-up, distributional coalitions and government as determinants of economic growth or decline in industrialized democracies', *British Journal of Sociology* 37(2), 194–218.

Williams, R. (1963) *Culture and Society 1780–1950*, Penguin, Harmondsworth.

Williams, R. (1973) 'Base and superstructure in Marxist cultural theory', *New Left Review*, 82, Nov.-Dec.

Williamson, O. (1975) *Markets and Hierarchies*, Free Press, New York.

Winkler, J. (1974) 'Corporatism', *Archives Européennes de Sociologie* 15.

Wright, E. (1978) *Class, Crisis and the State*, New Left Books, London.

Wright, E. (1985) *Classes*, Verso, London.

Wrong, D. (1961) 'The over-socialized conception of man in modern sociology', *American Sociological Review* 26, 183–93.

Yankelovitch, D. et al. (1983) *Work and Human Values*, Aspen Institute, New York.

Yoshimoto, M. (1989) 'The postmodern and mass images in Japan', *Public Culture* 1(2), 8–25.

Zelizer, V. (1978) 'Human values and the market: the case of life insurance and death in nineteenth century America', *American Journal of Sociology* 84(3), 591–610.

Zelizer, V. (1979) *Morals and Markets: The Development of Life Insurance in the United States*, Columbia University Press, New York.

NAME INDEX

283

SUBJECT INDEX